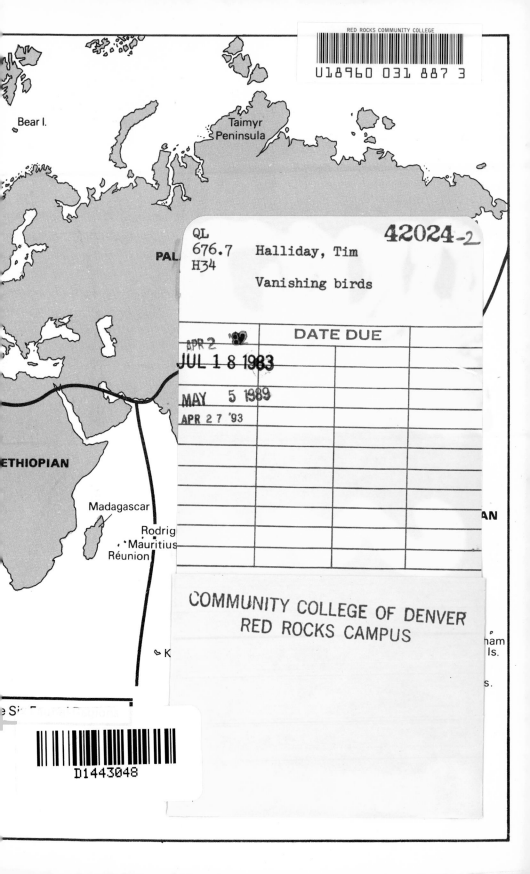

VANISHING BIRDS

Vanishing Birds

Their Natural History and Conservation

TIM HALLIDAY

FOREWORD BY BRUCE CAMPBELL

HOLT, RINEHART AND WINSTON
NEW YORK

Library of Congress Cataloging in Public ation Data
Halliday, Tim, 1945-
  Vanishing birds.

  Bibliography: P.
  Includes index.
  1. Rare birds.   2. Birds, Protection of.
I. Title.
QL676.7.H34   598.2   77-19010
  ISBN 0-03-043561-7

First Edition
Printed in Great Britain

To the memory of my father,

JACK HALLIDAY

Foreword

THERE have been a number of books about the decrease or extinction of birds throughout the world, but most of them have been written from an historical angle, faithfully charting the process of decline with a wealth of chronological detail.

Tim Halliday, while giving his full quota of historical facts, has taken an essentially biological line. As a specialist in animal behaviour by no means confined to birds, he approaches the problem from this point of view and shows how species have failed in modern times to meet the challenge of man's impact on the environment because of 'weaknesses' or specializations in their ways of life. These specializations may be due to ecological factors, such as adaptation to an island environment, or to their method of reproduction, as in his comparison of what are called the r and K strategies, shown contrastingly by, for example, the titmouse on the one hand and, on the other, by the large birds of prey and sea birds.

Such terms may seem rather formidable to the layman, but he need have no fears; the author's style is calculated to be 'understanded of the people' and those who wish to follow up more specialized aspects have notes and a bibliography for each chapter at the end of the book to guide their further reading.

The book opens with a necessary chapter on the evolution of birds, which began 165 million years ago and in the course of which unnumbered species appeared, flourished and vanished. 'Clearly', as the author puts it, 'extinction is a natural part of the evolutionary process.' But man has brought to it a factor of acceleration that has led to the present critical situation in which many species face extinction long before their due time.

The second chapter brings out this aspect very well, summarizing the variety of ways in which a bird's future may be put in jeopardy, from accidental drowning in fishing nets to predation by mammals introduced on remote islands and finally by the attentions of egg-collectors and skin-hunters, as happened to the Great Auk, whose fate is among those described in Chapter 3.

The next four chapters range geographically; one is devoted to island birds, perhaps the most menaced group of all; another to the peculiar situation in New Zealand where methods both ingenious and heroic are being applied to restore the status of some unique birds. The chapters on North America and Europe cover continents where birds have been most studied and where a responsible attitude might be expected to have developed first; it is somewhat humbling to find how slow progress has been and how many species are still at risk.

Finally, there is the chapter on conservation in which Tim Halliday sets out clearly the problems that have to be faced when the will to conserve is there; the snags, for example, that underly the apparently promising technique of captive breeding for reintroduction to the original habitat. The pros and cons for conserving wild life are also examined closely and to me the author's arguments for the ecological case are convincing: we are all in it together.

It is unusual to find a professional biologist who is also an artist of great ability. There is no doubt that an author who can illustrate his own text is at a great advantage; when these illustrations are beauti-fully designed as well as making their biological point, there is an unexpected bonus. Tim Halliday has not been afraid to chance his arm too, as in his suggestion of how Great Auks used to fish. How much better to show them in action instead of as obvious copies of stuffed specimens.

I believe this extremely thoughtful book will have a considerable impact on attitudes to wild life conservation in general, and I feel honoured to have been asked to write a foreword to it.

April 1977   BRUCE CAMPBELL

Acknowledgements

IT has been my good fortune to have been able to carry out the research for this book in the Alexander Library of the Edward Grey Institute of Field Ornithology in Oxford and I would like to thank Dorothy Vincent and Anthony Cheke, past and present librarians, for all the help they have given me. I am indebted to Euan Dunn, Nick Davies and Nigel Collar for helpful discussions and for providing me with much useful information. Others who generously gave me factual material are Wilma Crowther, Tony Hallam, Bill Hardy, Peter Jenkins, Janet Kear, D. V. Merton, and Bernard Stonehouse. S. D. Housden of the Royal Society for the Protection of Birds and Miss S. Sweeting of the International Council for Bird Preservation kindly provided information and literature about their respective organizations. Robert Ditchfield, Diana Saville, Sheila McIlwraith and Jan Widdows have provided encouragement since the book was first conceived. I am indebted to Margaret Willes for the patience and consideration with which she has handled the production of this book. I am most grateful to Richard Cassels and Nick Davies for reading and making valuable comments on parts of the book and to Maggie Norris who typed the manuscript. My particular thanks go to Bruce Campbell who, as well as contributing the Foreword, has read the entire manuscript and has given me the benefit of his great experience, making many valuable suggestions. Finally, I would like to thank my wife, Carolyn, for her critical comments on the early drafts and for her unfailing support throughout.

Contents

List of Illustrations

LIST OF MAPS

Preface

—————⊰⊱—————

THE history of man's cultural and technological evolution is punctuated by the destruction of innumerable species of animals and plants. The unparallelled evolutionary success of the human species has been primarily due to man's capacity to modify his own environment, enabling him to invade and successfully colonize all parts of the world. Many animal species have been drastically reduced or exterminated through direct hunting by man, as he has continually sought new sources of food and clothing. In addition, through his varied efforts to create an ideal environment for himself he has destroyed or altered the environments of other species, forcing them to adapt so that they can coexist with man or driving them into a precarious existence in remote refuges and sometimes ultimately to extinction. While mankind has become particularly aware of this process in recent years, as accelerating population growth and industrial development combine to devour natural habitats and to generate pollutant waste, it is clear that man has been driving species to extinction since long before the industrial era. Many of the unique birds of New Zealand, for example, were exterminated or drastically reduced by early Polynesian invaders long before the arrival of the European settlers.

The extinction of species is of course not confined to the recent period of the earth's history in which man has been a dominating influence. In the evolutionary story of all forms of life competition between different species is a recurrent theme and countless forms, now known only from fossils, have been eliminated by the advent of other forms more successful at exploiting the environment. The cultural evolution of man, however, has been a more rapid and wide-ranging development than any other change that has occurred in the evolution of life on earth, affecting virtually all forms of life and taking place at a rate much faster than that at which most species can adapt. Thus, whereas the evolutionary pressures generated by the slow-acting changes occurring during the greater part of the evolutionary process tended to produce a variety of new species that replaced the old, the sudden changes caused by man tend to destroy species so quickly that no new forms can evolve to replace them.

There are those who regard these developments in a mood of fatalistic pessimism. While there is little reason to be optimistic that the process of extinction of our fellow creatures will be arrested in the near future, it is not the purpose of this book to dwell overlong on the sad history of extinct and endangered species of birds. This book attempts a constructive approach, my purpose in analysing the causes of past extinctions being to point the way to practical measures that may be taken in the future to halt the process of destruction. I shall describe in some detail a number of species of birds whose existence is in danger and discuss what might be done, and what in many instances is being done, to prevent their total disappearance. In recent years there has been a widespread and encouraging upsurge of interest in all aspects of conservation and wildlife protection as awareness of the plight of many species in the face of the threat from human development has increased. At the present time countless people around the world, both professional scientists and amateur enthusiasts, are engaged in the fight to slow the rate at which natural habitats are destroyed and species are exterminated. This book discusses some of the techniques that have been developed for the protection and preservation of birds with a view to assessing the prospects for the success of the conservation movement.

This book is not intended to be exhaustive; it does not contain an account of every extinct and endangered bird species. I have been selective in my choice of the species I discuss, preferring to deal with a few species in depth rather than provide a comprehensive account.

My aim in this approach has been to establish some general principles, to identify the causes of extinction and the means by which it may be prevented in the future.

Another aim of my selective approach to this subject is to attempt, through both word and picture, to bring the species I discuss to life in the mind of the reader. To many the image of an extinct or very rare bird is that of the stuffed museum specimen gathering dust or of a sad bundle of feathers huddled in a cage at the zoo. I have attempted to reconstruct, both from contemporary accounts of extinct species made when they were alive and by inference from many aspects of their remains, an image of the sort of life led by the species that I discuss. I hope that after reading this book the reader will have a fuller and richer picture of the Great Auk, the Dodo, the Passenger Pigeon and many other birds than that provided by a museum specimen or by the more scholarly and technical ornithological texts.

Behind every discussion of conservation lies the basic question, why should we bother to preserve other species? This book is intended to make a contribution towards answering this question. By attempting to bring to life some extinct species and by my account of those species facing a similar fate I hope to underline what has been lost and what is likely to be lost to man in terms of priceless aesthetic and scientific material. Most readers of this book will not need to be convinced of the aesthetic and scientific arguments for conservation, but it has to be recognized that to the vast majority of mankind such arguments have no significance whatsoever. The final chapter of this book includes a discussion of what I believe to be a more compelling argument for the preservation of other species. Every species that man exterminates is a symptom of the changes he is making in the world environment. Such changes, if they are allowed to continue unchecked, must ultimately lead to man's own extinction.

A recurrent theme throughout the book is the island and its significance in biological theory, in conservation and in the evolutionary history of birds. Islands are frequently inhabited by species that are quite unique to them and it was an awareness of this phenomenon, notably in the Galapagos, that was an important influence in the development of Darwin's theory of evolution. The great majority of extinct and endangered birds are insular species; clearly they are more vulnerable than continental species to the various causes of extinction. In recent years there has developed a new branch of ecology called Island Biogeography which is important not only to our understanding of how many and which species are found on a given island, but also in conservation and wildlife management. Any nature reserve is effectively an island surrounded by urban or agricultural habitats hostile to most species. An understanding of the dynamics of insular communities is vital if we are to design wildlife reserves that will successfully contribute to the survival of endangered species. Finally, an island can be regarded as a model ecosystem, a microcosm of the larger, worldwide community of species. By understanding the forces that regulate the stability of the smaller island community we may hopefully establish principles that will ultimately enable us to regulate our own stable world ecosystem. During the course of human history man's view of his own significance has continually been diminished so that we can now see our planet as a tiny dot in the vastness of space. This insignificant speck is itself an island, an island which supports a confined community of interdependent animals and plants of which man now finds himself the custodian.

This book is about birds; very similar books, developing the same themes, could be written about mammals, amphibians, insects, microbes and plants. Perhaps the greatest task facing mankind is to find a way to reverse the current trends by which we continually diminish the complexity and variety of our environment and instead devise a culture which can live in a stable balance with other forms of life. I hope that this book makes some small contribution towards the achievement of such a radical change.

I

The Evolution of Birds

THERE are about 8600 species of birds living in the world at the present time. A few of these species are flourishing and are increasing in numbers; many are holding their own, but many others are declining and a few are on the verge of extinction. To us the species seem to be a permanent entity; the living birds have remained essentially the same in appearance and habits since the beginning of human history. However, just as a photograph captures only a single moment in a person's life, so the period of human civilization is an infinitesimal part of the process of bird evolution which had its beginnings 165 million years ago. It is customary to liken the evolutionary process, in which a few ancestral forms give rise to several living species, to the growth of a tree, in which the outermost twigs represent the most recently evolved species. The species are grouped on the basis of their similarities and differences so that, just as a number of twigs are all connected to the same major branch, so groups or families of species are joined by their common descent from a single ancestor. The analogy with a tree is a limited one; in terms of the living species of birds the evolutionary tree has only a crown of terminal twigs. The greater part of the tree, its trunk and branches, has vanished in the past and we can only reconstruct how it might have been arranged by examining the affinities of the families of twigs. Here and there an occasional fossil may help us to connect the branches correctly.[1]

Trees grow, and as they grow terminal twigs become major branches and new twigs are formed, so that during its life a tree bears many more twigs than it ever has at any one time. Likewise, in the evolution of birds the 8600 species that now inhabit the earth are only a tiny fraction of the total that have existed since bird evolution began. Attempts to calculate the total number of bird species, using our knowledge of the fossil record, have produced figures ranging from 150,000 to 1,634,000, a discrepancy that shows how difficult it is to make estimates from the scanty fossil evidence available.[2] While we may never know with any accuracy how many species of birds have existed, it is clear that innumerable species have appeared, flourished and vanished during bird evolution.[3] Clearly extinction is a natural part of the evolutionary process. As this book is about birds that have recently become extinct, or may be about to do so, it is important to consider the role that natural extinction has played in the past to establish the extent to which modern extinctions are a continuation of the natural process or, alternatively, a manifestation of human civilization. The fact that some living species are flourishing while others are in decline suggests that some species may be more prone to extinction than others. An analysis of the evolutionary process, and the role played by natural extinction, may give us some clues as to why some species seem to be more vulnerable than others.

The evolutionary story of the birds begins in the Jurassic period, when the whole appearance of the world was radically different from what we see today. The major continents that we know today did not exist as such; there were just two huge continents, which we now call Laurasia and Gondwana. The world climate was warmer and more equable than it is today and the vegetation consisted of varieties of ferns and conifers. The deciduous trees and flowering plants that are so dominant a feature of the modern world had not yet evolved. The dominant form of animal life was the reptiles; this was the age of the dinosaurs. We tend to think of the dinosaurs as huge Brontosaurs and Tyrannosaurs, but the majority of them were small creatures, among them a group of slender, long-tailed animals called the Coelurosaurs that ran about on their hind legs. There is no doubt that the birds are descended from reptiles; both lay much the same kind of egg, which provides the embryo with a complete life-support system within a protective shell, both possess scales and there are many skeletal similarities. Of all the many sorts of dinosaurs the Coelurosaurs have most in common with the birds. Although the most obvious feature of birds that differentiates them from reptiles is that they have wings with which they can fly, in fact the birds were not the first animals to evolve flight; there were two other 'experiments' with flight going on at the time the first birds were evolving. These were the Dawn Lizards, which possessed greatly elongated ribs carrying a flap of skin on each side of the body, and the Pterodactyls, which had wings consisting of skin stretched across elongated fingers. Both were probably only able to glide in the manner of a hang-glider; they had to clamber to the top of a cliff or a tree in order to become airborne. While both these groups of flying reptiles flourished for millions of years, they eventually died out, perhaps in the face of competition from the more successful birds.

The crucial innovation that gave the ancestral birds a competitive edge over the other flying creatures was the feather. Feathers are derived from the scales of the Coelurosaur ancestors, which gradually became longer and divided into separate parts and which developed muscles at their base so that they could be moved independently of one another. Feathers gave the early birds a vital advantage in that between them and the skin was trapped a layer of air which effectively insulated the body from the vagaries of the temperature of the outside world. While the reptiles were cold-blooded and were only able to be active when the air about them was warm, the birds were able to control the exchange of heat between their bodies and the air by altering the positions of their feathers and so became warm-blooded and able to be active in all weathers. In addition, the bird wing was less vulnerable to damage than the membranous sails of the Dawn Lizards and Pterodactyls, which would have been useless if they had been torn. If a bird loses a wing feather the wing does not lose its rigidity in the way a torn reptilian wing would have done since the other feathers retain their stiffness.

Among the fossil remains from the Jurassic period is a pigeon-sized bird called *Archeopteryx*, a creature that provides a perfect missing link

1. Archeopteryx, *the earliest fossil bird, from the Jurassic period*

between the Coelurosaurs and the modern birds.[4] In common with the reptiles, *Archeopteryx* possessed teeth, a long tail and a generally light, spindly skeleton. Its affinities with the birds are shown by the possession of feathers and feet adapted for perching. In other respects, such as the size of its skull, its overall build and its beak, it is intermediate between the reptiles and the birds. It is rare in palaeontology that so ideal a clue to the course of evolution is found. It is unlikely that all the modern birds are direct descendants of *Archeopteryx* since the twenty-five million years that separate it from the next fossil birds we know do not seem sufficient time to account for the many differences between them. *Archeopteryx* may represent just one of a number of lineages of early birds that were evolving during the Jurassic. It seems likely that *Archeopteryx* was an arboreal bird, using the claws that it carried on the front edge of its wings to clamber up among the branches of the giant ferns and coniferous trees that flourished at that time, running along the larger branches on its powerful hind legs and using its outstretched wings to glide down to the lower branches of neighbouring trees. (The young of a living bird, the Hoatzin of South America, have claws on the front edge of their wings which they use for climbing about in the trees.) *Archeopteryx* cannot have been capable of powered, flapping flight in the manner of modern birds as its breastbone was too small and fragile to carry the large muscles necessary for beating the wings, and the wing bones themselves were too weak to sustain the forces that would have been exerted on them during flying. It has been suggested that these wings may not have evolved as a means of flight at all, but as a device for catching prey. They could have been used as two large brushes for gathering in insects that were then snapped up in the bill.[5]

Just as a human invention, such as the wheel, leads to the development of a profusion of further inventions, so a successful evolutionary innovation may give rise to a diversity of new forms that make use of it in different ways. This process is called adaptive radiation and it is well illustrated by the evolution of the birds.[6] The descendants of *Archeopteryx* and its contemporaries, which almost certainly lived in the primeval forests, have successfully colonized every conceivable type of habitat, so that birds are to be found in every corner of the world, be it land or sea, arctic icecap or tropical forest. The ancestral birds possessed teeth and probably fed on insects and other small animals. Among the modern birds, none of which have teeth, we find not only insectivores but flesh-eaters, seed-eaters and nectar-drinkers and many other types whose dietary specialities are reflected in, for example, the wide variety of bill shapes that they show. By the end of the Cretaceous period, some sixty-four million years ago, it is estimated that there were about 2000 species of birds. Most of the fossils from this period are of water birds very similar to some modern birds; there were grebes, cormorants, pelicans, flamingoes, ibises, rails and sandpipers. The scarcity of fossil remains of land birds from this period does not mean that few existed, rather that aquatic habitats are more suitable for the formation of fossils than the dry land. The process of radiation and diversification continued so that by the end of the Miocene era, about thirteen million years ago, there were around 11,000 species. This period represents the

2. Hesperornis, *a fossil bird from the Cretaceous period*

zenith of bird evolution; since then the number of species in the world
has been declining.

Many of the fossil birds of which we have remains were very large.
In the Cretaceous period there lived a diving bird called *Hesperornis*
which was over six feet long and possessed teeth and huge paddle-like
feet. In the Eocene period the North American plains were the home of
Diatryma, a heavily-built, ostrich-like bird, standing over seven feet
tall with a head the size of a horse's and a massive hooked beak.
Diatryma was a carnivore and seems to have adopted the same habits
as the extinct predatory dinosaurs, but in its turn it was eventually
replaced by carnivorous mammals which evolved at a later date. In the
Miocene era there were giant penguins standing over five feet tall,
some two feet taller than the Emperor Penguin, largest of the living
species. But these giant birds are in no way representative of fossil
birds, most of which were similar in size to their living equivalents.

3. Diatryma, *a fossil bird from the Eocene period*

What they illustrate is a tendency, shown by other animal groups such as the reptiles and the insects, to give rise to lineages that evolve ever-greater size.[7] In most cases this trend reached its peak in the past, so that these gigantic fossils are larger than any equivalent species alive today. As we shall see later in this chapter, there are good reasons to suppose that large animals are more likely to become extinct than smaller ones.

Essential to any discussion of evolution is an understanding of the process of speciation, by which new species are formed from old. A species is defined as a population of essentially similar organisms which freely breed with one another, but which do not breed with members of other such groups. For an ancestral species to give rise to two or more new species it must first become separated into isolated sub-populations. Each population undergoes adaptation through natural selection to the environment in which it lives and, since each is likely to be in a somewhat different environment, they will evolve in different ways and gradually become differentiated from one another. This divergent evolution will only occur if the separation between the two populations is total; any interbreeding between them will result in a tendency for their differences to become 'diluted'. However, at a certain stage in this process the differences between the sub-populations will have become so great that, should interbreeding occur, the hybrid offspring will be at a disadvantage, being inadequately equipped to survive in either environment. In these circumstances natural selection will favour the evolution of isolating mechanisms, often in the form of courtship behaviour, which preclude interbreeding. Ancestral species may become divided by the formation of any geographical feature that restricts movement across it, such as mountain ranges, large expanses of water and ice sheets. A common way in which isolation occurs, especially among birds, to whom wings have given the power of long-distance dispersal, is when a sub-population of a mainland species colonizes an island on which evolutionary changes take place independently of those occurring in the ancestral mainland population. Throughout its long history the surface of the earth has been constantly changing, with new continents, mountain ranges and seas being created and transformed, producing pockets of unexploited environment which are open to invasion by populations from existing species.

An excellent example of evolutionary opportunism is provided by the Blue Chaffinch on the Canary Islands. This species is clearly descended from the European Common Chaffinch but differs markedly in colour, being almost entirely blue and lacking the pink breast of the common form. It also differs slightly in its overall size and in the shape of its bill. It appears that a population of the mainland species, which inhabits both deciduous and coniferous woodlands, invaded the Canaries at some time in the past and became adapted to the coniferous forests that cover much of these islands. In doing so they diverged from their ancestors in habits, anatomy and colouration. When, at a later date, a second invasion by the mainland form occurred, the new colonists occupied only the areas of deciduous woodland, being unable to compete with their descendants in the coniferous forests.[8]

The twin evolutionary processes of adaptive radiation and speciation, on the other hand, are nowhere better illustrated than in groups of birds that have colonized remote archipelagoes. Indeed, it was a group of small birds that have colonized the Galapagos Islands that largely inspired Charles Darwin in his formation of the theory of evolution through natural selection. These birds, called Darwin's Finches, now comprise fourteen distinct species, all derived from a common finch-like ancestor which at some time made the 600-mile crossing from the South American mainland to the Galapagos and the Island of Cocos.[9] On each of the islands sub-populations of this ancestral species evolved independently, diverging most strikingly in their feeding habits as manifested in the form of their beaks. There are now six distinct types, including heavy-billed birds that eat seeds, long-billed insect eaters and a remarkable chisel-billed woodpecker that uses a cactus spine to extricate insects from crevices. In the course of time some of these species made the crossing from their original island to other islands, so that today most islands are populated by more than one species. However, the more remote Cocos Island, 600 miles to the north of the Galapagos, contains only one species, the Cocos Finch. An even more impressive example of this kind of evolution is provided by another archipelago, the Hawaiian Islands, where the original colonists, one or two species of North American honeycreeper, were the ancestors of no less than twenty-two distinct species. These have specialized in a variety of dietary habits, and include nectar, fruit, seed, nut, caterpillar and insect eaters.[10]

The biological significance of islands does not only lie in the way they so vividly illustrate important aspects of evolution. They are also remarkable for the fact that they are often the home of species that are quite unlike birds found elsewhere. Such species are usually highly endemic; that is, they are confined to one or a very few islands, are specially adapted to the particular conditions that prevail there, and are thus unable to survive and flourish elsewhere.[11] Birds, with their superior powers of dispersal, have frequently colonized islands which are too isolated from the mainland to be invaded by other forms of life, especially mammals. In many such species the power of flight, which was so advantageous on the mainland where it made possible dispersion over a wide area and very effective escape from predators, became redundant. Many island birds, notably several species of rails and the extinct Dodo on Mauritius, became flightless, with their wings greatly reduced in size. Such a trend was possible on islands because of the absence of the ground-living predatory mammals that were present in their ancestral mainland home. The reason why the tendency to lose the power of flight would be favoured by natural selection under such circumstances is that the energy and resources saved by having smaller wings could be invested in other, positively advantageous ways, such as a larger body size.

A major change in the nature of the earth which has had a profound effect on the course of evolution is the phenomenon of continental drift.[12] The present alignment of the continents is the result of a process by which one huge continent, called Pangaea, broke up into smaller pieces which began to drift away from one another. Eventually some of these moving segments met one another and combined to form new, larger land masses. The break-up of Pangaea began some 200 million years ago and initially produced two large continents, Laurasia in the north and Gondwana in the south. As they separated these two masses also began to break up, Laurasia into two parts which are now North America and Eurasia, Gondwana into five parts, South America, Africa, India, Australia and Antarctica. Eventually North and South America became joined together, Africa combined with Europe and India coalesced with Asia. Australia and Antarctica moved away from the rest and have remained separated. While these moving continents remained isolated from each other evolution within them continued along independent lines. As a result it is now possible to divide the world into faunal regions or realms, each characterized by distinctive groups of species. These realms were first described in 1858 by P. L. Sclater, who noted discontinuities in the world-wide distribution of the families of birds. Later Alfred Russel Wallace pointed out that other animals, notably the mammals, showed similar anomalies in their distribution. When he crossed what is now called Wallace's Line between the Indonesian islands of Bali and Lombok, a distance of only twenty miles, he noticed a complete change in the species of birds and other creatures around him. There are six faunal regions and they correspond closely to the continental masses that resulted from the break-up of Laurasia and Gondwana (see map).

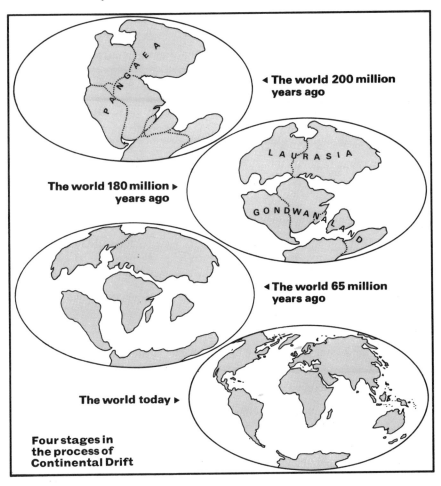

◄ **The world 200 million years ago**

The world 180 million ► years ago

◄ **The world 65 million years ago**

The world today ►

Four stages in the process of Continental Drift

The importance of continental drift in the evolutionary history of the birds can be illustrated by the vexed question of the evolution of the Ratites, a group of generally large, flightless birds that have many features in common but which live in widely separated parts of the world. They include the African Ostrich, the South American Rheas, the Cassowaries of New Guinea, the Australian Emu, the Kiwi and the extinct Moas from New Zealand and the extinct Elephant Birds from Madagascar. The many similarities in their appearance, morphology and habits tend to suggest that all are descended from a common ancestor, but if this is so, how did they come to be so widely dispersed?

Until recently there have been two principal theories. The first is that they did not have a common ancestor but that they each evolved from different forms, but along similar, convergent paths so that their similarities are due to their having been subjected to similar evolutionary pressures. The alternative theory is that they are derived from a single ancestor which, to have colonized such widely separated areas, must have been a flying bird. Then, in each area, flightlessness evolved independently but along similar, parallel lines. Recently Joel Cracraft has pointed out that both these theories, neither of which is very satisfactory, are based on the implicit, false assumption that the areas where Ratites are found today have always been in the same place. His theory is that the Ratites are all descended from a single, flightless ancestor which was widely distributed across Gondwana and that separate populations became isolated on each of the land masses that resulted from its breaking up.[13]

The theory of continental drift gives a new perspective in our view of the evolution of life on earth. We can see that at one time the world was an archipelago of continents on which evolution progressed in essentially the same way as it does on archipelagos of small islands like the Galapagos and the Hawaiian islands, though on a much larger scale. Continental drift has not stopped; even at the present time the gap between North America and Europe is widening at the rate of about one foot every hundred years.

The movements and realignments of the continents are not the only large-scale changes that have influenced the course of animal evolution. There have also been dramatic changes in the earth's climate. In the Miocene era, when bird species were most numerous, the world climate was so warm and equable that northern Europe was covered by tropical forest and, as the fossil record shows, hornbills and trogons flew over what is now Paris. Since then there has been a trend towards generally cooler and less equable climates and the deciduous forests have been compressed towards the equator. This process was accelerated in the Pleistocene period, twelve million to eleven thousand years ago, when there was a succession of ice ages in which huge glaciers moved southwards from the north pole and retreated again. The decline in the number of bird species since the Miocene can be attributed to these climatic changes and the changes in the world's vegetation that resulted from them. Tropical, deciduous forests support a much richer variety of species than do temperate habitats. At the present time the Neotropical region, which includes the vast but steadily disappearing tropical forests of South America, contains nearly three times as many species of birds as the entire Palaearctic region, whose area is many times larger but consists mostly of temperate and sub-arctic habitats.

Birds do not live in an environment that consists only of physical aspects such as geography and climate. They also have a biotic environment made up of many plant and animal species with which they have relationships such as those between predators and prey, parasites and hosts and between competitors for a resource, such as food or space. As new species evolve they impose selection pressures on existing species through such relationships, thus contributing to the continual process of change which is the spur to evolution. As we have seen, the giant fossil bird *Diatryma* probably became extinct in the face of competition from the newly-evolving carnivorous mammals.

The evolution of the birds thus has to be seen against the background of a constantly changing world. Geographical, climatic and biotic changes combine to create new conditions which tend to force existing species into extinction but which provide opportunities for exploitation by new forms. It is this continued process of change that has led to the extinction of the great majority of bird species that have inhabited the earth. In one sense many of these species did not become extinct. Those which, through adaptation to new circumstances, became transformed into new species, or which were ancestral to two or more new species, became extinct only in a superficial sense. The theory of evolution by natural selection is not about the survival of species; as formulated by Charles Darwin it is about the survival of individuals and their offspring. To be strictly accurate, it is not even about individuals, but about genes, the units of inheritance which are passed on from one generation to the next.[14] Genes express themselves by influencing the structure, physiology and behaviour of the individual animals that carry them, and the successful genes are those which influence their individual 'hosts' in such a way that they have more descendants than other individuals. Since these descendants will tend to carry the same genes as their parents, the number of successful genes in the population will increase. Ancestral species which give rise to new species may have vanished as a distinctive group of individual animals, but many of their genes will have been passed on to their descendant species. It is quite likely that the birds we see today carry identical genes to some of those carried by *Archeopteryx* 126 million years ago. Seen in this light, we can regard bird evolution as a process in which some successful ancestral genes, particularly those which determine such characteristics as wings, feathers and warm-bloodedness, have spread and multiplied by finding expression through a continually changing variety of forms. Sometimes these successful genes combined with others to form species which, like *Diatryma* or the more recent Dodo, failed to adapt to changing conditions and died out without giving rise to new forms. To return to the analogy with a tree, these represent terminal twigs which, like some of those on the tree, die and fall off before they become larger branches.

Biologists are so impressed by the intricate and precise ways in which animals have become adapted to their environment that they tend to assume that natural selection is a process which produces perfectly adapted species. J. B. S. Haldane called this Pangloss's theorem, after the character in Voltaire's *Candide* who continually intones that 'All is for the best in the best of all possible worlds.' It is wrong to assume that, because natural selection tends to produce perfect adaptations, animals are perfectly adapted in all respects. If they were there would be no evolutionary lineages ending in species which had no descendants. Natural selection produces adaptations which are advantageous to the individual's survival, and not necessarily to that of the species. The discrepancy between the kind of perfection that natural selection tends to produce and that which would prevent extinction exists because of the different time scales on which environmental changes take place. Many species are beautifully adapted to the rhythmic and predictable changes that take place during the lifetime of an individual, such as the rotation of the seasons and the rise and fall of the tides. The large-scale geographical and climatic changes I have discussed above are very long-term changes, acting over a period vastly greater than the lifetime of individuals. Since natural selection acts on the differential survival of individuals from one generation to the next it can only produce adapatations in response to environmental changes on a generation-to-generation basis. It cannot create adaptations for circumstances which will apply in the unforseeable future. Some lineages have been able to survive for millions of years on the basis of this generation-to-generation adaptive change; others have not. In the next part of this chapter I shall discuss why some species are better able to adapt to changes than others.

So far I have discussed the evolution of birds in a rather general way, without being at all specific about the ways in which species must alter in the face of environmental changes if they are to avoid extinction. Clearly, adaptive changes may occur in any aspect of a species' physical make-up, such as its beak shape or its colouration, or in its behaviour or physiology. Extinction, however, is a phenomenon that can be considered not only at the level of an individual's adaptations to its environment, but also at the level of the species population. In a population there is a continual turnover of individuals as young birds are hatched and reared by their parents while other birds die through predation, disease or old age. A viable population is one in which the reproductive rate, that is, the rate at which young birds enter the adult population, exceeds or is equal to the death rate. If the reproductive rate falls below the death rate the population will decline and will eventually become extinct. Reproductive rates and death rates are not random variables; they vary from species to species but are as much characteristics of species as bill shapes or colour patterns. If we are to understand the underlying causes of natural extinction we must discover why it is that some bird species have high, while others have low, reproductive rates, and why some species are typically long-lived whereas others are short-lived.

In the last few years these questions have been the subject of considerable analysis in the field of theoretical ecology in an attempt to express the relationships between birth rate, death rate, longevity, body size and efficiency of habitat exploitation in terms of evolution by natural selection. Selection favours those individuals whose inheritable characteristics enable them to leave more offspring than other individuals, that is, it favours the ability to achieve a large reproductive output. Broadly speaking, an animal may do this in two ways. It can devote most of its energy and resources to one large reproductive effort early in its life, or, alternatively, it can be long-lived and achieve a high reproductive output by breeding several times. In the language of theoretical ecology these two strategies are referred to as the r- and the K-strategy respectively.[15] We need not concern ourselves here with what r and K actually represent; suffice it to say that the r-strategy is that in which long-term survival is sacrificed for a large short-term reproductive output whereas the K-strategy is that in which short-term reproductive output is sacrificed for long-term survival. Which strategy the members of a species adopt depends on the general characteristics of their habitat. In temporary, relatively unstable habitats, such as land which is in the process of being overgrown by young bushes and trees, we find the r-strategists. These are opportunistic species who quickly invade newly-formed habitats. They are generally small birds, they breed early in life, they lay large clutches of eggs and they tend to die young. In stable habitats, in which food supply tends to be fairly constant, we find the K-strategists, large birds who breed several times but do not breed for the first time until relatively late in life. Since they have a low reproductive rate they have evolved adaptations that tend to minimize their death rates. They are long-lived and well protected against predators, partly by virtue of their large size, they show prolonged parental care of their young and they tend to be very efficient at finding their food.

This dichotomy can best be illustrated by means of extreme examples of each strategy. The European Blue Tit is an r-strategist. It is a small bird which utilizes a food source, the caterpillars of moths, showing dramatic year-to-year fluctuations. It breeds when it is one year old, lays a clutch of ten or twelve eggs and has a high chance of dying before the next breeding season. The California Condor is a K-strategist. One of the largest flying birds in the world, it does not breed for the first time until it is five years old; thereafter it breeds every other year, but lays only one egg each time. Individuals may live for fifty years and it has been estimated that it takes a pair of birds no less than twenty-one years to be certain of raising the two chicks that will eventually replace them in the population. Some albatrosses show similar life histories and do not breed until they are nine or eleven years old. Apart from these differences in their life histories, r- and K-strategists tend to differ in the extent to which they show specializations for one particular type of habitat. The European House Sparrow, a small r-strategist, is able to feed on a wide variety of foods, including seeds, insects and all manner of human debris. It is probable that this ability to eat almost anything has contributed to the considerable success with which the sparrow has invaded North America since its introduction in 1852.[16] In contrast, the albatrosses, extreme K-strategists, feed almost exclusively on squid and often have to fly vast distances to find them. So marked is the food specialization of the Everglade Kite, which lives almost entirely on one species of snail, that it even has a specially adapted hooked beak for extracting its food from its shell. (Plate II).

These differences in overall 'life-strategy' between species are profoundly important when we consider the extent to which any particular species is likely to become extinct. There are three reasons for supposing that K-strategists will be more vulnerable than r-strategists. Firstly, since they tend to be larger, each individual requires a large share of available food and space, with the result that, within a restricted area of habitat, the population size must be relatively small. Thus K-strategists tend to be intrinsically rare. Secondly, they have evolved low reproductive rates so that, should the population become depleted by some natural disaster, it will take a long time before its numbers can be built up again. If a second catastrophe follows a few years later the population may still be at such a low ebb that it is totally wiped out. Finally, and most important of all, a K-strategist species will be less able to adapt to a changing environment. It is a feature of sexual reproduction that the offspring all differ slightly from one another and from their parents. The more rapidly new offspring are produced, the more likely is it that some will appear with combinations of characters that are well-adapted to the changed environment. Thus the faster a species' reproductive rate, the more effectively it can keep pace with a changing environment. A K-strategist species is less likely to be able to produce new and different offspring at a rate fast enough to keep pace with environment changes.

The vulnerability of the K-strategist to rapid environmental change may be the reason for the rapid decline and extinction of the dinosaurs. They flourished during the Cretaceous area, a period of prolonged climatic stability, a condition which tends to favour the K-strategist. Many of the dinosaurs were very large, suggesting that selection along these lines was taking place. Towards the end of the Cretaceous the world climate became unsettled and more variable, a condition which typically favours r-strategists. The dinosaurs were apparently unable to adapt fast enough and so became extinct. The large fossil birds mentioned earlier may also have been K-strategists who became the victims of rapid environmental change.

Of course, in making this distinction between r- and K-strategists and the susceptibility of each to extinction I have made a number of sweeping generalizations; naturally, there are exceptions. The Fulmar, a large, slow-breeding, pelagic species from the north Atlantic, has shown a steady population increase over the last 200 years. This seems to be due to an increase in its food supply in the form of fish offal thrown out by the numerous fishing boats that frequent the north Atlantic. In contrast, the Passenger Pigeon of North America, which I shall discuss in Chapter 4, showed many of the characteristics of an r-strategist but rapidly became extinct in the face of human civilization.

In this chapter I have described evolution as a process in which there is a continual turnover of species as a result of the fact that the world environment has been continually changing. Each new species adapts to its own environment in its own way, according to the demands made by that environment, and, as we have seen, some environments lead to the evolution of adaptations that are advantageous to the individuals but which make the species as a whole vulnerable to extinction when those environments start to change rapidly. Two groups of species in particular are more prone than others to extinction, the highly endemic inhabitants of remote islands and the large, slow-breeding, often highly specialized K-strategists that have evolved in relatively stable environments.[17] It is significant that 91 per cent of the bird species that have become extinct since 1680 were the inhabitants of islands. Many of the most endangered species about which there is now so much concern are large birds such as the California Condor and Whooping Crane of

North America, some of the bustards from Europe and Asia and the Kakapo of New Zealand.

The environmental changes discussed in this chapter have been very long-term and, on human time-scales, extremely slow changes, such as the movements of the continents and changes in world climate. In the next chapter I shall discuss changes that have occurred at a vastly greater rate, the changes due to the activities of modern man. Human influences have not affected all species to the same degree; some have perished, others have declined but a few have actually increased in numbers. These differences are largely attributable to their evolutionary history, which has determined the extent to which they have evolved the capacity to adjust to changed circumstances.

2

Birds and Man

THROUGHOUT the history of human civilization the relationship between birds and mankind has been a complex and varied one.[1] In many cultures birds, with their ability to fly, have symbolized the essential freedom of the human spirit. Birds of prey have often been symbols of power and authority, doves have represented peace, and several species have been identified with deities. In ancient Greece the goddess Athena took the form of an owl and in Egypt the Sacred Ibis was the embodiment of Thoth, the god of wisdom and magic. In contrast, man has repeatedly exercised his destructive powers to exact the most appalling carnage among bird populations when he has found them a convenient source of food and other essentials. When the Polynesian islanders invaded and colonized New Zealand, for example, they found there a rich variety of birds they had never seen before. Many of these became incorporated in their mythology; others, particularly the Moas, they hunted for food and gradually exterminated. A similar dichotomy of attitudes exists today. In many parts of the world ornithology is a thriving pastime and considerable resources are expended in the conservation and protection of birds. At the same time whole industries are devoted to the destruction of those birds which are regarded as pests or which provide an economically viable source of food.

Man has achieved a position of virtual dominance over all the other species of animals. This success is seen both in the phenomenal growth of the human population and in man's ability to colonize almost all parts of the earth. This capacity arises largely from man's unique combination of intelligence and ingenuity which together enable him to modify practically any environment to suit his own requirements. In this chapter I shall discuss some of the ways in which man, particularly during the spread of Western civilization, has changed the world environment. For the most part this process has been a destructive one and has been at the expense of the majority of species of animals and plants. Sometimes the confrontation between birds and human interests has been direct, for example when birds are killed to provide food or clothing. More often man's influence has been indirect, through his manipulation of the environment which may affect birds in many varied and complex ways. The impact of primitive man on the environment was generally slight, man simply assuming the role of a predator, and many primitive societies have lived for thousands of years in a stable co-existence with other creatures. More recently, however, and particularly since the industrial revolution, human population growth and technological developments have increased man's powers of exploitation and the balance between man and nature has been destroyed.

In some instances the changes wrought by man have actually been of benefit to birds. Human societies generate vast quantities of waste and some species, notably some of the gulls, have shown a spectacular population increase in recent years, probably as a result of this addition to their normal food supply. In towns and cities gardens create a varied environment in which many species are able to breed successfully, but it is unlikely that gardens support as many birds, in terms of either individuals or species, as did the natural habitats that they have replaced. Agriculture also provides opportunities for some birds which, as we shall see later in this chapter, often become serious pests.

The bird species most important to man as a source of food, chickens, turkeys, ducks and geese, are now largely domesticated and are produced by sophisticated agricultural techniques. However, in many parts of the world wild birds still play a vital part in the domestic economy. The most commonly exploited species are large birds which form dense breeding colonies, since these provide a maximum return for a minimum of effort. Many seabirds fulfil these requirements and throughout the world auks, penguins, shearwaters and albatrosses have for hundreds of years been harvested by local inhabitants for their meat, eggs, feathers and oil. In some places traditions have developed by which the over-exploitation of seabird colonies is avoided. For example, on the Faeroes and formerly on St Kilda, where puffins and guillemots have long been collected, only a certain number are taken each year and the population has been maintained at a fairly constant size. Around Lake Myvatn in Iceland, where large numbers of ducks congregate to breed, eggs are collected in very large numbers, but farmers have evolved a policy of leaving four eggs in each nest. In other places man has not been so prudent and farsighted and the scale of his depredations has been staggering. In 1857 an estimated half a million penguins were killed for their oil on the Falkland Islands. Around 1900 Japanese fishermen killed more than five million albatrosses on Bonin Island in the Pacific. Some of the figures for egg-collecting are equally dramatic. In 1901 630,000 eggs of the Jackass Penguin were collected on islands around the South African coast. In 1935 it is estimated that 300,000 eggs of the Black-headed Gull were sold in one British market. Exploitation on this scale cannot be sustained for long if populations are not to be destroyed, and most of these species are now protected. However, it is estimated that at the present time approximately 100 million songbirds are killed each year in Italy alone.

The controlled, farsighted harvesting of birds like that practised by the inhabitants of St Kilda and the Faeroes seems to have developed in small, rather isolated communities where man is more aware that the resources of nature are not infinite. When men have explored and colonized new and larger areas they have tended to adopt a less prudent policy towards species that have provided their food. The Great Auk, which nested in colonies on a number of desolate islands in the North Atlantic, was butchered by fishermen, for whom it provided a vital source of fresh meat. The early colonists of North America so devastated the huge breeding colonies of the Passenger Pigeon that from being one of the most abundant species in the world it became extinct in a period of less than 150 years. A similar departure from accepted practice was shown by the British colonists in many parts of the world. They took with them their taste for hunting and shooting, but they tended to forget conservationist practices such as the observance of a close season on game birds.

In primitive societies the hunting of birds may be a serious business, the meat acquired thereby being a major component of the diet. In more advanced societies there are many alternative sources of food to that gained by hunting and improved weapons have made it possible to kill many more birds than are required to maintain a balanced diet. In its modern forms hunting is a recreational activity, and its original purpose, that of acquiring meat, has receded in importance. Some species of birds have become extinct or severely reduced in numbers by the activities of hunters. The extinct Heath Hen of North America and the Pink-headed Duck of India were both wiped out largely as a result of over-hunting and at the present time the bustards of Europe, Africa and Asia are threatened by illegal hunting. In the developed countries hunting has become a highly sophisticated and economically important business but its overall effect on wildlife need not be detrimental. Whatever one may think about the ethics of blood sports, they do have a beneficial effect on wildlife in that many game species and their habitats are carefully conserved in order that there will be enough birds to shoot at. However, the balance between careful game management and over-exploitation is a delicate one and the reckless use of modern hunting techniques can threaten a species' survival. There has been considerable concern in America over the practice of shooting birds from aircraft, which negates any chance the bird might have had against the gun through flight. Another problem is the shooting of birds during migration. A number of species migrate along well-defined narrow flight paths, so that during migration the observer gets a greatly inflated view of their numbers, and this has encouraged the view that shooting cannot adversely affect their numbers. The Eskimo Curlew and the Whooping Crane of North America, both migrating species that are now extremely rare, have been reduced in numbers largely as a result of being hunted during migration. An indirect hazard to birds resulting from hunting is lead poisoning, which has been found to affect ducks which ingest lead shot when they are

4. American Egrets

feeding from the bottom of ponds where it has accumulated during
duck-shoots.

Falconry is a very specialized form of hunting in which birds of prey
are trained to catch game birds. This ancient art was developed in the
Middle East and has since spread to Europe and America. Recently
there has been a resurgence of interest in falconry and this has created
a serious threat to several species of birds of prey whose numbers are
already greatly reduced as a result of a variety of other factors. Eggs and
nestlings are taken from nests, illegally in many countries, and sold to
falconers who are often prepared to pay very high prices for them.

A number of species of birds have been hunted for their feathers to
satisfy the sartorial requirements of the rich. At one time the demand
for ostrich feathers was so great that it became economically viable to
farm ostriches. Today, when ostrich feathers are no longer fashionable,
some 25,000 ostriches are reared and slaughtered each year in South
Africa for their skin, which is made into handbags and other accessories.

The American Egret was at one time severely endangered as a result of being hunted for its plumes; in 1902 nearly 1½ tons of feathers were sold to milliners in London. Fortunately a change in fashion came soon enough and today this beautiful bird is fairly common again. In Iceland the collection of down from the nests of Eider Ducks is carefully controlled by law. The Great Auk was not so fortunate; in the later years of its decline it was being slaughtered principally for the sake of its feathers, which were used to stuff bedding.

Perhaps the most indefensible form of direct killing of birds is that carried out by some ornithologists, or at least people who profess a keen interest in birds. There is still a highly lucrative trade in the skins and eggs of very rare birds. The danger of this sort of collecting is that the pressure on a species increases as it becomes rarer. The great ornithologist Walter Lawry Buller collected large numbers of New Zealand birds in the nineteenth century and concentrated particularly on the rarer species.[2] He saw that they were rapidly declining in numbers and his aim was to preserve as many museum specimens as possible before they became extinct. The philosophy of some nineteenth-century ornithologists is well illustrated by A. W. Crichton's book *A Naturalist's Ramble to the Orcades*, published in 1866, from which the following is a characteristic sample:

> About the centre of this peaty but partly-cultivated vale I crossed a little burn whose waters bubbled onwards to the loch, and here I had the pleasure of obtaining in very perfect plumage a pair of that very delicately pencilled bird the redshank (*Totanus calidris*). The male bird arose very suddenly some distance before I approached the stream, and, having received my charge of small-shot, flew in widening circles, apparently untouched, higher and further up the valley, and then fell, burying its crimson beak in the soft soil. It would have ill become me, after thus ruthlessly desecrating their domestic hearth, to have left his now sonorous mate to endure the cares and sorrows of disconsolate widowhood; so after indulging a lengthened observation of her beautiful airy unlaboured mode of flight, I raised my second barrel and consigned her to a timely and inglorious decease.

The general attitude of ornithologists to birds has changed dramatically over the years and this destructive approach is mostly a thing of the past. Largely influenced by the writings of pioneer ethologists like Konrad Lorenz and Niko Tinbergen, the modern ornithologist tends to be more interested in the behaviour of birds in their natural surroundings and less in collecting skins and eggs. However, the hunting of rarities remains a problem and must be countered by constant vigilance. Each year in Britain the Royal Society for the Protection of Birds brings a number of prosecutions against illegal collectors. The breeding sites of very rare species are often closely guarded, or else their whereabouts are kept secret.

Another practice which is detrimental to bird populations and which, like the collecting of specimens by ornithologists, is the unfortunate result of a demand created by those who apparently love and are interested in birds, is the collecting of birds for keeping as cage pets or zoo specimens.[3] The problem with the trade in live birds is that it depletes wild populations to an extent that greatly exceeds the number of birds that actually find their way into cages and aviaries. Birds caught in the wild generally do not take kindly to capture and there are frequent accounts in the press of large numbers dying as a result of bad treatment in transit on aircraft. One of the most highly coveted cage birds is the brilliant red Cock of the Rock from the northern Andes and it has been estimated that for every one that safely arrives at its destination, no less than fifty others perish.

Apart from killing birds for his direct gain, man frequently destroys them where he regards them as competitors. Throughout the world man has changed the face of the land, destroying the natural vegetation, so as to convert the land to agricultural use. While this has destroyed the habitats of indigenous birds it has created new habitats which other species are ideally equipped to exploit. Modern agricultural trends are towards the creation of monocultures, large areas of land given over to the growing of a single crop, which maximize the efficiency with which the land is used. Monocultures provide large areas of uniform and abundant food which are ideal for exploitation by small, migratory, fast-breeding species of birds, the r-strategists described in the previous chapter. These species are specially adapted to be able to locate new

5. The Cock of the Rock

areas of suitable habitat and to colonize them rapidly. Their natural predators are usually slow-breeding species unable to increase in numbers at the same rate and so an unchecked population explosion occurs and the birds become serious pests. In South and East Africa the Weaver Finches have built up such enormous flocks that they have caused the total failure of crops with a resulting famine among the human population. Other birds capable of this sort of large-scale destruction include pigeons, starlings, finches and parrots. In North America the early colonists felled the forests of the east and turned the land over to farming. The endemic Carolina Parakeet became a serious pest in orchards and gardens and its extinction is probably largely due to persecution by farmers. However, direct killing is rarely a successful way to combat these pest species, since the survivors are often able to make the most of the opportunity created by man, increasing their breeding output and replacing the birds killed. There is a trend towards the development of more subtle biological techniques such as the

6. The Kea (after a photograph by Eugen Schumacher)

broadcasting of recorded alarm calls to dispel orchard pests and the use of trained falcons to combat bird flocks around airfields.

Unfortunately, many species have acquired totally unjustified reputations as competitors against human enterprise. Birds of prey are widely persecuted by game-keepers because they frequently eat game birds, despite the fact that their impact on game populations is probably slight and that they mostly take the weaker birds. In New Zealand there is a remarkable species of parrot, the Kea, which has a hawk-like bill. This has acquired an erroneous reputation as a killer of sheep and is frequently shot by farmers.[4] A great deal of research is required to identify those species that really do constitute a threat to agriculture and to find effective means by which they may be controlled without adversely affecting species which cause no damage.

While direct destruction by man has been a major factor in the decline and extinction of some bird species, the greatest human threat to birds generally is the destruction and modification of their habitats.

In colonizing new areas man has radically altered the face of the country-side. Britain, for example, was at one time almost entirely covered by forests; even the downlands of the south and the highlands of Scotland, which we now regard as areas of natural habitat, were once covered by trees. Such dramatic changes, though they may take hundreds of years, are too rapid for bird species to be able to evolve adaptations to the new conditions. Deforestation is perhaps the most dramatic change wrought by man; the greater parts of the huge forests that once covered most of Europe and the eastern part of North America have been destroyed. The greatest area of forest remaining is in the Amazon basin of South America and this too is now under threat. Another type of habitat that supports a large number of bird species is the wetland and throughout the world areas of marsh and swamp have been drained and filled in so that they can be used for farming and building. The vast prairies of North America have largely been converted into farm-land and with them have gone all but a handful of American Bison and the now extinct Heath Hen, which both once inhabited the prairies in huge numbers. Other manifestations of human civilization such as overhead power cables, the nets of fishing boats, farm machinery and even sonic booms claim the lives of innumerable birds. The accidental spillage of oil kills thousands of seabirds every year, as does industrial smog in cities. None of these factors in themselves constitutes a major threat to any bird species. What they do is to exacerbate an already serious situation and to reduce the chances that bird populations which have been depleted by other factors will be able to recover.

Perhaps the most widespread and insidious threat to bird life to have resulted from man's manipulation of nature is the use of pesticides such as DDT, DDD and Dieldrin. Though these chemicals are applied to crops in very small concentrations, they constitute a severe danger to wildlife because they are not broken down but accumulate in the environment and particularly in the bodies of animals. Animals cannot excrete these toxic substances but instead deposit them in their fat reserves. Predators that eat them take them over and likewise accumu-late them in their fat. In a food chain in which the predators of smaller species are themselves the prey of larger species the concentrations of pesticide derivatives increase at each link up the chain. On Clear Lake in California the pesticide DDD was applied to counter a plague of gnats. It accumulated in the microscopic plankton which forms the diet of small fish which are in turn eaten by grebes. The grebes, which were all but wiped out, were found to be carrying DDD in their bodies in concentrations 80,000 times greater than that in which it had first been applied to the lake. In strong doses these pesticides cause death through their effects on the nervous system. In smaller quantities they reduce the animal's reproductive capacity by causing sterility, the death of embryos and the formation of eggshells so thin that they break under the weight of the parent bird. Most birds store up fat before breeding and then use their fat reserves to provide the extra energy required for rearing their broods. As the fat is used up the toxins accumulated in it are released into the bird's system so that they affect the bird at the most damaging time.[5]

The most notable victims of pesticide poisoning have been the birds of prey. Following the end of the Second World War a dramatic decline in the numbers of several species of hawks and falcons, and particularly of Peregrine Falcons (Plate I), was noted in both America and Europe. No reason for this decline could be detected until in 1958 a British ornithologist, Derek Ratcliffe, observed that many Peregrine nests contained broken eggs and that the parents often ate their eggs.[6] He noted that the decline in Peregrine numbers had begun about the time that DDT and other pesticides first came into widespread use and that it was most dramatic in those parts of the world where pesticides were being applied most intensively. His initial supposition was that egg-eating was a behavioural disorder caused by pesticides attacking the nervous system. Subsequently he showed that the eggs were not deliberately broken by the parents but were crushed during incubation because they had abnormally thin shells.[7] They were eaten an entirely natural response to the fact that they were broken. Since then a great deal of research has been done into the precise way DDT and similar chemicals affect the physiology of birds. They produce their symptoms by causing the bird's liver to secrete enzymes which break down the female sex hormone oestrogen. The reduced oestrogen levels in the blood that result cause a general depression of breeding activity in the form of delayed egg-laying and reduced clutch size. DDT interferes with the hormonal system that controls the deposit of calcium in eggshells and it is this effect which results in the thin-shelled, fragile eggs that collapse under the weight of their parents.[8]

Birds of prey are particularly at risk because they are at the top of the food chain, at each link of which the concentration of toxic substances is increased. Predatory species that live off marine life are similarly affected by pesticides. Because they are not broken down by natural processes pesticides are washed off the land into rivers and the sea, where they accumulate in fishes. The Brown Pelican and the Osprey around the North American coast have been severely depleted by the same thin-eggshell syndrome that has afflicted terrestrial birds of prey. Appreciable quantities of pesticides have even been found in Antarctic penguins, thousands of miles from the areas where they were first applied to crops. As well as pesticides a number of other man-made chemicals pose a similar threat to wildlife. In particular, polychlorinated biphenyls are widely dispersed compounds that are formed when plastic is burned. These also cause depressed breeding activity and thin-shelled eggs in birds. There is widespread concern about the build-up in the environment of compounds containing heavy metals like lead and mercury which have a variety of toxic effects on animals and man. The ramifications of the harmful effects of chemicals on birds can be very complex. There is some concern at the present time over a decline in the numbers of the Red-breasted Goose which breeds in Siberia. Red-breasted Geese typically nest close to the nests of Peregrines and other birds of prey where they apparently gain some protection from predatory animals, which are eaten by the Peregrines. The Peregrine's decline must have greatly reduced this protection and may thus be the indirect cause of the Red-breasted Goose's predicament.

Our concern over the harmful effects of pesticides should not be confined to birds. Man, being an eater of meat, is himself at the top of the food chain and consumes toxic chemicals in high concentrations.[9] As yet no harmful effect on man has been demonstrated, though it has been suggested that pesticide poisoning may cause cancer or the kind of hormonal disturbance that it produces in birds. Even those who are not particularly concerned about endangered species like the Peregrine

7. *Red-breasted Geese*

Falcon should not be indifferent to their fate because their decline is a symptom of the way man is poisoning his own environment.

The history of pesticides and their effects on wildlife dramatically shows how dangerous human manipulation of the environment can be when its full consequences are not understood. There are many other ways in which man, through carelessness or ignorance, has brought about changes in the habitat that have had catastrophic effects on bird life. Wherever men have colonized new areas of the world they have taken with them a variety of animals such as dogs, cats, rats and pigs. When these are introduced to places where they are not indigenous they can cause havoc among endemic species which have not evolved adaptations to counter their predatory activities. Such damage is especially severe on islands, many of which have never been colonized by mammals and where the birds that colonized them have often lost any adaptations against mammalian predators that they might have possessed. Cats were introduced to Herokapare Island off New Zealand in 1931 and have reduced the population of birds from an estimated 400,000 to a few thousand, totally exterminating six species that previously bred there. In 1918 rats became established on Lord Howe Island to the east of Australia as the result of a shipwreck and they have been responsible for the extinction of eight bird species. On Laysan Island in the Pacific rabbits have caused the extinction of five species that were found nowhere else by destroying most of the vegetation on which they depended. One of the most remarkable cases is that of a species of wren which was found only on the tiny Stephens Island off New Zealand. The entire population of this bird was eliminated during the year 1894 by a single cat belonging to a lighthouse keeper.

Introduced animals do not always prey upon the indigenous birds but may cause just as much damage as competitors for food or nest sites. Because of their remoteness and small size islands tend to contain fewer species than are found on the continents. Continental species evolve in an environment supporting many species which create a selection pressure that favours the evolution of greater efficiency in, for example, finding food, leading to an increased capacity to compete successfully with species of similar habits. When they are introduced to islands continental species tend to be very successful because they are more competitive than the endemic species which have evolved in a less demanding environment. In fact the situation is more complex than this because the introduction of alien species is only one of many concurrent changes that have taken place on colonized islands. When man colonizes an island he destroys the natural vegetation and converts the land to agricultural use. The success of introduced species such as starlings and sparrows on many islands is probably mainly due to the fact that they are ideally equipped to colonize man-made habitats. An analysis of the status of introduced species in New Zealand suggests that only a few have significantly invaded those areas of original habitat that remain unspoiled.[10] Introduced competitors are not always birds. Alien herbivores like rabbits, goats and sheep have severely depleted the vegetation of many islands, destroying the food supply of the indigenous birds. The Blue Duck of New Zealand, which feeds on small aquatic animals, is now an endangered species and its numbers may have been reduced largely as a result of the introduction of trout, which have a similar diet.[11]

As well as bringing predators and competitors to the areas he colonizes man also carries with him a number of diseases. In 1826 the Night Mosquito was accidentally introduced to the island of Maui in the Hawaiian group.[12] This is a carrier of bird diseases including avian malaria, to which the indigenous birds have evolved no immunity. As a result several species which were unique to the Hawaiian islands became extinct and now most of the surviving endemic species are found only at altitudes greater than 2000 feet; above this altitude the mosquito cannot survive.

There is no doubt that it is the spread of Western civilization across the world that has been the cause of most of the extinctions that have occurred in the last 300 years. The earliest extinction which can be dated with any accuracy is that of the Dodo of Mauritius, which died out around 1680. Since then about 130 species and local races of birds have been exterminated. The rate at which they disappeared accelerated as man's activities intensified, reaching a peak around the turn of the century.[13] The worst period was between 1885 and 1907, when no less than twenty-four species and fourteen races were finally wiped out. In recent years the rate of extinction has slowed down and no species has definitely become extinct since 1945. This apparent improvement is no cause for complacency or optimism and is probably due only in a small degree to a more conservationist attitute to birds. What has happened is that man has eliminated the most vulnerable species and those that are left are species more resistant to his activities. It is virtually certain that a number of birds will become extinct in the next few years. Several species now have tiny populations of less than 100 birds which could be destroyed at any time by some sudden natural or man-made disturbance of their habitat. The total population of the North American Whooping Crane was seventy-three birds in 1974, the California Condor numbers around sixty individuals, the Kakapo of New Zealand is down to around twenty and the Mauritius Kestrel, probably the world's rarest bird, has a total population of nine, of which seven are wild and two are in captivity.

The birds that are most vulnerable to man's activities are those that live on islands; as we have seen, nearly all the birds that have become extinct in modern times were species or races that existed only on particular islands. Island species are vulnerable for certain biological reasons. I have already mentioned their tendency to lose adaptations such as the power of flight which protect them from predators. In addition they may have lost the ability to compete successfully with introduced species of similar habits. They are also vulnerable for the purely practical reason that it is relatively easy for man, especially on small islands, to spread his activities over the whole of a species' range. Species living on continents may be just as unable to coexist with man but they are often able to survive in isolated refuges where man has not intruded.

Enough is known about the history of the birds that have become extinct in the last 300 years to say that for at least half of them their demise is attributable to man, through direct hunting, destruction of their habitat or through the impact of his 'camp followers'. Of the rest, we cannot be certain why they died out, though it is likely that changes brought about by man were largely responsible. It must be remembered that extinction is a natural part of the evolutionary process and a few of these species may have died out as the result of naturally occurring changes in their environment.

This chapter has not presented a very edifying picture of man and his attitudes towards other species. Mankind has simply exploited birds whenever they have been of use to him for food, personal adornment and sport, and he has displaced them wherever it has suited him to destroy their habitat for his own purposes. These abuses cannot be attributed to a minority of humans but are symptomatic of a deep-seated attitude to animals that underlies man's view of nature. In a recent book in which he discusses the more offensive forms of man's exploitation of animals, such as their use in scientific experiments and their treatment in factory farms, Peter Singer analyses the history of this basic attitude.[14] He characterizes the human approach to animals as 'speciesism' and equates it with the racism and sexism which exist within our species.[15] Speciesism is the implicit assumption of superiority over other species and of the right to exploit them for our own ends.

This attitude is more prevalent in Western society than in many other cultures; the Hindus, for example, hold all animals to be sacred and are vegetarian. It is thus not surprising that Western civilization has been responsible for the destruction of more species than any other culture. Singer traces the development of speciesism in the West from such Ancient Greeks as Aristotle and from the Old Testament through Christianity, to the point where it is now an entrenched and pervasive influence in our treatment of other forms of life. He goes on to argue that speciesism is discredited on ethical grounds, largely as a result of what we now know about our close affinity with animals as a result of the development of evolutionary theory. We can no longer regard animals as having been specially made for our convenience and comfort by a generous creator. In recent years there has been a shift away from this anthropocentric view towards a feeling that man has a responsibility towards his fellow creatures. This change is only partly due to a change in our ethical values, but is more the result of a realization that the world does not contain infinite resources and that our survival and that of other species are intimately associated. I shall discuss the ethics and practicalities of conservation more fully in the last chapter.

3

Three Case Histories of Extinction

IN this chapter I discuss in some detail the natural history and extinction of four birds that have disappeared in the last 300 years. Together their histories illustrate most of those biological features resulting from the evolutionary process which can make some species more vulnerable than others and which I discussed in Chapter 1. They also reveal the many and varied effects that human activities have had on their environment, as discussed in Chapter 2. Two of these birds, the Dodo and the Great Auk, have become classic examples of extinct species; the third species, the Pink-headed Duck, will be less familiar to most readers. In the section on the Dodo I also discuss its less-celebrated close relative, the Solitaire. This selection of just a few of the many species that have recently become extinct is obviously somewhat arbitrary, but together they provide a marked contrast in their general habits and way of life. The Dodo and the Solitaire were each confined to a single island and perfectly illustrate the vulnerability of insular species to human invasion. The Great Auk was a wide-ranging pelagic bird, but one which congregated to breed in great numbers on a few remote islands in the North Atlantic. The Pink-headed Duck lived in the heart of India and its story shows how even continental species may be susceptible to extinction. These four birds became extinct at widely-spaced intervals, the Dodo in 1681, the Solitaire around 1791, the Great Auk in 1844 and the Pink-headed Duck around 1940. Together they show that man's destruction of the environment has been continuous throughout recent history and that extinctions which occurred early in the development of Western civilization have done little to modify man's activities and attitudes.

The Dodo and the Solitaire

The Dodo has become the epitome of the extinct bird; with its large, clumsy build and grotesque appearance it embodies all that one might expect of a primitive bird, outdated by the elegant and sophisticated flying creatures of the present day. As we shall see, the Dodo was not primitive in the sense of being ancestral to modern birds but was simply a product of the evolutionary pressures that can operate on remote islands. The Dodo is the earliest instance of an extinction for which there are reasonable eye-witness accounts; it died out around 1681, some 170 years after it was first described by a European. Our present knowledge of the Dodo is the result of careful detective work, principally by H. E. Strickland and A. G. Melville, who in 1848 published a book called *The Dodo and its Kindred* in which they carefully assessed all the evidence that had been passed down over the years.[1] This evidence came from three sources, eye-witness accounts by sixteenth- and seventeenth-century explorers and travellers, drawings and paintings made by contemporary artists and a few bones and other relics that are the remains of live specimens that were brought to Europe to be exhibited.

The Dodo inhabited the island of Mauritius in the Indian Ocean. This is one of three islands, all of volcanic origin, which are rather remote from one another and even further from the nearest substantial land mass, Madagascar. The other two islands in this group, the Mascarenes, are Rodriguez and Réunion, both of which were also inhabited by large, flightless birds, the Solitaires, which became extinct in the eighteenth century. The fact that Dodos and Solitaires occurred in the same group of islands and were both large and flightless

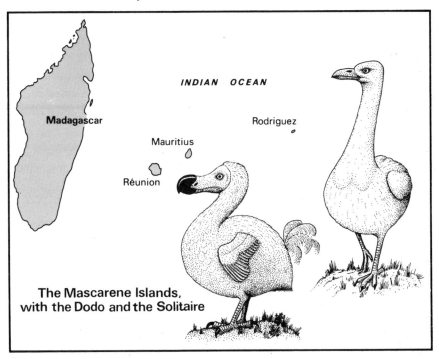

INDIAN OCEAN

Madagascar

Rodriguez

Mauritius

Réunion

The Mascarene Islands, with the Dodo and the Solitaire

has led many ornithologists to regard them as close relatives. As I shall discuss later, this may not be correct.

A large and heavily-built bird, the Dodo is thought to have weighed up to fifty pounds. Its plumage was loose and wispy, more like the down of a chick than feathers, and was grey on the body, whitish on the belly and dark grey on the thighs. Its face was quite bare, with greyish skin, and its huge hooked bill was grey at the base and yellowish at the tip. In most of the drawings that exist of the Dodo, its tail is depicted as a clump of wispy white feathers positioned rather high on the back. The yellowish wings are generally shown hanging rather loosely at the side; quite inadequate for flight, they may have been used in fights with rivals. The Dodo's very large yellow feet had black claws. All the early chroniclers agree that its meat was tough and unpleasant, though the breast was considered acceptable. The name Dodo seems to be derived from the Dutch name 'Dodars', which itself may be a composite of *dodoor*, meaning a sluggard, and *dodaers*, meaning a lubber. The early Dutch sailors were clearly not impressed by their agility.

The Mascarenes, with their thickly wooded mountains and hills, have been compared with Eden. They were probably visited from very early times by Arabs, who apparently never established a settlement there. The islands were discovered by the Portuguese explorer Pedro Mascarenhas in 1507. In 1598 a group of Dutch explorers led by Jacob Cornelius van Neck took possession of one of the islands and gave it the name Mauritius. A contemporary print shows van Neck's men 'revelling in the abundance of this virgin isle'. Here they found a profusion of fish, birds and fruits with which to provision their ships and wood to carry out repairs. An account of this visit records a variety of animals including 'walckvogel', meaning 'disgusting birds', whether in reference to their appearance or their flavour is not clear. In the next twenty years the island was visited frequently by Dutch ships and large numbers of Dodos were caught and salted down. The sailors did not have everything their own way; in one account there is a description of the grievous wound a Dodo could inflict with its bill. It seems fairly clear from these early travellers' chronicles that pigs and goats were introduced to Mauritius in 1602, presumably to establish a population of these animals that could be used for food at a later date.

In 1627 Mauritius was visited by an Englishman, Sir Thomas Herbert, who found the island uninhabited by man and who was impressed by the Dodo's melancholy look and distasteful meat. Herbert may have been the source of one of the museum specimens now in Britain. A Frenchman, François Cauche, visited Mauritius in 1638 and left us the only account of its nesting habits. He described a nest and a single egg the size of a Cape Pelican's, about four inches in length. In 1638 a live bird that had been brought back by one of these visitors caused quite a sensation when it was exhibited in London; this bird may have provided the remains now to be found in Oxford. In 1644 the Dutch began to occupy the island, setting up a penal colony and systematically felling the forests and turning the land over to cultivation. In 1681 a visit by a British ship under Captain William Talbot provided the last account of the living Dodo. Benjamin Harry wrote of 'Dodos whose fflesh is very hard' and also of 'many wild hogs' and 'munkeys of various sorts'. These animals, all introduced by man, appear to have had a spectacular population explosion in an environment quite devoid of any endemic mammals, and it is their presence as well as that of man himself, which is generally blamed for the rapid decline of the Dodo. We can be fairly sure that the Dodo was extinct by 1693; in that year François Leguat, of whom we shall hear more later, came to Mauritius and compiled an extensive list of the endemic birds which includes no mention of the Dodo.

Such, then, is the documentary evidence about the Dodo. Many of the early chroniclers illustrated their writings with sketches, most of which were probably made from memory, and do not give us a reliable impression of what the Dodo looked like. Some of the live birds that were brought back to Europe were drawn by skilled artists, the most notable of whom was a Dutchman, Roland Savery, who drew and painted the Dodo several times, once including it in a picture along with a number of still living birds which are drawn with great accuracy. However, even Savery contributed to our confusion about the Dodo's appearance. In a drawing discovered since Strickland and Melville's book was published he shows three Dodos, all with webbed feet.[2] The foot now in the Science Museum in Oxford shows no sign of any webbing between the toes and so this seems to be an aberration on Savery's part.

There are remarkably few museum remains of the Dodo; Strickland and Melville described only three, a foot in the British Museum, a cranium in Copenhagen and a foot and a head in Oxford. The Oxford relics have an interesting history; they existed as part of a complete, stuffed specimen mentioned in the catalogue of Tradescant's Museum for 1656. It was bequeathed to Elias Ashmole, the founder of the Ashmolean Museum, where it survived until 1755. By this time it was in an advanced state of decay and the Chancellor of the University and other museum trustees ordered it to be burnt. Some more enlightened person rescued a foot and the head, one side of which was carefully dissected by Dr Acland in 1847. In 1866 George Clark, who for some years had scoured Mauritius in vain for Dodo relics, discovered a large number of bones at the bottom of a swamp.[3] There was clearly great

enthusiasm to find more such remains; in 1885 Mr J. Caldwell, a
resident of Mauritius, reported that one of his men had found several
bones in a cave. These proved to be turkey bones and it seems that Mr
Caldwell, who was an old and ailing man, had been duped by a
'cunning Creole'.[4] A complete skeleton of a Dodo, made up from the
remains of several individuals, is to be found in Durban Museum.

From these various sources of evidence we can gain a reasonable
picture of what the Dodo looked like, but we know virtually nothing
of the sort of life it led. Its beak seems to have been adapted for shelling
and eating fallen fruit or for breaking up the roots of plants. Because of
its size, it must have been an entirely ground-living bird. Its great
weight would have precluded it from perching on any but the largest
branches of trees and its tiny wings were quite inadequate for flight.
The fact that Mauritius is a volcanic island that rose from the sea bed
and was never attached to any other piece of land means that the
Dodo's ancestor must have flown there; the distance from the mainland
is so great as to make the accidental crossing of flightless ancestors on
some sort of raft most improbable. In an environment where there
were no mammalian predators the ancestral flying colonists gave rise
to a lineage in which flight was gradually lost as body size increased
and terrestrial habits evolved. The finding of Dodo bones at the
bottom of a swamp and Savery's drawing of the Dodo with webbed
feet have suggested to some that it was a marsh dweller, but neither
clue can be considered good evidence of this. In an analysis of the
evidence published in 1953, Hachisuka suggests that the Dodo existed
in two forms, a lean, non-breeding phase which existed through the
hot period from October to March, and a fat, breeding phase found in
the cooler period from March to September.[5] He also draws attention
to the variation in bill size in the many drawings that exist of the Dodo
and suggests that it may have possessed a horny bill covering which,
rather like that of the puffin, was shed outside the breeding season.

It seems certain that it was the loss during its evolution of any
defence against predators that was the ultimate cause of the Dodo's
rapid decline. Not only was it hunted by man, even though its meat was
considered poor fare, but the animals that man introduced, the pigs,
goats, cats and monkeys, probably preyed on its eggs and chicks. In

addition the early settlers felled large areas of forest, destroying its habitat.

The principal ornithological interest of the Dodo is in the question of its relationship to other families of birds. At first it was suggested that it might be related to other flightless groups, such as the penguins, auks and ostriches. The penguins and auks can be discounted, for in these groups flightlessness evolved quite independently as an adaptation for diving. The ostriches show some superficial resemblances, particularly in their plumage, but there are a number of osteological differences; for example the ostriches lack a backward-pointing fourth toe, which the Dodo certainly had. Another suggestion, based on the appearance of the beak, was that the Dodo was related to the birds of prey and was some kind of 'terrestrial vulture', feeding on carrion and rotting fruit. Again there are too many skeletal differences for such a relationship to be plausible. In their analysis Strickland and Melville suggest a relationship with the pigeon family and present an impressive array of similarities between the Dodo and the pigeons. In the East Indies there are a number of ground-dwelling pigeons, notably one called the Toothed-billed Pigeon, which have a heavy hooked bill and feed on fallen fruit; these species have not, however, lost the power of flight. More recently it has been suggested that the Dodo is a relative of the rails, a family that has invaded many remote islands and which has given rise to a number of flightless forms.[6] In the absence of anything other than skeletal remains of the Dodo it is unlikely that the question of the Dodo's relationship to other birds will ever be resolved to everyone's satisfaction.

It is common in writings about the Dodo to see it described as degenerate, over-specialized or maladapted, as if it were some aberrant result of the evolutionary process. This is a totally misconceived idea; there is only one criterion of evolutionary success, survival, and the Dodo certainly survived and flourished for many millions of years. The fact that it was destroyed by human intervention in its habitat does not make it an evolutionary failure. If man destroys the earth in a nuclear holocaust is he to be called maladapted because he cannot survive high levels of radioactivity? The Dodo is an example of the economy of energy and resources that the process of natural selection

8. Heads of the Dodo (top) and of the Tooth-billed Pigeon from Samoa

brings about in animals. When the Dodo's winged ancestors arrived in Mauritius they entered a habitat where there were no predators and where there was an abundant supply of food at ground level. Flight was now redundant and natural selection favoured those individuals who invested less of their resources in wings than in other features required for a terrestrial life. The loose, downy plumage of the Dodo is cited as an example of an evolutionary trend called paedomorphosis, whereby features characteristic of the embryonic or juvenile stages come to persist into the adult stage. The Dodo did not need sleek feathers for streamlined flight and so selection favoured those that tended to retain the downy feathers of the nestling phase which were probably less energetically expensive to produce but quite sufficient for maintaining a steady body temperature. It has been suggested that man is paedomorphic in that he has retained the hairless skin characteristic of infant apes into the adult stage. Natural selection is a process whereby animals acquire and maintain features that adapt them to their environment. As we saw in the first chapter, the selection process can keep pace with environmental changes, provided that these are gradual. What natural selection generally cannot do is equip an animal for changes that occur quickly, such as those that occurred on Mauritius after the arrival there of man.

The island of Rodriguez, which lies 365 miles to the east of Mauritius, was the home of the Solitaire. Almost everything we know about this curious bird comes from the detailed chronicle of the travels of a Frenchman, François Leguat. He was the leader of a group of Huguenot refugees who fled France to avoid religious persecution and who settled in Rodriguez in 1691. They seem to have made a comfortable life for themselves there but left in 1693 and sailed to Mauritius; it has been suggested that they went in search of female companionship. They did not find it on Mauritius, where they received a very hostile reception and were jailed for some time by the Dutch governor. Eventually Leguat made his way home and published an account of all his travels in 1708. Leguat and his men gave the Solitaire its name because it was rarely to be found in groups but was usually encountered on its own; the birds seem to have been spaced out in this way through territorial behaviour.

The Solitaire was much the same size as the Dodo, adults weighing between forty and fifty pounds, but it was more like a turkey in appearance. It was tall, with a long neck, a head smaller than the Dodo's and a smaller and less hooked bill. Leguat writes admiringly of its stately, elegant walk and its immaculately preened plumage, a marked contrast to the clumsy, unkempt Dodo. The feathers on the body were hair-like, probably like those of the Kiwi, while those on the legs were said to resemble neat rows of scallops. Leguat's drawing of the Solitaire shows two curious bulges at the base of the neck whose smooth whiteness he compares to the fine bosom of a woman. (In their translation of his account Strickland and Melville are rather bashful at this point and translate *sein* as 'neck'.) The males were said to be generally grey in colour, paler below and darker above, while the females apparently varied, some being 'fair', others brown. Their diet consisted of leaves and fruit, including dates. They built a huge nest, some eighteen inches high, out of palm leaves and are reported to have laid only a single egg. The Frenchmen found them excellent eating, especially between March and September, when they were very fat. They were not easy to catch in the forest, where they were fast and agile runners, but they were quite easily run down if they were forced into the open. A curious discovery was a stone in the gizzard of every bird, even the youngest nestling, apparently too large to have passed down the gullet. The French settlers used these stones as whetstones for sharpening their weapons and tools; what function they served in the bird's gizzard, and how they got there, remains a mystery. Leguat also remarks upon the hard swelling the size of a musket ball at the joint of the wing and describes how these were used in fights between birds.

The most interesting part of Leguat's account is his description of the Solitaire's territorial behaviour. E. A. Armstrong has pointed out that, while there had been fragmentary accounts of territoriality in birds dating back as far as Aristotle, Leguat's is the earliest description that incorporates almost all of the typical features of this kind of behaviour.[7] The territory was apparently 200 yards in radius, with the nest at the centre. Both members of a pair defended it, the male taking on male intruders, the female other females. Defence was not entirely a matter of fighting but was also achieved through a dramatic display in which a bird pirouetted for four to five minutes, at the same time whirring its wings violently to produce a rattling noise that could be heard 200 yards away, equivalent to the radius of the territory. If a dispute escalated into a fight the wings were used to beat the opponent, as they are by many living birds, and the bony lumps at the joints would have made them very effective clubs. Some of the wing bones that are now in museums have healed fractures, indicating perhaps that these fights were violent affairs. Leguat suggests that the male's territorial display, as well as warning off intruders, may have attracted females; this is often the case in territorial species. The main purpose of this territoriality, however, seems to have been the defence of the food supplies contained within the nesting area. The young bird was apparently dependent on food provided by its parents for several months and the defence of an adequate food supply would have ensured that they successfully reared their fledgling. Territorial behaviour is a subject of great interest to ornithologists and ethologists today and Leguat's account is remarkable in that it describes so many features of territoriality that are now well-established phenomena.

Leguat describes another very curious pattern of behaviour, in which the parent birds escorted their newly-fledged chick to a gathering of other Solitaire families. There the chick became attached to a mate, and the newly formed pair remained together thereafter. This 'marriage ceremony', as Leguat describes it, is quite unlike any known behaviour in any other species; and, as it is accompanied by a lengthy discourse on the virtues of matrimony, one must assume that his imagination got the better of him. What he probably saw was some sort of social aggregation behaviour at the end of the breeding season, perhaps a crèche of the sort formed by Eider Ducks, flamingoes and some penguins. Some authors have pointed out that much of Leguat's narrative has obviously been gleaned from the writings of other travellers and naturalists, and that this fact raises doubts as to its veracity.[8] Indeed, it has even been suggested that François Leguat is himself a fictional character. However, there do not seem to be good grounds for dismissing most of his account of the Solitaire as fabrication; his descriptions of the bird agree very well with skeletal remains that have been found on Rodriguez and it is unlikely that he could have invented so plausible a description of territorial behaviour when it had not been described previously.

Apart from Leguat's account we know nothing of the living Solitaire and we do not know when or why it became extinct. A second-hand report suggests that it still existed in 1761, though in very small numbers. Quite large numbers of Solitaire bones have been found in ravines and caves on Rodriguez, suggesting that in its heyday it was quite a common bird. It is generally believed to have become extinct around 1791.

If we know little about the Rodriguez Solitaire, we know even less about the apparently similar birds that inhabited the third island in the Mascarene group, Réunion, formerly called Bourbon. An English naval officer who visited Réunion in 1613 described a huge turkey-like fowl with white plumage which the crew collected for food. William Bontekoe, a Dutchman, visited the Mascarenes in 1618 and likened a bird he saw on Réunion to the Mauritius Dodo. This account has been questioned; Bontekoe was the sole survivor of the blowing-up of his ship and he wrote his account some time later from memory.

In 1668 a Frenchman called Carré described a bird of solitary and secretive habits which he called a Solitaire; its plumage he describes as beautiful and yellowish and it was apparently good to eat. In 1669 a French colony was established on the island and one of its members described two birds, one white with black tips to the wings and tail, the other bluish in colour. These birds seem to have survived until the middle of the eighteenth century.

Both Strickland and Melville and Hachisuka in their analyses of the various evidence conclude that Réunion was inhabited by two species, one Dodo-like, the other a Solitaire. Many of the eye-witness accounts agree that there were large white birds on Réunion and Hachisuka describes a white Dodo and a Solitaire in which the male was brown and the female white.[9] No bones of either bird have been found on Réunion, and since many of the contemporary accounts are contradictory and may reflect a confusion in the minds of their writers between different birds and different islands, we should perhaps be sceptical about the existence of such birds on Réunion. The persistent accounts of white birds may indicate that somewhere in the Mascarenes there existed albino individuals of either the Dodo or the Solitaire.

The question of the relationship between these two giant birds, like the speculation about their evolutionary origins, may never be satisfactorily resolved unless a good deal more evidence comes to light. Though both birds show some affinities with the pigeon family, there are many differences between them in their skeletons, their appearance and apparently in their way of life, suggesting that they must have evolved independently of one another for many millions of years. They may have had a common ancestor but, since the Mascarene Islands were never joined by a land bridge, it must have arrived independently on the different islands. It is equally possible that the Dodo and the Solitaire had different, though perhaps related, ancestors who colonized different islands at different times.[10]

The story of these two remarkable birds provides an object lesson in the vulnerability of remote islands to human invasion. The Mascarene group provide a classic example of an island bird fauna consisting of a few, rather specialized species that have lost many of the adaptations found in mainland birds which live in more complex and more varied communities. In particular the Mascarene birds had evolved in the absence of mammalian predators, had lost any defensive adaptations their ancestors might have had and were hopelessly ill-equipped to meet the challenge of man and his various mammalian camp-followers.

The Great Auk

Forty miles to the east of Newfoundland lies Funk Island, a flat, desolate islet some 800 yards long and 400 yards wide. Funk Island is a breeding haven for thousands of seabirds, particularly guillemots and gannets, who crowd together shoulder to shoulder to lay their eggs and rear their chicks on the bare ground.[11] 'Funk' means evil odour, an allusion to the stench generated by the estimated 100 tons of dung produced by the birds each day during the breeding season. The dung is washed by the rain into the sea, which becomes putrid and discoloured but which sustains a community of tiny organisms, supporting in turn the fish upon which the birds feed. The island is covered by a layer of soil, several feet thick in places and honeycombed by the burrows of thousands of puffins. This soil is the accumulated debris of countless generations of seabirds that have bred on Funk Island and much of it consists of fragments of bones and crushed eggshells. Here and there there are darker layers, consisting of the ashes and charred remains of a bird that once bred on Funk Island but which is now extinct, the Great Auk (Plate III). The puffins and the guillemots have inherited Funk Island from the Great Auk and the soil in which they nest bears testimony to what was once one of the great breeding grounds of this species and to the destruction that was wrought upon it by man. Islands like Funk Island, far from the mainland, provided safe havens where the Great Auk could breed, just as they do now for other seabirds. Safe, that is, until man conquered the sea and discovered such islands and the rich harvest they could gather there.

The Greak Auk, also called the Garefowl, was the original penguin.[12] There are two possible derivations of the word 'penguin'. One is that it is derived from two Welsh words, *pen* meaning head and *gwyn*

meaning white, a reference to the two white patches at the base of its
bill. This is considered unlikely by some authorities on the grounds
that it was probably never a common bird around the Welsh coast.
The alternative is that the name was coined by Portuguese and Spanish
explorers who derived it from the Latin word *pinguis*, meaning fat.
The very large fat deposits under its skin would have been familiar
to early sailors who used Greak Auks to provision their ships.

It was a large bird, standing some two and a half feet tall; both sexes
were black on the back and tail, white on the breast and belly and
brownish on the sides of the head, chin, throat, and wings. The bill
was large with a series of grooves on its upper portion which increased
in number with age, mature birds having eight to ten. In their summer
plumage both sexes had a large white spot between the bill and the eye.
With its sleek, black and white plumage, erect stance and tiny wings
it was remarkably like the penguins that are so popular an attraction
in zoos around the world. For a bird of such large size, its wings were
very small, reflecting the fact that it was quite incapable of flight. The
wings were, however, used in swimming under water, as they are by
the penguins and the smaller living auks. There was a marked contrast
between the Great Auk's clumsiness and vulnerability when it was on
land and its speed and agility in the water. Many contemporary
accounts describe how difficult it was to catch a Great Auk in the water;
it could easily outpace a rowing boat and could remain submerged for
several minutes at a time. Great Auks fed on fish, a habit for which they
must have needed considerable speed and manoeuvrability under water.
They probably spent much of their lives at sea ranging widely in search
of fish and they were recorded by early sailors from points across the
whole of the North Atlantic. Each spring they converged on small
offshore islands around Scandinavia, Britain, Iceland and Newfoundland to form pairs, lay a single egg and raise their chicks. Their eggs
were of a conical, or pyriform shape, very like that of the guillemot,
Such a shape means that when the egg starts to roll it does so in a tight
circle, making it less likely to fall off a narrow rock ledge.

In its heyday the Great Auk was probably a common bird, occupying
the same position in the community of animals in the North Atlantic
as the medium-sized penguins do in the southern oceans. During the

9. Great Auks diving for fish

second great ice age, when its range was probably pushed southwards by the ice sheet, it was found as far south as Gibraltar, where it appears to have been eaten by Neanderthal men some 20,000 years ago.[13] Its decline, which was gradual at first, began as soon as stone-age men began to live near the sea and to gather their food there. Great Auk bones have been found in the refuse tips or middens of stone-age men in Scotland which date back some 4000 years, and similar remains have been found in Ireland, Denmark, Iceland and along the New England coast of North America. An early chronicler of the Great Auk was Symington Grieve, who in his book of 1885 describes his excavations of a cone-shaped mound called Caisteal-nan-Gillean, meaning 'castle of the servants', on Oronsay in the Inner Hebrides in 1879.[14] This mound, which he considers was left by Danish and Norwegian invaders, contains charcoal, charred fire-stones and Great Auk bones. The mound also contains red deer bones, which became increasingly rare towards the top of the mound, suggesting that the settlers gradually

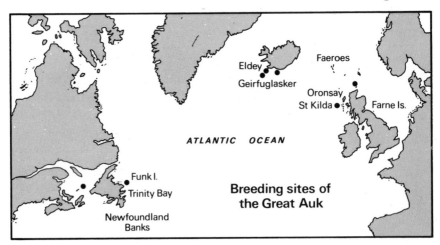

exterminated them from the island. Such finds provide a picture of early European men as wanderers who used their ability to cross the sea in boats to colonize islands and to live there by exploiting the animals they found. The same pattern of life was probably being carried on by the early inhabitants of North America and Newfoundland and it is thought that the Red Indians used their canoes to collect birds from offshore islands.

Great Auk remains have been found in ancient kitchen middens at mainland sites on both sides of the Atlantic, in America as far south as Florida. We cannot be sure whether these finds indicate that Great Auks nested on the mainland at one time or whether they were somehow caught at sea or collected from offshore island colonies. Only a few breeding colonies are known and these are all on offshore islands (see map). Many seabirds are remarkably conservative in their breeding habits, returning to the colony where they were raised to breed. Gannets, for example, form huge colonies on relatively few North Atlantic islands, leaving apparently suitable islands quite unoccupied; the Great Auk may have been similar in this respect.

The Great Auk was such a hopelessly clumsy and slow-moving bird when it came ashore to breed, and its eggs were so easily collected, that it would have been eradicated from its breeding sites on or near the mainland at an early stage. Its large size and tasty meat made it a most attractive and convenient source of food. Gradually, as man's mastery of the seas increased, he roamed more widely in search of new territories and sought out new supplies of food to sustain him. The more remote breeding havens of the Great Auk came within the range of early sailors and began to suffer the same fate as the mainland breeding colonies. Funk Island, which appears to have been discovered around 1170 by Norse explorers, is shown on a map dated 1505 and is called Y-dos-aves, meaning 'island of birds'. A distinguished early visitor was Jacques Cartier, the founder of Canada, who collected auks to feed his crew in 1534. Its exploitation by sailors probably began soon after; in 1578 no less than fifty English and 350 French and Spanish ships are reported to have provisioned there. Funk Island with its supply of fresh meat proved a godsend to the crews of ships in the days when sailing meant weeks or months away from port on a diet of salted food. Richard Whitbourne in 1622 praised 'God [who] made the innocencie of so poor a creature . . . such an admirable instrument for the sustention of man'.[15] Among the many visitors to Funk Island were European fishermen in search of shoals of fish. The appearance of Great Auks swimming in the water was an indication that they had reached the Great Newfoundland Bank, a rich source of fish, and the helpless birds on Funk Island provided a vital source of food enabling them to reprovision their boats for the long haul home. The Great Auks were literally herded together and driven across gangplanks into boats. Those not eaten immediately were salted down for the voyage.

The last recorded sighting of a live Great Auk in mainland Britain was in the 1760s. J. Wallis in 1769 wrote that 'The Penguin, a curious and uncommon bird, was taken alive a few years ago in the island of Farn, and presented to the late John William Bacon Esq. of Etherston, with whom it grew so tame and familiar that it would follow him with its head erect to be fed.'[16] Such accounts create a picture of a bird whose naivety in the presence of man reminds us once again of the living penguins.

Around 1785 there began a trade which greatly exacerbated the destruction of the Funk Island breeding colony. Great Auks began to be killed more for their feathers than for their meat. They were herded into pens, clubbed to death and thrown into vats of boiling water to loosen their feathers, which were presumably used for stuffing bedding.

There was no wood with which to build fires and so the bodies of other Great Auks were used, the fat in them providing an excellent fuel. The blackened, bone-filled patches of soil still to be found on Funk Island are the legacy of this appalling trade.

It was not only on Funk Island that Great Auks were exploited for their meat and feathers; the people of Iceland visited the Geirfuglasker, or Garefowl skerries, around their coasts. In 1808, during the Anglo-Danish war, Baron Hompesch set sail in the British privateer *Salamine*, captained by one John Gilpin; they kidnapped a pilot in Faeroe and forced him to guide them to the Geirfuglasker off Cape Reykjanes in South-west Iceland.[17] There they conducted a seemingly aimless destruction of Great Auks and their eggs before returning home.

The last record of living Great Auks in Orkney or Shetland is of a pair killed in Orkney in 1812 whose remains are now in the British Museum. In 1821 the last bird to be recorded on St Kilda was captured alive and was kept tied up for three days before being beaten to death, suspected of being a witch. In 1828 the last Great Auk to be recorded in the Faeroes was killed.

In 1830 the rare and now widely-scattered Great Auk suffered a catastrophe of a quite different kind. One of the islands off Cape Reykjanes in Iceland, indeed the one that afforded them a relatively safe breeding site since it was the furthest from the shore and the approach to it by boat was extremely hazardous, vanished beneath the sea in a volcanic eruption. Thereafter the Icelandic populations had to breed mostly on Eldey Island, also called the Mealsack because of its shape and its white cap of guano. This is nearer the coast and relatively accessible and for many years the population there was exploited by the Icelanders.

In 1834 a live bird was captured in Waterford harbour in south-west Ireland; this was the last unequivocal sighting of the Great Auk in the British Isles. The first sign of any alarm at the rapid decline of the species came in 1838 from Danish ornithologists who warned that it was in imminent danger of extinction. However, by 1841 the last Great Auk had been destroyed on Funk Island. In 1844 a pair were found on Eldey Island off Iceland, sitting on a rocky ledge. They were beaten to death in the last act of man's extermination of the

Great Auk. These birds had been intended for a collector who had commissioned the expedition, but they were in fact sold to the son of the pilot who had been kidnapped thirty-six years earlier by the *Salamine*, and he subsequently sold them to an apothecary in Reykjavik who stuffed them.[18]

There were many reported sightings after 1844, including that of a pair of birds in Belfast Lough in 1845. For the most part these were discounted by ornithologists; at that time it was considered necessary to produce proof of a new sighting in the form of a corpse or an egg, a practice not very conducive to the preservation of rare birds. In 1852 Colonel Drummond-Hay, who became the first president of the British Ornithologists' Union, sighted what he identified as a Great Auk near the Newfoundland Banks, in one of the earliest accounts of binoculars being used in the study of birds. He also reported a corpse being found in Trinity Bay, Newfoundland, in the following year.[19] Symington Grieve dismisses these reports, apparently because no specimen was produced, but Drummond-Hay's account shows that he took great care to distinguish the bird he saw from the Great Northern Diver, with which it was often confused, and it is quite possible that his claim to be the last man to see the Great Auk alive was justified.

It is clear from this historical account of the decline of the Great Auk that the principal cause of its decline was direct destruction by man. Its vulnerability to human exploitation was largely due to a number of features it had acquired during its evolution as adaptations to its habitat and way of life. It was larger than the other auks, enabling it to exploit larger fishes; to survive in the cold arctic waters it had evolved, like the penguins, a large subcutaneous layer of insulating fat. Together, these features made it an attractive source of food. It bred on small, remote islands where there were no predators and so had evolved no defensive adaptations, either for itself or for its young. In common with many large birds it probably did not breed in its first few years and when it did it laid only a single egg; there must thus have been an intrinsically low rate of recruitment to the population, making it more vulnerable to persistent human predation.[20] At one time it was clearly a highly successful species with a vast range, but wherever it came into contact with the expanding human population it was rapidly wiped out. After the early displacement of the Auk from its inshore breeding sites, it was just a matter of time before the development of human technology opened up its more remote breeding havens.

The Great Auk played a vital part in the expansion of human civilization from Europe to America, by providing a food source for explorers and fishermen. Later its exploitation became a matter of simple economics. Its meat and its feathers could be sold and so could the oil extracted from the subcutaneous fat. The early inhabitants of St Kilda stuffed the fat into the stomach, smoked it and sold the resulting concoction, called Giben, on the mainland as a cure for rheumatism and a variety of other ills. Populations that become small, and particularly those that have a low intrinsic recruitment rate, are very vulnerable to random catastrophes. The volcanic eruption that destroyed one of the Great Auk colonies off Iceland in 1830 seems to have hit the species at the worst possible time in its decline. The Auk's increasing rarity merely meant that one form of commercial exploitation gave way to another, for trophy hunters and collectors now went after the eggs and skins and sold them at higher and higher prices. In 1912, many years after its demise, a Great Auk's egg was sold in London for 220 guineas, an indication of the sort of value that rarity can confer upon a simple egg.[21]

Why should we mourn the passing of the Great Auk; what is it that we have lost? The principal ornithological interest of the Great Auk lies in its adaptations for underwater swimming and in the way that these appear to have paralleled those of the penguins. All the penguins come from the southern hemisphere; the Great Auk was found only in the North Atlantic. In a remarkable instance of convergent evolution the auks and the penguins, which are descended from the gulls and the petrels respectively, have evolved similar habits, shape and colouration quite independently of one another and at opposite ends of the earth.[22] The penguins have gone further along the path of flightlessness in that they are all incapable of flight; of the auks only the Great Auk was entirely flightless. The living auks represent a compromise between aerial flight and underwater swimming. For mechanical reasons this compromise imposes strict limits upon the body size that they can attain and all the living auks are smaller than any of the penguin family.

As a bird becomes larger, its volume and weight become greater as a cubic function of its length and breadth. For this reason larger birds must have larger wings in proportion to their body size than smaller birds so as to provide the uplift required to keep them airborne. However, under the water large wings would be disadvantageous, since they would make the bird less manoeuvrable in the denser medium. A large flying-and-diving bird would thus require an impossible combination of large wings for flight and small wings for diving. Of the auks, only the Great Auk paralleled the penguins and evolved a body size greater than that for which both flight and underwater swimming are possible. The Great Auk was the same height as the living Gentoo Penguin, which is midway up the penguin size scale; the Emperor Penguin stands forty-eight inches tall. Why the trend towards large size and a greater emphasis on diving rather than flying should have been more extreme in the southern oceans than in the north is not clear, but there is a much greater area of sea relative to the land in the south and this may have favoured the evolution of birds more specifically adapted to an oceanic life.

There are many lessons that we can learn from the sad history of the Great Auk. It provides a classic example of how human exploitation, gradual at first and then accelerated by economic factors, can so reduce a species' numbers that it becomes vulnerable to natural catastrophes and subject to the special risk that rarity brings from collectors. There are many birds that have an essentially similar life-style, pelagic species that come ashore to breed in dense colonies where they are vulnerable to human exploitation, particularly because they provide such easy pickings. The gannet of the North Atlantic is a species that at one time suffered heavily from human exploitation but which is now in a very healthy state.[23] In the 1830s there were an estimated 300,000 gannets breeding in the North Atlantic; through egg collecting, especially on islands in the St Lawrence, this was reduced to some 100,000 birds by the end of the nineteenth century. In this century, partly because of a more conservationist attitude and partly because of the availability of other food sources, human predation has largely ceased and the population has steadily risen. In the southern oceans penguins of several species were collected for their meat, their skins and

their oil.[24] South American Indians raided offshore islands, and as
Europeans colonized New Zealand, Australia and South America
they too exploited the penguin breeding colonies. In 1891 an oil factory
was set up in the Macquarie Islands between New Zealand and Antarctica. This was closed some twenty-five years later largely as a result of
public outcry at quite erroneous reports that penguins were being
boiled alive. Gradually a more conservationist attitude to penguins has
developed. In 1909 the International Ornithological Congress urged
Australia and New Zealand to cease oil production based on penguins;
in the same year the penguins of South Georgia were given full legal
protection. The Falkland Island penguins, which had been exploited by
the islanders for many years, were given partial protection in 1864 and
total protection in 1914. The Macquarie Islands were made a wildlife
sanctuary in 1919 and the Kerguelen Islands in 1924. Finally, the
Antarctic Treaty of 1959 afforded protection to penguins breeding
there. So the penguins, which have so much in common with the
Great Auk, have been spared a similar fate. It was the Great Auk's
misfortune to be, from man's point of view, the ideal food supply in
the right place at the right time. When the North Atlantic was being
opened up by man the prevailing attitude was that wildlife was
provided for man's use by a benevolent creator. By the time the
southern oceans began to be developed, animals and birds were regarded more as fellow creatures and public opinion simply would not
tolerate the kind of carnage suffered by the Great Auk.

The Pink-headed Duck

The area around the lower reaches of the Ganges and Brahmaputra
rivers, previously called Bengal, now Bangladesh, is one of the most
densely populated parts of the world. In the nineteenth century Bengal
was a largely unexplored wilderness whose rich and exotic wildlife
attracted British colonialists seeking a substitute for the hunting and
shooting which was so popular a pastime at home. It was extremely
difficult country to cross, with areas of thick, tall grass intersected by
innumerable slow-moving expanses of water. The grassland was the

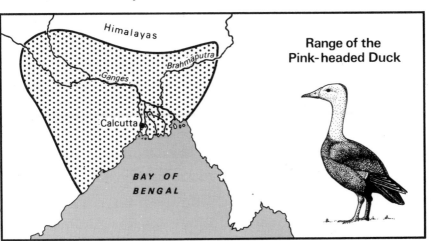

home of the tiger, the chief target of the sportsmen who used elephants to cross the difficult terrain and to provide a vantage point above the grass. The streams and pools were infested by crocodiles, which, with the tigers, were chiefly responsible for the fact that this country had previously been virtually unexplored by man. The limpid waters were largely covered by pink and white lotus flowers and were the home of innumerable species of water fowl which provided another target for sportsmen. The most beautiful and the rarest of these waterfowl was the Pink-headed Duck. (Plate IV)

Although it became extinct comparatively recently, very little is known about the Pink-headed Duck. The fact that there are less than eighty skins in museum collections throughout the world, despite a number of concerted attempts to obtain specimens around the turn of the century, suggests that it was never a common species.[25] It was unique among ducks in having a bright pink head and neck, described by one author as the colour of fresh blotting-paper.[26] The rest of the plumage was brown, except for a pink and white patch, called the speculum, on the wings. In flight the pale pink of the underside of the wings contrasted strongly with the dark brown of the body. Male and female were essentially similar in appearance, though the female's head and neck were less vividly pink than the male's. It had a long, slender neck and appears to have fed both by dabbling in the water surface and by diving beneath the water 'as neatly and as long as a Pochard'.[27] In the breeding season, which began in April, Pink-headed Ducks were usually seen on their own or in pairs while at other times they gathered in small flocks of up to about ten birds. They built a nest in a clump of grass some distance away from water and laid a clutch of up to nine white eggs, which were remarkable for being almost perfectly spherical in shape. From the accounts of naturalists and sportsmen it appears that both male and female attended the eggs and one observer described a female performing an injury-feigning display, apparently in an attempt to draw him away from her nest. Such behaviour is common among ground-nesting birds.

One of the earliest descriptions of the Pink-headed Duck in its natural habitat is provided by F. B. Simson, writing in 1884.[28] He gives a vivid account of how a group of sportsmen, mounted on elephants, moved through the grass and the pools, putting up all sorts of wildfowl at which they could shoot. They were highly delighted to have bagged a few Pink-headed Ducks, simply because they were the rarest of the waterfowl. They were not usually eaten, being considered the least tasty of all the ducks. They must still have been relatively abundant at this time, however, for bags of up to six birds were frequently sold in Calcutta markets. In the early part of this century some concern for the species began to build up as it became more and more rare, though in 1923 J. C. Phillips suggested that its rarity might be more apparent than real and might simply reflect the unwillingness of hunters and collectors to explore the more remote areas still infested by tigers and crocodiles.[29] His optimism was misplaced; J. Bucknill, writing in 1924, reported on an expedition into Bengal to look for the Pink-headed Duck which did not succeed in finding a single specimen.[30] He considered that at that time it was on the verge of extinction. However, in the following year a number of specimens were captured alive and were shipped to Britain, where they joined the collection of Alfred Ezra of Foxwarren Park.[31] The last reliable sightings in the wild were made in 1935 and 1936 and around this time further introductions were made to Ezra's captive stock. Though they flourished in captivity, some of them living for more than ten years, they never bred, and the last of them died in 1944. In 1956 the capture and killing of Pink-headed Ducks, and the collection of their eggs, were declared illegal; but by this time they were almost certainly extinct.[32] A concerted attempt by the Bombay Natural History Society in the 1950s to obtain sightings was entirely fruitless.[33]

It seems certain that a principal factor in the decline of this beautiful bird was hunting. Always a rare species, it was particularly sought out by sportsmen simply because of its rarity and its unusual colouration. The effect of hunting was exacerbated by the fact that the colonial hunters apparently tended to ignore the close season on wildfowl shooting, which was observed at home as a measure to protect ducks during the breeding season and so avoid over-depletion of the population. In addition the Pink-headed Duck was threatened by the steady destruction of its habitat. As the human population of Bengal began to grow, areas of grassland were cleared and cultivated and the pools and streams were drained and filled in. Gradually this natural wilderness, with its wildfowl, crocodiles and tigers, was pushed back by the advance of human civilization. In view of its apparent readiness to settle down in captivity it might have been saved from extinction by being bred under artificial conditions. However, the techniques of captive breeding, which have recently proved so valuable in the conservation of endangered wildfowl, had not been developed at that time.

The relationship of the Pink-headed Duck to other ducks is uncertain.[34] In many of its habits and in some features of its anatomy, particularly the form of its feet, it resembles the dabbling ducks, a group that includes the familiar mallard. However, the anatomy of its windpipe and the fact that it appears to have been an accomplished diver suggest that it had affinities with the diving ducks; these include the pochards, for one of which the Pink-headed Duck was frequently mistaken. It may be that it was a direct descendant of an ancestral form which gave rise to both these large groups of ducks.

This singular and beautiful bird is but one of a number of species from the Oriental region which have been exterminated or severely threatened by the advance of human civilization. Jerdon's Courser, a relative of the plovers, and the Himalayan Mountain Quail, both inhabitants of hilly country, are now extinct. The Great Indian Bustard that once roamed the vast open plains now exists only in a few isolated populations and the colourful Western Tragopan, a kind of pheasant

10. The Western Tragopan

which lives in dense forests, is also nearly extinct. All these birds, like the Pink-headed Duck, were game birds and suffered severely at the hands of hunters. Illegal shooting is still a problem in the conservation of the Great Indian Bustard. However, the blame for the decline of these species cannot be entirely attributed to sportsmen; all have suffered severely from a reduction in the extent of their former habitats as a result of the conversion of land to agricultural use, the destruction of forests and the draining of marshes. The Bengal Tiger, the most magnificent of the inhabitants of the homeland of the Pink-headed Duck, is also declining as a result of habitat destruction and may soon have to be classified as an endangered animal.

The Pink-headed Duck also symbolizes a type of habitat, the wetlands, which is in great danger of being destroyed and about which conservationists are now greatly concerned. Throughout the world there are many large areas of low-lying, waterlogged country which provide a habitat for whole communities of animals that can exist nowhere else. Many of the world's waterfowl are entirely dependent on such areas. There is severe pressure on wetlands since modern technology has made it comparatively easy to drain them or fill them in and so 'reclaim' the land for human use. The Pink-headed Duck was just the first species to disappear as a result of the gradual and inexorable destruction of the unique wetlands of Bengal.

With these three case histories I have tried to illustrate a central theme of this book, that the extinction of a species is usually the result of an interaction between certain features of that species' biology and any of a number of environmental changes brought about by man. The Dodo and Solitaire had adapted to a remote island home where there were few predators by losing the power of flight and any sort of effective defence against predators. As a result they were highly vulnerable to direct destruction both by humans and by the predatory mammals that accompanied them. The Great Auk had the misfortune, as a result of its large size, its flightlessness and its gregarious habits, to provide man with an ideally exploitable food supply which was in the right place at the right time. As it became rare collectors of ornithological relics and a random natural catastrophe in the form of a volcanic eruption combined to finally exterminate it. The Pink-headed Duck appears to have been a species of rather specialized habits which was never common. Its unusual plumage made it a favourite target of the sportsman and hunting, combined with the destruction of its wetland habitat, brought about its demise.

This examination of species that differed markedly in their habitats and ways of life shows that there is no simple answer to the question of what kinds of birds are especially vulnerable to extinction. So many and varied are the adaptations of different species of birds to their environments that it is difficult to predict where and how the many facets of human civilization will have their effects and which species will be most affected. If we are to learn anything from the sad history of these species and so prevent others from becoming extinct in the future, it is surely that we need a much deeper understanding of the way many factors combine to influence the balance between the death rate and the reproductive rate of a given species.

4

Extinct and Endangered Birds of North America

THE North American continent encompasses the Nearctic faunal region, which is one of the two products of the break-up of the northern supercontinent Laurasia. Extending from the high arctic latitudes to the tropics, this region contains very large areas of a number of contrasting habitats. Since it became separated from the other land masses evolution has taken place independently of the rest of the world except for the occasional invasion of forms from the Neotropical and Palaearctic regions, with which it has been connected at times by land bridges. Among the families of birds that had their origins in North America are the wrens, the mocking birds and the grouse, some species of which have successfully invaded other faunal regions. Among the dominant features of North America are the forests that once covered the entire eastern half of the continent, as coniferous forest in the north, merging through deciduous woodlands into tropical forest in the deep south. In the middle of the continent is a huge area of open, sparsely-wooded habitat, with grassy prairies in the north and arid desert in the south. The west of the continent is dominated by the Rocky Mountains, home of the California Condor, and their thickly vegetated coastal plain. This pattern of three basic habitat types, each running north to south, is broken up by the Great Lakes in the north and the major river systems like that of the Mississippi, around which are extensive areas of wetland habitat.

The endemic human inhabitants of North America are the many tribes of Indians.[1] So dramatic and so rapid have been the changes in the natural environment wrought by European man since the early seventeenth century that it is difficult to tell what impact if any the Indians had on the indigenous bird life of North America. They certainly took a number of species for food, and killed others for their feathers, but it is unlikely that they had any significant effect on their populations. Though they sometimes burnt the undergrowth to clear the ground, there is no indication that they altered the natural habitat to an extent that would have threatened the survival of any of the birds. Of all the species that have become extinct or very rare in recent times, none appears to have done so as a result of the activities of the Indians.

The colonization of North America by Europeans began in the north-east and radiated westwards and southwards across the continent. The early settlers established an agricultural society based on that of their homelands and the clearing of the great eastern forests to create fields for crops and livestock has been the most dramatic single change wrought by man in this area. It is estimated that the forests covered 431 million acres in 1600, just before the arrival of the first colonists; now there are only 19 million acres. When later they colonized the midwest, the settlers adopted a different method of farming, that of ranching cattle on the vast prairies. Wherever wetlands constituted a barrier to the expansion of the human population they have been drained. The draining of the great Iowa marshes in the late nineteenth century was probably the major factor in the decline of the magnificent Whooping Crane which once bred there. These changes in the countryside of America were essentially the same as those that had been brought about in Europe hundreds of years earlier. However, because of the rapid increase in the human population due to the high level of immigration from Europe, and because the colonists were able to use relatively advanced agricultural techniques that had been developed over many years in their homelands, the face of the countryside in America was altered very much more rapidly than it had been in Europe. The virgin forests and plains of North America were rich in a

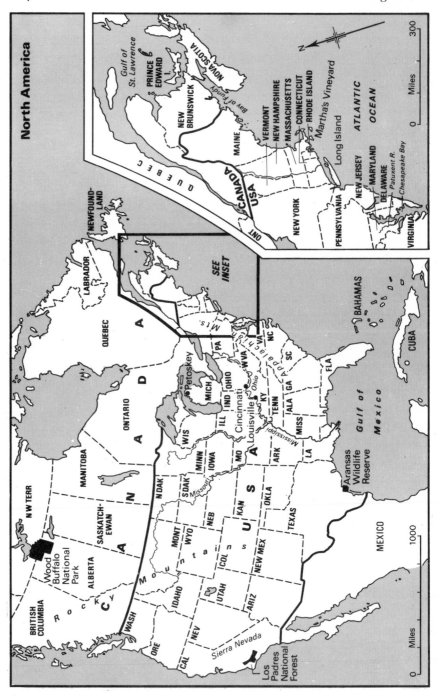

North America

variety of mammals and birds which provided an easy supply of food and hunting was an important part of the pioneer colonists' domestic economy. They ate Passenger Pigeons, wild turkeys and Heath Hens in such quantities that they sometimes complained about the monotony of their diet. Even today hunting is a very much more widely-practised activity in America than it is in the Old World, where the sense of a link with a pioneering past is not so strong.

One of the most spectacular features of North American bird life is the annual migration made by a number of species between their breeding grounds in the north and their wintering areas in the south of the continent, or even further afield in the West Indies or South America. These migratory habits have evolved as a response to the dramatic seasonal fluctuations in climate that occur at northern latitudes and they enable the birds concerned to live in favourable habitats at all times of the year. Some species migrate in great flocks and travel along traditional flight lines, like those up and down the east coast and along the Mississippi valley. Because of their densities and of the predicta-bility of the timing and route of their movements, these flocks are at great risk from hunters. A number of America's rarer species, notably the Whooping Crane, which winters on the Gulf of Mexico, and the Eskimo Curlew, which travels between Labrador and Argentina, have been severely reduced in this way.

We are fortunate that the early changes in the American countryside and the effect that they had on the bird life were carefully observed and recorded as they happened by a number of contemporary writers and naturalists. Foremost among these were the two great founders of American ornithology, Alexander Wilson and John James Audubon.[2] Though they shared a common goal, to record in word and picture every species of American bird, the two men could not have been more different in temperament. Wilson, who was born into an impoverished family in Paisley, Glasgow in 1776, trained as a weaver and was a promising poet. Imprisoned for publishing a poem attacking the owners of the weaving mills, he emigrated to America after his release. He became a school teacher but his friends, who found him morose and introspective, suggested that he take up the study of birds. This he did in 1803 and he soon embarked on a huge undertaking, a ten-volume book called *American Ornithology*. Though having only rudimentary experience as a naturalist, he carried out all his own meticulous and remarkably accurate observations as well as doing many of his own engravings. He had great difficulty in finding patrons to support his work and, when he died of dysentry and a chill in 1813 at the age of forty-eight, only eight volumes of his great work had been published.

Audubon, the illegitimate son of a French sea captain and a Creole woman, was born in Haiti in 1785. Between the ages of four and eighteen he lived in France, where he studied art for a time under Jacques Louis David, painter to the court of Napoleon. When he emigrated to America in 1803 the western frontier of the new colony was the Ohio River. He combined the pioneer spirit of the New World with a flamboyant, romantic personality acquired in the Old and was a colourful, extrovert figure. At the beginning Audubon's attitude to birds was that of the gun-carrying frontiersman. 'I call birds few when I shoot less than one hundred per day,' he once said. In 1810 Wilson came to Audubon's somewhat rundown general store in Louisville, Kentucky, and showed him his engravings and manuscripts. At this time Audubon had given little thought to publishing his own work, but seeing Wilson's material apparently spurred him to better it. He embarked on a most ambitious and lavish work, *The Birds of America*, and a five-volume *Ornithological Biography*, both vividly illustrated in his unique and dramatic style. He obtained much of his patronage for these books in Europe, where his flamboyance attracted much attention and where his paintings were highly acclaimed. Both works were completed, in 1838 and 1839 respectively, and he then embarked on a book on American mammals which was uncompleted when he died in 1851. As he worked on his books and witnessed the slaughter of countless birds and the devastation of the forests his attitude to wildlife changed. He spoke out against the destruction of the natural habitat and its birds and his heritage is the National Audubon Society, which today works for the conservation of America's birds and wildlife in general.

Wilson's writings give us as good an account as we can get of the American scene before it was so radically altered. Audubon bears witness to the changes that occurred in the first half of the nineteenth century. During his life the number of states grew from seventeen to thirty-one and their area expanded from the Ohio River to the west coast, though he himself never travelled west of the Rockies. When he arrived in America the great forests of the east were largely intact and the Passenger Pigeon and Carolina Parakeet occurred in huge flocks; when he died both were on the verge of extinction, largely as a result of the destruction of the forests. While Audubon has always been more widely known than Wilson, it is generally considered that the latter's observations of birds are more accurate and less tinged with romanticism.

The great oak and beech forests that once covered most of the eastern part of North America were the habitat of the Passenger Pigeon, a species whose history provides the most spectacular and remarkable example of extinction due to man's impact on the environment.[3] In the first 200 years of European colonization of North America the Passenger Pigeon must have seemed the most unlikely candidate for extinction. Its enormous flocks and breeding colonies were one of the most dramatic phenomena of the animal world and it may well have been the most numerous species of bird that has ever existed on earth. It took the white man only 300 years to exterminate it and its dramatic decline over the last fifty years of its existence is one of the most puzzling events in ornithological history. Like almost all recent extinctions that of the Passenger Pigeon seems to have been due to a combination of some curious features of its biology and of direct and indirect pressures exerted by man.

The Passenger Pigeon was a slender, elegant bird with long wings and powerful breast muscles that equipped it for prolonged and fast flight (Plate V). It was beautifully coloured with a slaty-blue back and deep pink on the breast. It was highly gregarious and formed enormous flocks which travelled at great speed over the countryside in search of food, roosted together at night and, in the spring, formed gigantic breeding colonies or nestings. The flocks were itinerant, remaining in one area only as long as there was a sufficient supply of food. So large did some of these flocks become that they darkened the sky for hours or even days at a time as they passed overhead. The wind that the pigeons created as they flew over at an estimated sixty miles per hour spread a chill over the area and their droppings peppered the ground like hail, leaving a characteristic odour. Audubon witnessed a flock in Kentucky in 1813 which passed through the area continuously for three days and he estimated that at times pigeons passed over him at a rate of over 1000 million birds in three hours. Alexander Wilson arrived at an estimate for a single flock of over 2000 million birds. These flocks were up to three or four miles wide and as many as 300 miles long and they twisted and turned like a snake as they went. It has been suggested that the early settlers coined the name Passenger Pigeon because these flocks resembled trains, but, since the name predated the building of the railroads, it perhaps referred to their spectacular migratory habits.

At night the great flocks descended to roost, often in places that they had used many times before in previous years. As more and more birds came in to land large branches and even whole trees collapsed under their weight and crashed to the ground. In the confusion many pigeons were killed. If a roost site was used frequently the accumulation of pigeon dung on the ground became several inches thick and so toxic that it killed the vegetation, including the trees. The principal foods of the pigeons were beech nuts, acorns and fruits of other deciduous trees. They would also eat wheat and on occasion they would descend on recently sown fields and devour the seed. It was partly the devastation caused by pigeon flocks that led to the invention of the seed-drill which pushes seeds into the soil where birds like pigeons cannot find them. Yields of nuts from beech and oak trees are highly variable from year to year and from one locality to another and it appears that the Passenger Pigeon's gregarious and itinerant habits were adaptations that enabled it to locate and capitalize on those areas where tree productivity was highest.

In the spring the great flocks settled to breed in a site near a good supply of food. The nesting colonies were ribbon-shaped, three or four miles wide and up to forty miles long. Within this area every tall tree contained several nests, with up to 100 nests in a single tree. These very large nestings were apparently not annual events but appear to have occurred sporadically, presumably when there was a combination of a large pigeon population and a local abundance of food. The nests were simply a crude tangle of twigs lodged in a fork and were so flimsy that the egg could be seen through them from below. It appears certain that only one egg was laid per pair. Both parents incubated the egg and, after it had hatched on the fourteenth day, both cared for the chick or squab until it was about five weeks old. It was reported by many observers that the parents then deserted the squab and sometimes actually ejected it from the nest, having fattened it up by intensive feeding, but this behaviour may have been the result of excessive disturbance by humans.[4] The nest relief behaviour when one parent took over from the other seems to have been highly synchronized throughout the colony so that mass movements of birds occurred between nine and ten o'clock in the morning and again between two and three o'clock in the afternoon. This behaviour may have been an adaptation against the many predators, such as birds of prey, that tended to congregate around pigeon nestings. Some predators are known to be more successful when attacking single prey and are confused by large numbers.

The descriptions of Passenger Pigeon courtship suggest some interesting departures from the behaviour patterns usually observed in pigeons. No doubt these evolved as a result of the Passenger Pigeon's highly gregarious breeding habits.[5] There was little of the elaborate male display of many pigeons; rather the male pressed himself up against the female in a more tactile, less visual pattern of courtship. In this way interference in courtship from neighbouring birds was probably reduced. The calls were louder and more strident than the soft cooing sounds of most pigeons, presumably an adaptation that enabled individuals to be heard above the cacophony in the breeding colony.

The breeding biology of the pigeon family is unique among birds in that the parents feed the young on a kind of milk which is secreted in their crops. Unlike mammalian milk this is produced by the male as well as the female. Most pigeon species lay a small clutch of one or two eggs and this probably reflects the fact that their diet is relatively low in nutritional value, making it difficult for them to produce large amounts of high-quality milk.[6] The Passenger Pigeon was no exception to this pattern with its single egg. Records of two eggs in a nest are probably due to some females 'playing cuckoo' and laying their eggs in another pair's nest; this is known to happen in some existing colonial-nesting species.

There is something of a paradox in the Passenger Pigeon's great abundance and an apparently low fecundity. Contemporary accounts suggest that in the bedlam of the nesting colonies there was high mortality among both adults and squabs; while some of this was probably due to human disturbance, much of it must have been the natural result of so many birds being in such close proximity. In any case, fecundity must have been severely limited if each pair produced no more than one offspring in a season. To have maintained such huge populations and to have generated the dramatic local population explosions that occurred from time to time Passenger Pigeons must either have been very long-lived, so that they bred in several successive years, or they must have bred several times in each year. Some accounts suggest that the latter was the case and it is suggested that after leaving their first nest and squab the parents moved to a new nesting colony and started again, and that they may have nested up to three or four times in a season.[7] Birds kept in captivity were able to breed as many as seven times in a year. With its itinerant habits and capacity to generate large numbers the Passenger Pigeon showed features typical of an r-strategy species. Such species generally have a high fecundity which, if not achieved by a large clutch size, is brought about by breeding several times in a season.

The highly sociable life-style of the Passenger Pigeon had its attendant hazards and wherever large numbers congregated to feed, roost or breed many were killed in the mêlée. One of the causes of mortality in the huge flocks was mass drowning, which was observed on the Great Lakes and in the Gulf of Mexico. Generally flocks seem to have avoided flying over large areas of water and instead skirted around them, but occasionally they were driven off course by bad weather and thousands perished. There are also descriptions of flocks descending on to lakes to drink and of the early arrivals being drowned when their fellows landed on their backs. In view of these and other risks there must have been some powerful advantage afforded to individuals within flocks, otherwise such a high degree of gregariousness would not have evolved. It is now well established that for many birds feeding on plant food which is unevenly distributed in the environment, flocking is advantageous in that it increases the chances that an individual will locate a new supply of food. Many species of birds nest in dense colonies and the advantage of such behaviour may again be that it facilitates the finding of food, or that, as we have already seen, it provides a defence against predators. Whatever the advantages of social behaviour to the Passenger Pigeon they appear to have far out-weighed the hazards. It was noted by early American ornithologists that breeding success among birds that for some reason nested on their own or in small groups was extremely low compared with that observed in the great nestings.

Long before the arrival of European colonists the Red Indians had been hunting the Passenger Pigeon for food. From some accounts it seems that they took care not to disturb breeding birds in case they failed to return in later years, but simply collected birds and squabs that had fallen to the ground. They apparently took only enough to supply their immediate needs and can have made virtually no impact on the pigeon population. Later, when white men offered them money for pigeons they adopted more destructive practices.

The earliest account of the Passenger Pigeon by a European is that of Jacques Cartier, who saw them flying above Prince Edward Island in the Gulf of St Lawrence in 1534. When the colonization of America began in the early seventeenth century the first settlers quickly made use of so abundant a food supply. The adults were considered reasonably palatable but the fat, tender squabs were very highly regarded. They were eaten fresh or, following the custom of the Red Indians, were preserved by smoking. In the early days enough could be collected simply by visiting the roosts and nest colonies and collecting the birds that were killed naturally in the general confusion. Gradually, as the human population increased, professional hunters and trappers devel-oped more and more sophisticated techniques for taking the pigeons. When flocks flew low over the ground large numbers of birds could be knocked down with long sticks and as many as a hundred could be reaped from a single discharge from a shotgun. Other techniques in-cluded felling the trees in which the pigeons were roosting or nesting, suffocating them by burning grass or sulphur beneath them or leaving out alcohol-soaked grain and collecting up the intoxicated birds. The slaughter that was carried out at roosts and nestings filled Audubon with amazement and disgust but he considered that the Passenger Pigeon was so numerous that its numbers were not adversely affected. The most sophisticated and effective method of harvesting the pigeons was by trapping.[8] A small area of ground near a roost or a breeding colony was baited with grain or with salt, of which pigeons were very fond. The lure of the bait was enhanced by means of live pigeons whose eyelids had been sewn shut and who were tethered to a perch, called a stool, which could be moved in such a way that they fluttered their wings as if alighting on the bait. These were the 'stool-pigeons' that gave rise to the figure of speech. On one or both sides of the bait was a large net on a frame which was held back under tension. When sufficient birds had landed on the bait the trap was sprung by the trapper, who was in a hide nearby. A single trap could catch up to thirty dozen pigeons at a time and a double trap is said to have once caught 1332 birds at a single attempt.

Pigeon trapping became a lucrative business, even though the price per bird was only a cent or less. A single trapper could catch as many as 24,000 birds in ten days and at one of the last of the really large nestings in 1878 at Petoskey, Michigan, which covered about 100 square miles, one man made $60,000, which represents a turnover of some three million birds. In the late nineteenth century there were about 5000 professional pigeon trappers who kept each other informed about flock movements and who converged on a roost or nesting as soon as it began to form. The pigeon trade was given a boost in the 1850s when the railroads were built, speeding up the lines of trade between the heavily populated eastern seaboard states and the midwest. As the east was colonized and the forests were felled the pigeons became less abundant and large flocks rarer, but with the coming of the railroads the trappers could collect in the largely untouched forests further west and ship the corpses to New York and other eastern cities. There was also a trade in live birds, which were used as targets in New York shooting galleries.

In the 1880s it began to be realized that the Passenger Pigeon was declining fast and a number of states introduced laws designed to curb the activities of the trappers. These proved to be totally ineffective, simply because they were rarely enforced, and the pigeon decline continued. The species disappeared first from the north-east states, then from the middle Atlantic states and the central states and finally from the states around the Great Lakes. In Massachusetts the last large nesting was observed in 1851, and the last nest in 1880; the last record of any kind was in 1894. In its last refuge in Michigan the last nesting was in 1886, the last nest was recorded in 1894 and the last undisputed sighting of a wild bird was in 1889. Between 1910 and 1912 substantial rewards were offered for confirmed sightings of wild pigeons but by then the species was apparently extinct in the wild. A number of groups had been set up in captivity and these bred successfully for several years until they became so inbred that they ceased to produce fertile eggs. One such collection was kept in Chicago by C. O. Whitman, whose observations of the behaviour of pigeons were one of the pioneering studies in the science of animal behaviour.[9] One of his birds was transferred to Cincinnati Zoo and this, a female called Martha, was the last Passenger Pigeon. It died in 1914.

The final decline and disappearance of the Passenger Pigeon was remarkably rapid. The nesting at Petoskey in 1878 was big enough for three million birds to pass through the hands of one dealer and yet thirty-six years later the species was extinct. The speed of this decline was such that it seems to have taken people almost by surprise. Certainly, the processes of law lagged hopelessly behind events. In 1907 a law was passed in New York to prohibit the use of live pigeons as targets in shooting galleries but by this time the species had probably ceased to breed in the wild. A number of theories were put forward to account for the pigeons' disappearance. It was suggested that they had been struck down by some disease, perhaps one introduced with European pigeons, but there is no evidence for this. Natural catastrophes such as storms were invoked but these could hardly have wiped out the entire population. Another theory was that human persecution had forced the birds to attempt to breed further north, where they were unable to rear their young successfully; again, there is no evidence for this.[10] The most fanciful theory was that the entire population had migrated to South America. So graphic and horrifying are the accounts of human destruction of pigeons and so great were the numbers involved in the pigeon trade that it is tempting to attribute the Passenger Pigeon's decline entirely to persecution by man. Clearly, such intensive killing must have severely depleted the population, but it is unlikely to have accounted for the final demise of the species since such pressure would have relaxed when it became rare and hunting was no longer economically viable. Likewise, the wholesale destruction of the great oak and beech forests must have greatly reduced the population that the area could support; but even to this day there are large areas of woodland that produce heavy acorn and beech-nut crops that could probably support substantial numbers of pigeons. It seems probable that some other factors contributed to the final stages of the Passenger Pigeon's decline when direct human pressures had generally relaxed.

The clue to this mystery may well lie in the Passenger Pigeon's highly gregarious habits. We will never know what benefit it derived from congregating in such large numbers; but whatever the advantages were, it is reasonable to assume that, at least within limits, they increased as the flock size increased. For Bank Swallows it has been found that the breeding success of individual pairs of birds is higher in large colonies than it is in small ones and among colonial gulls it is higher in the crowded centre of a colony than it is at the periphery.[11] A species will become extinct when the death rate exceeds the breeding rate. We may suppose that there was a critical colony size below which there were not enough birds present for the advantages of social nesting, whatever they were, to encourage a breeding rate higher than the mortality rate. Man did not need to wipe out every last pigeon to make the species extinct; he had only to reduce its numbers until it could no longer form colonies larger than this critical size and the species would have been doomed. By concentrating their efforts on the larger nestings and roosts hunters ensured that the pigeon population became dispersed and unable to form large colonies.

Some authors have suggested that the Passenger Pigeon was doomed to extinction because of certain 'biological defects' such as the flimsiness of its nest, its small clutch size and the way so many died in their great gatherings.[12] It was even suggested that it was a 'degenerate' species for which extinction was a natural fate. Such attitudes, as I tried to show in the first chapter, betray a misunderstanding of the way evolution takes place. At first sight a flimsy nest and laying only one egg do not seem to be compatible with the idea that natural selection favours those individuals who have the most offspring. However, such phenomena have to be understood within the context of the animal's whole life history and habits. It was evidently a more successful strategy to raise one fledgling at a time, and to do so quickly, than to attempt to raise more (which would probably have taken longer), perhaps because of the transitory nature of the pigeon's food supply. Clearly, these apparent 'defects' were advantageous to the Passenger Pigeon; in terms of sheer numbers it was one of the most successful species that has ever lived. It was man, through his exploitation and destruction of the natural environment, who turned advantages into liabilities.

Two other American species, the Night Heron and the Canvasback Duck, also used to breed in dense colonies where they were heavily exploited by hunters.[13] Both species have apparently evolved more solitary and dispersed nesting habits and their numbers have increased as hunting them has become less easy. We can only speculate as to why the Passenger Pigeon did not undergo a similar change; perhaps it had gone further along the evolutionary path to sociality and could not reverse the process in so short a space of time.

There are many lessons to be learned from the sorry history of the Passenger Pigeon. It serves to remind us of the dangers of hunting, of habitat destruction and of allowing human greed to go unchecked, but perhaps most important of all, it shows that there is no obvious population size above which a species is safe. Even an apparently common bird can quickly become extinct. The populations of some species have recovered after falling to a handful of individuals but the Passenger Pigeon may well have been doomed, for the reasons I suggested earlier, even while it was still fairly common. If this theory is correct we should be particularly careful to protect those species that form large breeding colonies. Even though the size of some colonies may suggest that a species is in a healthy state, it may be very close to some unknown critical point below which the death rate will exceed the reproductive rate. The real lesson of the Passenger Pigeon story is that we can learn little of a species' status from simple numbers; we have to understand many aspects of its biology before we can decide if it is in danger of extinction or not.

The decline of the Passenger Pigeon was almost exactly paralleled by that of another bird which was once a prominent feature of the eastern forests, the Carolina Parakeet.[14] This, the only species of parrot ever to have inhabited North America, was, like most parrots, vividly coloured, its brilliant green wings, tail and body contrasting with a red and yellow face mask (Plate VI). It occurred as two races or sub-species, the typical form living in the eastern states and the slightly larger and less vividly coloured Louisiana Parakeet being found to the west of the Appalachian Mountains. It was very unusual among parrots in apparently being able to live at northerly latitudes and flocks were even observed flying when the land was deep in snow in Albany, New York. There are reports that it became torpid during very cold weather, remaining in its roosting place in a hollow tree, but suggestions that it hibernated over the winter are almost certainly unfounded. Like the Passenger Pigeon the Carolina Parakeet was a highly sociable bird. It flew about the forests in fast-moving flocks, darting in and out among the trees making raucous calls. It was not, however, a migratory species, individuals tending to remain in their home area for life.

The typical home of the Carolina Parakeet was in the tall, moss-covered sycamores, buttonwoods and cypress trees that bordered the rivers and grew in the swamps of the eastern and southern states. Here they bred and roosted at night but they often ranged further afield in search of their food. Their diet was primarily the seeds of cypresses, maples, elms and pine trees. They were also very partial to the fruits of the cocklebur, a very common and vigorous weed that proved to be a serious pest to the settler farmers. They were very wary birds and a flock would circle several times around a likely feeding place before finally settling. If they were alarmed they flew off and rarely returned that day. This cautious behaviour was in marked contrast to their re-sponse when a member of a flock was injured or killed. Then they would gather around their comrade, apparently in an attempt to assist it. They were most active in the early morning and again in the evening when they foraged for food, and generally spent the middle of the day high in the trees where their quiescence and green colouration made them inconspicuous. At night they roosted together, usually in cavities in the trunks of old trees, clinging to a vertical surface with their claws and beaks. If the flock was large those who could not find space inside the tree clung in a similar manner to the bark outside.

It seems likely that these parakeets also nested socially. Both Audubon and Wilson reported that groups of birds laid their eggs together at the bottom of cavities in trees, but other observers described flimsy nests built in groups at the ends of the branches of cypress trees.[15] They bred readily in captivity, producing white eggs, but they were inattentive parents and very few young were successfully reared by captive birds. Their natural sociability expressed itself in captivity and they showed much distress if one of their cage-mates was removed. Their bright colours made them very popular as cage birds, though Audubon wrote that 'their screams are so disagreeable as to render them at best very indifferent companions', and he was unable to teach them to speak. He claimed, however, that they could be tamed 'by being frequently immersed in water'.[16]

The demise of the Carolina Parakeet was principally due to its becoming a serious pest in the fields, orchards and gardens that replaced much of its natural habitat. Its habit of foraging in flocks meant that it could devastate a crop in a very short space of time. Parakeets were very partial to unripe fruit, particularly citrus fruits, and were extremely destructive. Those fruits that they did not eat they simply tore off and tossed to the ground, apparently for the fun of it. Mulberries, pecan nuts and grapes were treated in a similar fashion. They also devastated stacks of grain, which would become covered by a flock as if, in Audubon's words, 'a brilliantly coloured carpet had been thrown over them'.[17] Not surprisingly the farmers hated them and shot them relentlessly. Against the gun the parakeets' habit of gathering over a fallen comrade proved disastrous. Once one had been shot, the others congregated over it and were shot in their turn until little or nothing of the flock remained.

This apparently suicidal behaviour must have been of some advantage under natural conditions or it would not have evolved. Some species of mammals, notably dolphins and elephants, have been reported to come to the aid of a sick or injured individual. Such altruistic behaviour, in which one animal puts itself at risk while conferring benefit on another, poses a problem for students of the evolution of behaviour. The theory of natural selection states that characteristics will be selected for only if they confer some advantage on the individuals showing them; how then can a behaviour trait which apparently is disadvantageous to the performer be selected for? This problem is resolved in most cases by the argument that it need not be only the individual that benefits but the individual and its close relatives; that is, other animals that have many genes in common. Thus, by giving assistance to relatives, a helper actually helps to propagate his own genes in succeeding generations. We will never know how closely related parakeets were to other members of a flock, but since their flocks were often very large this 'kin selection' effect is not likely to have been the evolutionary basis of this curious behaviour. Many instances of apparently altruistic behaviour have, on close examination, turned out not to be altruistic at all and the Carolina Parakeets' habit of gathering around a stricken companion may well have been an example. A number of animals are known to be attracted towards their predators, particularly after a kill has occurred, and the significance of this behaviour has been studied in Herring Gulls.[18] It may serve two functions. Firstly, it may enable individuals of the prey species to acquire information about the appearance and behaviour of the predator which will stand them in good stead when they encounter it in the future. Secondly, the presence of a large flock may deter or confuse the predator, making it less likely to kill again immediately. A number of predators such as foxes and hyenas will, given the opportunity, kill several prey in quick succession, even though they eat only one or two of them at that time. It seems likely that the parakeets' habit of gathering at a kill was some sort of adaptation to minimize the effects of natural predators, but against armed human ones it became a fatal liability.

As well as being shot by farmers as a pest, the Carolina Parakeet was collected in large numbers as a cage bird and was widely shot for sport, though it cannot have presented much of a challenge. As in the case of the Passenger Pigeon these pressures, severe though they were, do not seem sufficient to account for its total disappearance. Much of its habitat was destroyed by deforestation but substantial areas of riverine forest still exist to this day. One interesting theory about its decline involves the honey bees which were introduced from Europe by the settlers.[19]

These tend to nest in holes in trees, the very places where parakeets roosted and perhaps nested, and the bees may have prevented them from using the holes. In addition, honey-collectors felled many of the older trees to get at the bees' nests, further reducing the number of available sites for the parakeets. The gregarious habits of the Carolina Parakeet are reminiscent of those of the Passenger Pigeon and it is possible that it too died out simply because it became so rare and so dispersed that it could not form groups of a size that was viable.

In its heyday the Carolina Parakeet was found throughout the southern and eastern states. The heart of its range was the heavily wooded river valleys in the area from eastern Texas, through Florida to southern Virginia, but it was found as far north as Maryland, New York and Wisconsin and as far west as Colorado. Its decline seems to have closely followed the spread of colonial settlement. By the late nineteenth century it existed only in isolated populations and by 1891 there appear to have been only two locations where it survived in any numbers, one in Florida, the other in Oklahoma. E. M. Hasbrouck, writing in that year, predicted, with remarkable accuracy, that it would survive for only another twenty years.[20] The last specimen to be obtained in the wild was collected at Paget Creek, Florida, in 1901 and the last wild sighting was probably that at Lake Okeechobee, also in Florida, in 1904. It survived for some years in captive populations, the very last one dying, like the Passenger Pigeon, at Cincinnati Zoo in 1914. There were a number of sightings reported after that date, including one as late as 1938 at a swamp in South Carolina, but these are likely to have been of other, similar-looking species that were introduced into America from Central America and the West Indies.

The Passenger Pigeon and the Carolina Parakeet had much in common in terms of their general habits and their respective declines were synchronized to a remarkable degree. The last specimens of each species to be taken in the wild were collected within three years of each other and their very last representatives died in the same year, 1914. This similarity in history must surely remove any doubt that the decline of these two species was due to the same basic cause, the spread of European civilization across North America. I have discussed the Passenger Pigeon and Carolina Parakeet at some length, not only because more is known about them than about most extinct species, but also because they illustrate the important point that it is not only intrinsically rare species with restricted distributions, such as those living on remote islands, that are at risk in the face of human civilization.

It was not only the forests of the eastern parts of America that felt the impact of the changes brought about by the colonial settlers. The vast prairies of the midwest were also radically altered, both by the activities of hunters and by the spread of agriculture. Perhaps the most dramatic change in the fauna of this habitat was the almost total elimination of the Bison, which once roamed the prairies in huge herds but whose numbers are now measured in hundreds of animals, to be found only in special reserves. Among the birds, a similar fate befell the Heath Hen and the Prairie Chicken, members of a family of birds that had its origins in North America and which includes the grouse and ptarmigans.[21] There were four distinct forms, the now extinct Heath Hen and the three races of Prairie Chicken which survive to this day, though in pitifully small numbers compared to their previous abundance. Three of these are now generally considered to be subspecies or geographic races of a single species which once lived over virtually all parts of America east to the Rockies. The Heath Hen was found in the New England area, the Greater Prairie Chicken in the central states and in southern Canada, and Attwater's Prairie Chicken in the central plains of the south. The Lesser Prairie Chicken, which is classified as a distinct species, is found in the central southern states in an area centred on northern Texas.

It appears that even under natural conditions their numbers were liable to fluctuate violently within a given area so that where huge flocks occurred one year only a few might be seen the next. These changes were probably due to climatic variations, which tend to be more extreme in the middle of large continents, far from the stabilizing influence of the oceans. Heath Hens and Prairie Chickens both being ground-nesting species, a prolonged period of rain during the breeding season could flood the great majority of nests over a wide area. In a severe winter, such as that which has occurred in America in 1977, many would starve, cut off from their food supply by deep snow. In very hot summers bush fires devastated huge tracts of land, not only killing the birds but destroying their food supply and the under-growth which afforded them cover. They were well adapted to respond to these climatic catastrophes, however. They laid a very large clutch, up to seventeen eggs in the case of the Greater Prairie Chicken, which would increase the probability that at least one or two young would survive in bad years and which made possible the spectacular population explosions that occurred in good years.

Like many species of grouse, the Prairie Chickens gather to mate at particular localities called leks.[22] The males congregate first at traditional sites which are used year after year. Each lek is divided by the males into a series of small territories over which they compete fiercely, particularly those territories at the centre. The females come to the leks and the males all display vigorously to them, spreading wide their wings and tails and making a loud booming call by alternately inflating and deflating bright orange air sacs, one on each side of the head (Plate VIII). At the large leks that formed when Prairie Chickens were common the combined sound of hundreds of booming males was such that 'the very earth echoed with a continuous roar'.[23] The females tend to move to the middle of the lek so that the males who have claimed the more fiercely-disputed central territories mate with many more females than do the peripheral males. The lek is a social system that enables females to mate preferentially with the stronger, more dominant males in the local population. Not surprisingly, these noisy gatherings attract predators and when a hawk flies over a lek all the birds scurry for cover, re-convening when the danger is passed. After mating the females leave the lek and disperse to build their nests in thick clumps of grass. The males play no part in the building or defence of a nest or in the care of the young.

The Heath Hen and Prairie Chickens provided easy pickings for the pioneer colonist, who killed them in their thousands. Their flight was slow and laboured and they tended to gather in large groups, not only to mate but also to feed. They fell easy prey to introduced predators, particularly cats, and there is a good deal of evidence that they suffered from epidemics of diseases which may well have been introduced from Europe with game birds such a pheasants or with domestic poultry. Severe though these pressures were on the Heath Hen and Prairie

Chicken populations, the most important factor in their decline was the widespread conversion of their prairie habitat into farmland. Unlike many species of game birds they are apparently unable to flourish in anything other than undisturbed grassland.

The story of the decline and final demise of the Heath Hen in New England provides a classic example of the way several influences, some natural, others due to man, combine to destroy a population. In the early colonial days these birds provided an abundant source of meat and it is recorded that 'servants stipulated with their employers not to have Heath Hen brought to the table oftener than a few times a week'.[24] By 1830 the species had been eliminated on the mainland and there remained only a small population on Martha's Vineyard, an island that forms part of the state of Massachusetts. It is not clear whether Heath Hens occurred naturally on the island or whether they had been deliberately introduced at some time by man. In 1890 there were estimated to be 200 birds on Martha's Vineyard; this fell to less than 100 by 1896. In 1908, by which time there were only about fifty birds left, a 1600-acre reservation was established on the island. This was a highly successful venture and by 1915 the Heath Hen population had risen to 2000. In 1916, however, naturally occurring climatic changes completely altered the situation. In the summer a bush fire devastated the heart of the breeding area and this was followed by a severe winter whose effect on the population was exacerbated by the arrival on the island of unprecedented numbers of Goshawks that took many of the hard-pressed Heath Hens. The population was reduced to less than 150 birds and, to make matters worse, a disease called Blackhead broke out, having probably been inadvertently introduced with turkeys. By 1927 only thirteen Heath Hens were left, by 1928 there were only two, and in 1930 there remained just one member of what had once been a spectacularly abundant species. It attracted widespread attention from ornithologists and tourists who gathered to see it and at least once it narrowly escaped the ignominious fate of being run over by a car. This last of the Heath Hens seems to have survived until 1932.

In the latter stages of its decline the Heath Hen on Martha's Vineyard suffered from problems that often beset very small populations. The breeding rate became very low and it was found that many birds were sterile, probably as a consequence of excessive inbreeding. In addition there was a large preponderance of males in the population. Females, at their nests in the dense grass, were apparently more likely than males to be killed by grass fires during the breeding season. Under natural conditions, in which climatic catastrophes were a frequent occurrence, local populations which became depleted in this way would have been able to recover through the immigration of birds from neighbouring areas which had not been so severely affected. For the Martha's Vine-yard population of the Heath Hen there was no such salvation and its history illustrates how important it is that, if rare species are to be effectively conserved, attempts should be made to establish more than one population.

All the indications are that some of the Prairie Chickens may well follow the Heath Hens to extinction. All have suffered from the same combination of habitat destruction and hunting, exacerbated by in-troduced predators and disease, which destroyed the Heath Hen. The rarest of them, Attwater's Prairie Chicken, is now found only in a few isolated areas on the coastal plains of Texas. Though it has been afforded full legal protection which prohibits all hunting its numbers continue to decline. The Greater Prairie Chicken also survives in scattered areas in southern Canada, Oklahoma and Missouri, tiny relics of its once huge range. The fortunes of this race reached their nadir in the 1930s. Since then its numbers have generally increased, though with characteristic fluctuations, largely as a result of the establishment of several conserva-tion areas. The Lesser Prairie Chicken still occurs in all the states of its former range, though in small and generally dwindling isolated popu-lations.

While the decline of the Heath Hen was recorded down to the very last individual, very little is known about the first purely North American bird to become extinct in recorded history, the Labrador Duck.[25] The males of this species were strikingly patterned in black and white and it was, accordingly, also known as the Pied Duck or the Skunk Duck (Plate VII). The females were brownish-grey in colour with a large white bar on the wing which was conspicuous in flight. Virtually nothing is known about the habits of the Labrador Duck. Never a common bird, it apparently frequented remote islands and estuaries along the north-east seaboard from Labrador to Chesapeake Bay. It is thought to have bred in the remote wastes of Labrador and certainly bred on islands in the Gulf of St Lawrence, where its eggs were sometimes harvested by egg collectors. It was more likely to be seen during the autumn and winter, when small flocks gathered in the sandy inlets and bays of Long Island Sound, the Bay of Fundy and the New Jersey coast. Labrador Ducks had a large, curiously shaped bill. Nothing is known of their feeding habits but it has been suggested that they fed on small shellfish such as mussels. They were shot by hunters and could be bought in New York markets, though they were not considered to be good eating.

The decline of the Labrador Duck seems to have been rapid between 1840 and 1870; after 1860 it no longer appeared on the market stalls. The last authenticated sighting was made in 1875. The causes of its decline are as mysterious as was its way of life. The activities of hunters and egg-collectors have been implicated and it has also been suggested that it suffered as a result of a decline in its shellfish food supply perhaps due to pollution generated by the ever-increasing human population along the east coast.

Of the species I have discussed so far in this chapter, the Passenger Pigeon, Carolina Parakeet and Labrador Duck became extinct without any really concerted efforts being made to prevent their disappearance. The Heath Hen was offered protection on Martha's Vineyard but this was neutralized by natural catastrophes. There are a number of American species which are now extremely rare or whose numbers are declining rapidly. As a result both of a more conservationist attitude prevailing in America and of a much greater understanding of basic bird biology considerable efforts are being made to protect these endangered species. The results of these conservation schemes suggest that at least some of these species can be saved from extinction.

The Eskimo Curlew is one of the rarest and least-known birds in the world and appears to have been on the brink of extinction for many years. It was once an extremely abundant species whose flocks were so large that it acquired the name 'Prairie Pigeon', an allusion to the Passenger Pigeon. It has a remarkably itinerant life history which begins on its breeding grounds, the tundra of Alaska and western

11. The Eskimo Curlew

Canada. From there it migrates eastwards at the end of the summer, gathering in eastern Canada to fatten itself on berries and insects. It then migrates south down the eastern seaboard of America, across the Caribbean and down to the pampas of southern Brazil, Paraguay, Uruguay and northern Argentina, where it spends the winter. In the spring the cycle is completed by a northward migration through Texas and the midwest. During their migrations Eskimo Curlews are at the mercy of the weather, and the severe cyclones that sweep up the eastern coast of America and across the Atlantic probably accounted for the occasional sightings of the species in the British Isles in the second half of the nineteenth century. It was also during migration that Eskimo Curlews suffered most at the hands of man. They showed no alarm at the presence of humans and were shot in huge numbers as their flocks passed through the eastern coastal area in the fall and through the midwestern prairies in the spring. On Nantucket Island, Massachusetts, over 7000 were shot in one day in 1863. The New England colonists referred to them a 'Dough Birds' because of the great quantities of fat they had built up in their bodies prior to the southerly migration.[26]

Last seen on their breeding grounds in 1865, Eskimo Curlews have since been observed only occasionally and the species was once presumed extinct, as there were no recorded sightings in the fourteen years from 1945. Then, in 1959, it was seen again in Texas and has been reported regularly since then, suggesting that it may at least be maintaining a breeding population, though where this might be is a mystery.[27] The Eskimo Curlew is protected by law and shooting it is strictly prohibited. Until more is known about its present status, breeding grounds and movements no further practical steps can be taken to ensure its survival.

While the Eskimo Curlew is small and secretive enough to escape the notice of all but the most observant ornithologist, few could overlook another of America's rarest birds, the California Condor.[28] In the Pleistocene period, which ended around 11,000 years ago, this huge bird with its nine-foot wingspan ranged over the greater part of the continent, and its bones have been found among prehistoric cave deposits as far east as Florida. In the nineteenth century it was to be seen over a large part of eastern North America, throughout the Rocky Mountains and Sierra Nevada, but today it is confined to one small locality in southern California. The condor's decline was rapid and coincided with the settlement and development of the eastern states. By 1960 the condor population consisted of only sixty to sixty-five birds. The population fell to around forty in 1964 but since then it has slowly risen to between fifty and sixty in 1975. The primary cause of its decline has been the conversion of the land to agricultural use with a consequent reduction in the number of animal corpses on which it feeds. In addition it has always been highly prized as a hunting trophy and has suffered severely at the hands of sportsmen.

California Condors nest in caves among rocky crags and cliffs and may roam up to 200 miles from their nests in search of food. While their nesting habitat is now a sanctuary in the heart of Los Padres National Forest, it is not easy to provide effective legal protection for a species that ranges so far afield. As we saw in the first chapter the California Condor is a classic example of the long-lived, slowly-reproducing

12. The California Condor

K-strategist and its intrinsically low reproductive rate is the main problem facing conservationists.[29] It was estimated in the 1960s that an average of three adults were killed each year, mostly by illegal shooting, whereas the annual average number of young fledged was only two. Recognizing that it may never be possible to guarantee condors total immunity from hunting, conservationists have directed their main efforts towards trying to increase the reproductive rate. There has been some disagreement as to whether difficulty in finding sufficient food has limited the condors' ability to rear young. In the 1960s it was noticed that at one nest a young bird was raised in each of four successive years, whereas most nests produce young only in alternate years, and that this nest was situated in an area of unusually rich food supply.[30] Accordingly, carcasses of cattle and other suitable prey are now left out near nests to augment the natural food supply. This scheme has its critics, who point out that it may encourage condors to become tame and to lose the ability to find food for themselves, producing, in effect, a semi-domesticated species. It remains to be seen

13. The Ivory-billed Woodpecker

whether this scheme, combined with a programme to discourage hunters from shooting it, will save the California Condor from extinction and, if so, how dependent it will then have become on man's support.

Another species which is all but extinct is the Ivory-billed Woodpecker, one of the most beautiful and elusive of American birds.[31] This shared with the Carolina Parakeet the heavily forested habitat that once lined the rivers of middle and eastern America. A magnificent bird, with its black and white plumage, bright red crest and white bill, it is the largest of the American woodpeckers. It is a territorial species, each pair requiring a territory of about 2000 acres. It feeds on the wood-boring insects that infest recently dead trees; smaller, less powerful woodpeckers have to utilize softer, more rotten trees in a more advanced stage of decay. The Ivory-billed Woodpecker's decline has closely followed the development of the timber industry and was most marked in the period 1885 to 1900, when the timber trade was expanding very rapidly. In 1939 there were estimated to be about twenty-four breeding birds living in three localities in South Carolina, Texas and Florida. In 1968 the known population was just six breeding birds. There are still areas of suitable habitat and it may well be that the whereabouts of surviving Ivory-bills are being kept secret. During the later stages of its decline the Ivory-billed Woodpecker was greatly sought after by collectors of rarities and secrecy is probably the best defence against irresponsible hunters. So specific are the Ivory-bill's habitat require-ments that the only effective long-term conservation measure is to set aside areas of unspoiled river forest which alone can provide the fully-grown dead trees that the species needs. Such reserves would have to be extensive in view of the large areas required by each pair of woodpeckers. A Cuban subspecies of the Ivory-billed Woodpecker may already be extinct; its forest habitat has been extensively destroyed to make way for sugar-cane fields.

Though it is not yet nearly as rare as the California Condor or the Ivory-billed Woodpecker, there is considerable concern for the fate of the Duck Hawk, the American race of the Peregrine Falcon, a species which has a world-wide range. The epitome of a bird of prey, the Peregrine was once widespread in North America but has virtually ceased to breed there except in Alaska and Canada.[32] The cause of its decline has been pesticide pollution, which has had a catastrophic effect on its breeding rate, as described in Chapter 2. The first expressions of alarm at the disappearance of the species came in 1947. By the early 1960s the link with pesticides was clearly established but it was not until 1969 that the American government began to control the use of DDT. The vast forests and mountains of Alaska and Canada present a vision of pristine, unspoiled habitat, but even there the Peregrines are showing reduced breeding success, so pervasive is pesticide pollution.[33] Birds from these northern areas spend much of their winter further south, where they feed on contaminated prey.[34]

Ornithologists are now taking active steps to arrest the decline of the American Peregrine. Under the direction of Professor Tom Cade of Cornell University Peregrines are reared in captivity on uncon-taminated food and their offspring are later released into the wild.[35]

Such programmes are fraught with difficulties; not least is the problem that birds reared in captivity may not develop the skills in finding food and avoiding enemies that they will need to survive in the wild. Cade's solution to this problem has been to use the 'hacking back' technique of the falconer to help birds through the transition from captivity to freedom. Over a period of weeks young birds are encouraged to take more and more food for themselves. There is also the problem that birds reared in captivity will be too trusting of man and will fall victim to hunters, but this can be minimized by reducing their contacts with humans as far as possible. There are those who regard captive breeding schemes, not as conservation, but as unacceptable meddling with nature. All conservationists would prefer to see birds surviving without human intervention but captive breeding appears to be the only way to save some species and, if it succeeds in maintaining the American Peregrines until one day, hopefully, levels of toxic chemicals have fallen sufficiently for them to be able to maintain themselves, the exercise will have been fully justified.

Rarest of all the American birds of prey is the Everglade Kite, which is found only in the Everglades swamps of Florida. A census made in 1964 suggested that the entire population consisted of about fifteen birds, but a survey made four years later revealed between fifty and sixty.[36] Its decline to this perilous position is the result of highly specialized feeding habits. The Everglade Kite has a long, hooked bill which is specifically adapted for extracting from its shell one particular species of snail found in the Everglades. The snail has been greatly reduced in numbers by the wholesale destruction of its swamp habitat by flood control schemes, urban development and draining of the swamps to create farmland. The kite, unable to switch to alternative prey, has declined in numbers accordingly. Surviving breeding pairs show very low hatching success, possibly a consequence of the impoverished food supply or of inbreeding in the very small population. The nesting sites of the Everglade Kite are now the centre of a conservation area but the species can only be reliably saved from extinction if large areas of swampland habitat can be set aside for it.

Though the populations of American Peregrines and Everglade Kites have fallen to critical levels, they have not received as much

14. The Bald Eagle

public attention as a less threatened bird of prey, the Bald Eagle. This magnificent bird is America's national emblem and, as a result, the news that it was rapidly declining was met with widespread alarm. The Bald Eagle has vanished from many of its customary breeding areas, chiefly as a result of the loss of suitable habitats, but also through shooting by hunters. Until 1952 hunters actually received a bounty for killing them. In 1962 it was found that less than half of the known existing eyries produced any young at all.[37] This may well be due to pesticide poisoning. The decline of the Bald Eagle, more than that of any other American species, has given a great spur to conservation movements in America. The Audubon Society has embarked on a major campaign of research and education to try to save the eagle and has established agreements with many farmers and landowners whereby sanctuaries are set up.

The last American bird of prey I shall discuss is the Osprey, a species which, like the Peregrine, has a virtually world-wide distribution. It is not classified as an endangered species in America but its numbers are declining rapidly and in some areas where it was once common it has disappeared completely. This situation is due to pesticide poisoning and in the states of New York and New Jersey, where pesticides have been used extensively, the Osprey population is dwindling at the rate of 10 to 14 per cent each year.[38] A particularly imaginative study of the Osprey has been carried out on the Connecticut river, where a population numbering 200 pairs in 1940 fell to seventy-one pairs in 1960 and twenty-four pairs in 1963. It was clear that this fall in the population was principally due to reproductive failure, which was partly caused by the destruction of broods in nests built on the ground through both predation and flooding by occasional freak high tides. Elevated wooden platforms built along the river were quickly adopted by the Ospreys as nest sites and these losses were eliminated.[39] However, it was apparent that the low reproductive rate was mainly due to the typical symptoms of pesticide poisoning, infertility and crushed eggs. High levels of both DDT and polychlorinated biphenyls were found in eggs and chicks. Eggs from the Connecticut population and from nests in less heavily polluted Maryland were exchanged.[40] Connecticut eggs failed to hatch when tended by Maryland birds, whereas Maryland eggs were successfully reared by their Connecticut foster-parents. These results showed conclusively that the cause of hatching-failure was in the eggs and not in the behaviour of the parents. They also paved the way for an ingenious conservation technique. Ospreys, like many birds, will lay a second clutch of eggs if their first is lost or removed shortly after it is laid. This extra reproductive capacity can be exploited to swell the population. Eggs were removed from Maryland birds, who then laid and successfully reared a second brood; the original eggs were placed in the nests of Connecticut Ospreys as replacements for their polluted eggs. These were successfully reared so that the Connecticut population was once again producing young Ospreys. Unfortunately this technique does not solve the basic problem, which is the accumulation in the fish which Ospreys eat of large quantities of pesticides and other toxic chemicals. Unless pesticides are controlled this kind of manipulative conservation technique can only delay the inevitable extinction of the Osprey and other birds of prey.

Like the California Condor, the Whooping Crane is a very large bird which frequented the greater part of North America in the

15. *Whooping Cranes*

Pleistocene period but which now survives only in the smallest of relic populations.[41] It is a tall, long-legged white bird with black wings and a patch of red skin on the face. A native of wetland habitats where it feeds on crayfish, frogs and other animal life, it used to nest throughout the marshes that once covered a vast area from southern Canada to Minnesota and Iowa. Now it breeds only in the Wood Buffalo National Park in southern Canada. At the end of the breeding season Whooping Cranes migrate southwards to the coast of the Gulf of Mexico, where they are protected in the Aransas National Wildlife Refuge. These largest of American cranes vanished from most parts of America as they became settled and developed by man. The birds provided an easy target for the gun, especially during their migrations, and most of their original breeding range has been drained. By the beginning of this century the species was in dire straits and between 1922 and 1955 not a single nest was reported, except for some in Louisiana in 1939 which had vanished the following year. In 1955,

16. Kirtland's Warblers

however, the tiny breeding population in Wood Buffalo Park was discovered and it has been carefully guarded ever since. The wild population of Whooping Cranes has shown a steady increase, though with occasional fluctuations, from an estimated fourteen birds in 1938 to forty-three in 1967. In 1971 it stood at fifty-nine birds, only to fall to forty-nine in the next two years. Recently a captive breeding programme has been set up at Patuxent in Maryland.[42] Wild birds usually lay two eggs but successfully raise only one of them and so the policy of the Patuxent scheme has been to take eggs, one from each of a number of nests in Wood Buffalo Park, and to raise them in incubators. In this way the wild population should not be depleted. In 1974 twenty-one of the world's total population of seventy-three Whooping Cranes were living at Patuxent, where they had been raised. The next steps in the programme are to breed from these captive-reared birds and to release some cranes into the wild population. Every stage in the

Whooping Crane programme has first been tried out on another, less rare species, the Sandhill Crane. Attempts to introduce captive-reared Sandhill Cranes into the wild have not been successful and so it remains to be seen whether the Whooping Crane scheme will eventually lead to a substantial increase in the wild population.

A rare species which has been the subject of a quite different kind of conservation programme is Kirtland's Warbler.[43] This little yellow, brown and slate-grey bird nests in a very restricted area in the Jack-pine woodlands of Michigan and spends the winter in the Bahamas. It is very particular in its habitat requirements, nesting only in Jack-pine that is growing back after a bush fire and preferring trees that are between six and thirteen years old. It was first discovered in 1841 when a specimen was picked up on a boat passing between the Bahamas and Cuba, but it was not recorded on the mainland until 1851, when it was collected in Ohio; a nest was not found until 1903. In 1923 it was found that many of the warblers' nests were being parasitized by the Brown-headed Cowbird which, like cuckoos, lays its eggs in other species' nests to the detriment of the hosts' own broods.[44] This particular species of cowbird was not previously indigenous to Michigan but spread there from the eastern prairies as a result of the conversion of the land to agricultural use. Kirtland's Warbler had thus never evolved any counter-measures against it and so was affected more seriously than most of the cowbird's host species. It was estimated that the parasites accounted for the loss of 43 per cent of the warblers' eggs. In 1965 a campaign against the cowbird was mounted and large numbers were trapped and killed. Though the proportion of parasitized nests has declined, so has the size of the Kirtland's Warbler population.[45] It is not clear why this is, but it may be due to destruction of their wintering habitat on the Bahamas. Kirtland's Warbler, like the Whooping Crane, illustrates how vulnerable migratory species are to environmental changes and how difficult it is to protect them. They not only occupy two widely-spaced habitats but twice a year have to make the hazardous journey between them.

In this chapter I have described how the recent ornithological history of North America began with the destruction of some of its most prolific species. I have also discussed a number of species that are now

17. The Wood or Carolina Duck

severely threatened and have outlined what is being done to conserve them. I shall end on an optimistic note with the story of an American bird which was once in danger of extinction but which is now fairly common again. The Wood Duck, also called the Carolina Duck, is one of the most colourful of all ducks and is found in wildfowl collections throughout the world.[46] In America it was severely hunted and by the turn of the century was extremely rare. In 1914 it was thought to be extinct in the wild; there were probably fewer Wood Ducks in the wild than in captivity. A. C. White of Connecticut set up a captive breeding colony, actually importing his birds from a population in Belgium. The progeny of this colony were released into the wild, up to 400 of them each year, throughout the period 1922 to 1939. At the same time a total Federal ban on hunting and the provision of nesting boxes helped to re-establish the Wood Duck as a viable species among America's rich bird life. Let us hope that the Wood Duck is but one of many American species that will eventually be saved from extinction.

5

Extinct and Vanishing Birds of New Zealand

THE birds of New Zealand occupy a special place in ornithology, including as they do a number of species that are quite unlike any other birds found elsewhere in the world. A particular combination of geological, geographical and climatic influences has shaped a unique community of plants and animals.[1] There is a tendency for people in the rest of the world to think of New Zealand as a group of islands just off the coast of Australia. In fact the New Zealand archipelago is some 1200 miles from Australia's east coast, and this remoteness has been a major influence in the evolution of its birds. Apart from the two large islands, North Island and South Island, there is the smaller Stewart Island, which is separated from South Island by narrow straits, and the more remote Chatham Island, 500 miles to the east. In addition there are numerous offshore islands of various sizes and at varying distances from the larger islands.

The history of New Zealand began some 130 million years ago at the end of the Jurassic period and the beginning of the Cretaceous when a small segment of the great southern continent called Gondwanaland became separated and began to move away to the north.[2] Before the link with Gondwanaland was finally broken this small area of land was probably colonized by at least two types of bird belonging to the family

New Zealand

Hokianga

Cuvier I.

NORTH ISLAND

Wanganui

Stephens I.

Maud I.

Chatham Is.

Auckland Is.

SOUTH ISLAND

Chatham Island

Mangere I.

Murchison Mtns.
Kepler Mtns.

Dusky Bay

Fiordland

Stewart Island

of large, flightless Ratite birds which were distributed throughout Gondwanaland at that time.[3] The descendants of these two ancestral groups are the kiwis, which survive to the present day, and the moas, whose last representatives may have survived into the nineteenth century. The isolation of New Zealand at this early stage in the earth's geological history has had a profound effect on the nature and evolution of its fauna and flora. In particular it means that New Zealand has been largely unaffected by the major evolutionary developments that have taken place in the rest of the world. Most important of these was the great diversification of the mammals, which did not begin until sixty million years after New Zealand had become separated. As a result, New Zealand has never been naturally colonized by mammals, with the exception of a few species of bats which have flown there. The absence of mammals, as we shall see, has been a major influence in the evolution of New Zealand's birds. Other animals which have never found their way to New Zealand, except through the recent intervention of man, are snakes and true freshwater fishes.[4]

Another consequence of New Zealand's long separation is that some of the animals that live there now are essentially evolutionary relics, direct descendents of ancestral types that in other parts of the world have been replaced by more recently evolved forms. The most celebrated example of such an animal is the Tuatara Lizard, which is the sole living survivor of a whole family of reptiles whose many representatives were distributed throughout the ancient continents before they broke up. This animal is renowned for its well-developed pineal eye, a light-sensitive organ in the top of its head. New Zealand's three species of frog are likewise descended from very primitive amphibian stock. These ancient colonists have shown little tendency to give rise to new species so that New Zealand contains far fewer reptiles and amphibians than most areas of land of comparable size in the rest of the world.

The evolution of plant life in New Zealand has similarly been influenced by its primordial isolation. The proliferation of the flowering plants, which now dominate most of the world's vegetation, occurred, like that of the mammals, long after New Zealand had become separated. Some flowering plants did find their way to these remote islands, carried

there as seeds by the wind or by the sea, but those that became successful colonists represent only a tiny sample of the innumerable types that
are found elsewhere. The most important component of New Zealand's vegetation is the forest which once covered the greater part of
the archipelago and which contains some trees that are quite unlike
any found in the rest of the world. Among the more common trees
are the Kauri, which grows mostly in North Island and which can be
as much as 170 feet tall, and the evergreen New Zealand Beech, which
grows extensively in South Island. The absence of mammals profoundly
influenced plant evolution; elsewhere in the world many mammals
have evolved as herbivores and plants have become adapted accordingly. On New Zealand the only herbivores of any significance were the
moas and many of the endemic plants have never evolved adaptations
such as thorns which could protect them against the activities of brows-
ing mammals.

The section of Gondwanaland that broke off and drifted away so long
ago was like a half-filled Noah's Ark which took with it only a few of
the species living at that time and which left too early to take many of
the animals and plants that have since become a major part of the world's
fauna and flora. For birds this situation has created unique opportunities. Having the power of flight, they have been able to colonize New
Zealand on numerous occasions and, having established themselves
there, have become adapted to their new environment in ways which
reflect the absence of many of the animals that live in their places of
origin. The kiwis and the moas, alone among New Zealand's birds,
were probably passengers on the ark when it first became separated.
All the other species have arrived there at various times since. The
earliest of the colonists that have survived until recent times were birds
of three distinct types, now classified as three families, the wattlebirds,
the New Zealand 'Wrens' and the New Zealand 'Thrushes' or Piopios.
All three families are unique to New Zealand and their ancestors are
thought to have arrived from Australia or the East Indies about sixty
million years ago. Between then and the beginning of the Pleistocene
period about two million years ago many more colonizations occurred,
giving rise to at least twenty-five genera of endemic birds. The Pleistocene appears to have disrupted the process of colonization by which

18. A Moa

the New Zealand ark gradually became filled. It was a period of
extreme cold in which much of New Zealand was covered by glaciers
and many species were probably wiped out. Unlike the larger continents in the rest of the world, there were no adjacent areas of land with
more temperate climates in which New Zealand's birds could find
refuge. Many of the species derived from the early colonists disappeared
in the Pleistocene period and since then there has been a new wave of
immigrant birds which have moved into the vacant niches.

Most of the immigrants to New Zealand have been birds from Australia, the nearest large area of land, though some have also come from
the islands of the East Indies and a few from as far afield as the northern
hemisphere. It is thought that some of the ancestral bird types have
invaded New Zealand more than once. The New Zealand 'Robins'
and 'Tits' are believed to be derived from the same family of Australian
flycatchers, the robin stock having arrived first and become quite
distinct from its ancestors by the time of the second colonization which

gave rise to the tits. Likewise the flightless rail called the Takahe is thought to be an early descendant of the same ancestral stock which later produced another of New Zealand's rails, the Pukeko. For most of its long history New Zealand has been almost totally covered by forests and as a result the great majority of bird species that are descended from the early colonists are forest dwellers. Whereas New Zealand's land birds have adapted to the unique conditions prevailing in the forests and have consequently become so distinctive, the birds living around New Zealand's coasts are mostly very similar to, and often are the same as, coastal and sea birds found around Australia, Antarctica and the islands of the South Pacific.

It is not easy to reconstruct the history of New Zealand's birds, chiefly because there is a dearth of fossils. This is probably due to the fact that most of New Zealand has long been covered by forests which create acidic soils in which corpses decompose very quickly. There are many more fossil remains of the birds that have lived around the archipelago's coasts. For the most part the ancestry of the living birds has to be deduced by comparing the anatomy and habits of one species with another.

As we saw in Chapter 1, a frequent occurrence in evolution has been the tendency of ancestral birds that have colonized archipelagos to give rise to a variety of new species, each evolving independently on a different island. The classic examples of this process of adaptive radiation are provided by the birds of the Galapagos and Hawaiian islands. Though New Zealand is an archipelago, and has been for most of its history, there is little indication that a similar phenomenon has taken place there. Of the three ancient colonist families, the wattlebirds produced only three species, the wrens four and the thrushes or Piopios only two. The one real exception is provided by the moas, which are thought to have diversified into as many as twenty-five species.[5] It is possible that at one time there were many more descendants of the early immigrants but that the Pleistocene ice ages brought about their extinction.

The impoverished nature of New Zealand's fauna which has resulted from its isolation has been a major influence on the evolution of the habits and anatomy of the birds that have successfully colonized the islands. Many of the land birds have become flightless, or at least have reduced powers of flight, and many have become larger than their ancestors. Here again the loss of the ability to fly is apparently a direct result of the absence of mammalian predators. The kiwis, like the moas, were already flightless when New Zealand became separated and have lost all but the smallest vestiges of their wings. Of the descendants of the later colonists, the Takahe is flightless and the wrens, wattlebirds and Kakapo are only able to fly for very short distances. The relatively large size of many New Zealand birds is probably an adaptation to the colder climate compared with that of their ancestral home. There is an evolutionary rule, called Bergmann's rule, which holds for many types of animal, that at colder, higher latitudes animals tend to be bigger. This is because large animals are more efficient at retaining their heat than smaller ones due to their greater volume in relation to their surface area. This rule also applies within New Zealand; in those species which have distinct races or subspecies in the two main islands, the South Island race is generally larger than the North Island one.[6]

A curious feature of New Zealand's bird life is that it includes rather fewer species of endemic land birds than one would expect for an area of this size. This may be largely due to the fact that New Zealand is ecologically impoverished; that is, the small number of animals and plants that have successfully colonized the islands have created relatively few ecological opportunities for birds. In recent years the relationship between land areas and numbers of species has been examined by biologists, who have developed the theory of Island Biogeography. This is based on two simple observations: small islands contain fewer species than large ones and remote islands contain fewer species than those nearer a large land mass. I shall discuss some of the processes that are thought to underlie these correlations in the next chapter. New Zealand appears not to conform to the first of these rules; Tasmania, whose area is only a quarter of New Zealand's, contains one-and-a-half times as many species of land bird. On the face of it we might suppose that this discrepancy is explained by the second biogeographic rule: New Zealand contains fewer species because it is so remote and inaccessible. However, there are good reasons to suppose that, large as it is, the gap between New Zealand and neighbouring areas of land does not present too great an obstacle to birds. There have been innumerable reports over the years of sightings of species which have never been seen in New Zealand before and which apparently have found their own way there. By no means all of these incursions by alien species lead to successful colonization, that is, the establishment of a long-term breeding population. However, it is estimated that since the end of the Pleistocene period there have been about seven successful colonizations every century, which, in evolutionary terms, is a very high rate. One explanation of this is that the new colonists are taking the place of species that were wiped out in the Pleistocene.

The picture that emerges from this brief outline of the history of New Zealand's birds is of a motley group of species evolving along lines dictated by the archipelago's unique geographical and biological character. The general trend has been for the number of species to increase as it has been augmented by new colonists from elsewhere. This process of expansion received a severe setback during the Pleistocene ice ages. When more temperate climates returned the process of colonization resumed, only to be interrupted by a new and even more devastating development, the arrival of man.

There have been two quite independent human colonizations of New Zealand, each with profound effects on the indigenous birds.[7] The first was by Polynesian islanders, the founders of the Maori culture which dates back at least to the eleventh century AD. In the eighteenth century the Europeans arrived and the whole pace of change in the islands, which had been gradual over the previous 600 years, immediately accelerated. While it is fairly certain that the Maoris had an adverse effect on the bird life of New Zealand, both directly by hunting and indirectly on the habitat in general, it is also apparent that they had established the kind of symbiotic, live-and-let-live relationship with many of the birds which is often found in supposedly primitive societies. The arrival of the Europeans put an end to that. The wholesale changes in the environment wrought by the new colonists completely negated any conservationist policies that the Maoris had developed. It is not easy to determine from the available evidence to what extent species that have become extinct or severely reduced in the last few hundred years have done so as the result of Maori or European influence or, indeed, whether entirely natural environmental changes have played a part.

It is generally agreed that the Polynesian founders of the Maori culture arrived in New Zealand around AD 1000, though it has been suggested that there may have been colonizations before that date.[8] The most likely origin of these first settlers was in eastern Polynesia, particularly the Society and Marquesas Islands. The distance from there to New Zealand is some 3000 miles and it is improbable that the Polynesians sailed back and forth over so great a distance. It is therefore thought more likely that the original colonization was achieved by a single, one-way voyage and that the Maori civilization evolved in virtually total isolation from the ancestral way of life. The migration from Polynesia to New Zealand involved a considerable change in latitude and, consequently, in climate. Just as a bird that colonizes an island becomes adapted to the new conditions prevailing there, so the Maori culture represents the adaptation of a basically tropical way of life to more temperate conditions. The Polynesian settlers brought with them a number of their staple vegetables. Some, like yams and sweet potatoes, could be cultivated in the new climate; others, like bananas and coconuts, could not. Accordingly, the Maoris adopted some common indigenous plants as vegetables, notably the Bracken Fern, whose rhizome they used as a staple starch food. Their protein diet shows a similar compromise. They brought with them dogs, which provided not only meat but also skins for clothing, and supplemented their diet with fish, seals caught around the coasts and moas and other birds which they hunted on the coastal plains and in the forests. They also introduced the Polynesian rat or Kiore, whether by design or accident is not clear.

Two distinct phases in the evolution of the Maori culture have been differentiated by archaeologists. The first represents a shift away from the predominantly agricultural way of life of the Polynesian homelands to more of a hunting and gathering system in which cultivation of the land played a relatively minor role. This change was made possible by the relative abundance of indigenous animals, including birds. Later, and apparently in response to a decline in the numbers of wild animals, there developed in North Island the 'classic' Maori culture, which was based more on the cultivation of such vegetables as sweet potato and fern root. Because moa bones have been found among domestic remains dating from the earlier Maori culture, it has often been referred to as the 'Moa-hunter' culture, though this may give a rather misleading impression of the importance of moas to the early Maoris. Apart from those indigenous birds that they hunted for food, the Maoris used the feathers of a variety of birds to make cloaks and the tail feathers of the Huia as a badge of high rank. A number of species became incorporated into their mythology and religion and some of them were accordingly protected.

The Maoris are commonly blamed for the demise of the moas.[9] While there is no doubt that they did hunt and eat them, it is most improbable that hunting alone could have exterminated these once numerous birds. Excavations of ancient Maori living sites suggest that moas were not a mainstay of the early settlers' diet.[10] Fish, dogs and seals seem to have been the staple sources of protein, with moas probably being taken only when the opportunity arose. It is more likely that the Maoris' contribution to the decline of the moas was indirect. The dogs and rats that they introduced were the first carnivorous mammals to have set foot on New Zealand and they were presented with a host of bird species that built quite defenceless nests on the ground. It is probable that the extinction of the moas and the decline of several other species were principally due to the loss of their eggs and chicks through predation by these alien mammals. In addition the Maoris used fire to destroy substantial areas of the native forests to make way for farm land. Often the cleared land proved to be uncultivatable and became overgrown by Bracken Fern. However, the reduction in the forests due to the activities of the Maoris, though extensive, was small compared to the total area covered by forest at that time and cannot have contributed significantly to the reduction in numbers of the endemic forest birds. For whatever reason, a number of birds were on the decline when the second human invasion of New Zealand, this time by Europeans, began in the eighteenth century.

New Zealand was visited in 1642 by Abel Tasman, but its European history really begins in 1769, when it was visited by Captain James

Colour Plates

The Peregrine Falcon

The Everglade Kite

Great Auks

Pink headed Ducks

Passenger Pigeons

Carolina Parakeets

Labrador Ducks

H.C

Heath Hens

Huias

The Kakapo

The Takahe

The Mauritius Kestrel

The Kaui Oo

Nénés

Waldrapps

The Great Bustard

Cook in the *Endeavour*. Cook was deeply impressed by the new country, particularly by the 'forests of vast extent full of the straightest and cleanest and the largest trees we have ever seen'.[11] This was a reference to the giant White Pine or Kahikatea. Cook also remarked on the abundant bird life and on the deafening volume of its dawn chorus. By 1840 there was a population of about 2000 Europeans, mostly settled in the North Island. In that year an agreement was made with the Maoris and New Zealand became a British colony. In the next twenty years the European population grew to about 100,000. Then in 1861 a gold rush produced a further rapid increase to 400,000 people in 1881. Since then the population has grown steadily as a prosperous, basically agricultural economy has been developed.

The most important single change in the natural environment of New Zealand brought about by the expanding European population has been the destruction of the greater part of the indigenous forests.[12] When the Europeans arrived about 68 per cent of the islands' area was covered by forest; this is now reduced to around 14 per cent. The forests were felled for two reasons, to provide timber and to clear the land for agricultural use. The tall, straight trees were an ideal source of wood, both to build the houses required by the expanding colonial population and to export back to the Old World. In addition, the Kauri tree produced a valuable gum which was exported to be used in the manufacture of varnish. In the 1920s and 1930s large areas of the cleared land were planted with alien trees, particularly the Monterey Pine from California. To some extent the harvesting of these introduced trees relieved the pressure on the native forests but in 1971, by which time the plantations had mostly been cleared, the New Zealand government announced a plan to fell large areas of the evergreen beech forests to make wood pulp for export to Japan. This plan proposed the felling of an area equivalent to a strip one mile wide stretching from London to Bucharest. After tremendous public outcry the government announced a slightly reduced plan in 1973, but at the moment the future of New Zealand's remaining forests is still a matter for heated debate.

The felling of forests such as those in New Zealand has consequences far more profound and extensive than the mere loss of trees and the animals that live in them. The removal of trees completely alters the way water drains off the land and deforested areas have often become seriously eroded, the rain washing away the top-soil. This effect has frequently been exacerbated by allowing the cleared land to become over-grazed by sheep, which have destroyed much of the remaining vegetation. Mature forests are self-sustaining in that vital plant nutrients like nitrogen and phosphorus circulate within them and are not lost to the outside world. When trees are felled and taken away their store of these nutrients is removed and is not returned to the soil through the usual process of decay. Such plant foods as remain in the soil are gradually washed out by the rains. As a result deforested areas have gradually become less and less productive as agricultural land and farmers have increasingly had to resort to the use of artificial fertilizers to maintain their yields. Deforestation thus represents a major alteration of the environment, and when it is practised on the scale that it has been in New Zealand it should be a cause for concern far beyond the fact that it deprives many endemic birds and other animals of their habitat. Natural forests take literally thousands of years to reach maturity and when they are destroyed the stability that they bring to the environment cannot be quickly restored.

The European colonists brought with them a number of alien species that joined the Polynesian dogs and rats as enemies of the indigenous birds, as both predators and competitors. Predatory species that were imported included brown and black rats, dogs, cats, stoats, weasels and hedgehogs. These animals preyed not only on the flightless or feebly-flying birds but also on their eggs and young. A plague of rats that broke out on Stewart Island in 1963 all but wiped out the wrens, Saddlebacks and snipe that were previously fairly common there. Kiwis, though they are totally flightless, have been much less affected by these alien predators than other indigenous birds, but why this is so is not clear. Many species were introduced to provide the sport to which the settlers were accustomed and which they were denied by the absence of suitable endemic species. As well as birds such as pheasants, mammals like deer, wallabies and rabbits were imported for this purpose. These game species are all herbivores that both compete with native plant-eating birds and contribute to the general destruction of the natural vegetation. Other introduced herbivores include pigs, goats, sheep, cattle and horses. The Australian Opossum, introduced to provide fur, is particularly destructive because of its habit of eating the young shoots and leaves of trees and it has brought about the defoliation of large areas of forest. The success with which these many introduced mammals have taken to their new environment is due to the lack of any competition from indigenous mammals of similar habits.[13] The proportion of all introduced mammal species that have established viable breeding populations in New Zealand is twice that for introduced birds, which have had to face much stiffer competition from resident species.

The replacement of much of the natural forest by new agricultural and urban habitats has provided many opportunities for colonization by species of birds that inhabit such habitats outside New Zealand. Since the arrival of Europeans at least eight new species have become established of their own accord and a further forty-three have become resident following their introduction by man. Although a great many more alien species that found their way to New Zealand, with or without man's assistance, have failed to establish themselves, some of the recent colonists have become extremely successful. The Australian Silvereye, which first invaded in 1856, is now a very common bird in woodland and the Welcome Swallow, also from Australia, nests in large numbers on buildings and bridges. This invasion by so many foreign birds has led to frequent assertions that the decline of many of the endemic birds is due to their being excluded by 'more vigorous' invaders. This is probably a mistaken view.[14] Of the many species that have been introduced to New Zealand in the last 150 years, only a quarter of them are found in those areas of natural vegetation that still remain. All of these also live in man-made environments; there is not a single species that exclusively occupies natural habitats. There is in fact no clear evidence that introduced species have displaced or seriously competed with endemic species in their natural habitats.

The birds most severely affected by the various changes in New Zealand's natural history brought about by man have been those that have lived there the longest.[15] The moas were all but extinct by the time the Europeans arrived. Of the three families derived from birds that crossed the sea soon after New Zealand became separated, only isolated remnants remain. Two of the three species of wren and both the North and South Island races of thrush or Piopio are either extinct or probably so. Of the wattlebirds, the Huia is certainly extinct, the Kokako survives only in North Island and in very small numbers and the Saddleback is restricted to a number of small offshore islands. The kiwis are an exception in that, although they are the most ancient of the endemic birds, only one of their three species, the Little Spotted Kiwi, is considered to be in any danger. A number of New Zealand's older endemic species are declining, particularly on the larger islands, and their best chances of survival seem to be on the smaller offshore islands, some of which have been largely untouched by man and have escaped invasion by introduced herbivores and predators.

It is generally assumed that man, through the far-reaching changes he has brought about in New Zealand's natural environment, is primarily responsible for the decline or extinction of so many of its birds. However, there are those who think that natural climatic changes have also played a part.[16] They argue that the pattern of decline of several species has not followed the spread of human colonization as closely as one would expect if that were the most important factor. Since about 1800 it appears that a number of species have declined at a similar rate on the different islands despite the fact that human activity has not been evenly distributed between them. Nevertheless, while there is good evidence of significant climatic changes over the last several hundred years their effect has probably been slight compared to that of man's influence. Man has affected New Zealand's bird life in three ways, by hunting, by deforestation and by the introduction of alien species. Despite the fact that there are still some substantial areas of natural forest and the rarer birds are strenuously protected, many of them continue to decline. This suggests that the most serious of all human effects on the natural environment has been the introduction, deliberate or accidental, of mammalian species, particularly predators.

In the last 150 years some attempt has been made to ameliorate the critical position of many of New Zealand's birds by legislation.[17] Measures to control introduced mammals included a bill passed in 1844 to control dogs in towns and another introduced in 1876 that sought to control rabbits. In 1861 a bill concerning introduced game birds, fish and mammals was enacted, but its purpose was to protect them, not to curb them. The first endemic bird to be legally protected was the kiwi, in 1896. In 1907 the Tuatara Lizard and thirty-six of the endemic birds were afforded full legal protection and in 1921 this was extended to a further 132 species. In 1930 legislation to control introduced herbivores, which previously had been protected, was enacted and in 1953 the Wildlife Act gave full protection to all New Zealand's birds except for a few very common or pest species. Such legislation serves only to reduce losses through hunting, collecting and, to some extent, habitat destruction. There is probably little that can be done about the many introduced herbivores and predators that have so radically affected the endemic bird life and which are now widespread throughout the larger islands. Only on the smaller offshore islands is it feasible to eliminate introduced animals and to restore the natural habitat. As we shall see later in this chapter it is the imaginative use of such islands by the New Zealand Wildlife Service that offers the best prospects for New Zealand's beleaguered birds.

Much of what we know of the natural history of New Zealand's extinct and endangered birds comes from the writings of Walter Lawry Buller, a nineteenth-century naturalist whose position in New Zealand's ornithology is similar to that of Wilson and Audubon in America.[18] Born in 1838 at Pakanae in the Hokianga district of North Island, Buller was the son of a missionary priest who had come to New Zealand from Cornwall in 1836. A man of great intellectual gifts, he started out as a banker but went on to become a successful lawyer, magistrate and administrator. He was fluent in the Maori language and devoted much of his life to the administration of New Zealand's original colonists. His ornithological studies were brought together in *A History of the Birds of New Zealand*, which, beautifully illustrated by J. G. Keulemans, was published in 1873 and again in an expanded edition in 1888. Knighted in 1886 for his services as Commissioner for the Maoris, he moved to London in 1898, dying there in 1906. Buller's evocative writings give us a vivid account of New Zealand's forests and birds before their devastation by man had really begun. He has been criticized for the way he killed large numbers of birds for his collections, but, as we have seen, this was symptomatic of the general approach to natural history that prevailed at that time.

One group of birds that Buller never saw were the moas, which at one time were New Zealand's largest and, in some respects, most successful birds.[19] The great majority of their several species died out by the seventeenth century but there are some convincing eye-witness accounts from people who believe they saw one of the smaller moas during the late nineteenth century. What little we know about these curious birds is the result of careful detective work based on the evidence of a mass of bones found in swamps, sand dunes, caves and Maori kitchen middens. After much re-examination of this material, which was first described by Professor Richard Owen, it is now accepted that there were about twenty-five distinct species. Moas were completely flightless; they did not possess even the vestiges of wings and they clearly had much in common with other Ratite birds such as ostriches and emus. It is thought that they generally adopted the loop-necked posture of emus and cassowaries and not the straight, upright stance of ostriches and rheas. They had small heads, long, very powerful legs, rather loose straggly plumage and no tail feathers. They were entirely vegetarian, grazing on the grass of the coastal plains, and also eating the leaves and berries of bushes and shrubs. The biggest of the moas was up to ten feet tall, making it the biggest of all the Ratites. We shall never know precisely why the moas declined. As we have seen, it is not likely that hunting by the Maoris was entirely responsible though it may have been a contributory factor. Maori dogs and rats probably did more damage and several authorities agree that climatic variations and the botanical changes that resulted from them also played a part.

Though it is not in any danger of extinction, we cannot discuss the birds of New Zealand without mentioning the kiwi, that country's national emblem.[20] Kiwis, of which there are three species, are Ratite birds and are generally considered to be close relatives of the moas. However, they have followed a totally independent evolutionary path, and have been 'successful' in a quite different way. Whereas the moas diversified into many different species but eventually became extinct, the kiwis have specialized, have not diversified and survive to

19. *The Kiwi*

the present day. Though they are common. few New Zealanders ever see a kiwi, except in a zoo, They can be heard at night, uttering the call from which their name is derived, and a snuffling sound more characteristic of a mammal than a bird. In fact, the parallels between kiwis and mammals are many, suggesting the kiwis have adapted to the niche left totally vacant by the absence of any endemic mammals. They are flightless, nocturnal and secretive, relying more on a sense of smell unusually acute for a bird than on their rather ill-developed eyes.[21] They even have whiskers around the head just like those of nocturnal mammals. About the size of a hen, with feathers that are rather like coarse hair in texture, they search for their food with their long bills, which have nostrils at the tip. They will sometimes thrust the entire bill into the soil in pursuit of their insect prey. The most widespread species is the Brown Kiwi, found throughout all the main islands. The Little and Great Spotted Kiwi are found only in the South Island. All have healthy populations, except perhaps the Little Spotted Kiwi. They are apparently immune to the activities of introduced predators that have so devastated other flightless endemic birds. This may be because the kiwi's egg is exceptionally large for a bird of its size and may be too big for predators such as rats to handle. Also, young kiwis, in common with chicks of many ground-nesting birds, are mobile and alert very soon after hatching. Kiwis thrive in most areas of remaining natural forest. There are even signs that the Greater Spotted Kiwi is colonizing peripheral agricultural habitats.

Among the first birds to join the moas and kiwis in New Zealand after it had become isolated were the crow-like ancestors of the wattle-birds, a family unique to New Zealand that once included the Huia, the Kokako and the Saddleback.[22] Their name comes from the coloured, fleshy wattles that hung from the base of their bills. The Huia is now extinct but, thanks to Buller, we know a great deal about the habits of this beautiful and fascinating bird.[23]

The Huia was unique among known bird species in that the beaks of male and female differed markedly in size and shape, that of the male being straight and robust whereas the female's was long, delicate and curved (Plate IX). In all other respects the sexes were identical. It was a large bird, measuring eighteen inches in length, with glossy black plumage and a broad white band at the base of the tail. The bill was ivory in colour and the wattles at its base were orange. Even before it was threatened by the advent of Europeans the Huia was restricted to a rather small area in the heavily forested mountain ranges at the southern end of North Island. It nested in hollow trees and was generally to be seen in the lower branches of the beech trees or hopping about on the forest floor. Its wings were rather short and rounded and, with its fluttering flight, it looked rather like a giant black and white butterfly. Its name was derived from the most distinctive of its many loud calls. It was the Huia's misfortune that its beautiful plumage and call should have attracted the attention of both the Maoris and the European colonists.

The significance of the disparity between the beaks of the two sexes lies in a difference in their feeding habits. The Huia's principal food was the Huhu grub, the larva of a nocturnal beetle that lives in decaying wood and reaches the size of a man's finger. Buller obtained a live pair of Huias and kept them for a year in captivity, supplying them with rotten branches infested with Huhu grubs.[24] He found that the male and female employed quite different techniques to extract the larvae from the wood. The male concentrated on the most decayed timber, hammering it with his heavy beak in the manner of a woodpecker and chipping it away until the grubs were exposed. In contrast, the female concentrated her attention on more resistant wood, delicately probing with her bill into the crevices and tunnels made by the larvae. Once they had removed the grubs from the wood, the Huias clipped off the hard head and jaws and tossed up the succulent body so that it could be swallowed end-on. Buller described how the female frequently followed the male and explored for grubs in the wood that he had broken up, so that to some extent the male helped the female to find food. He dissected a male bird and found that, as in woodpeckers, the muscles of the head and neck were much better developed than in most birds. A recent analysis of the Huia's skull has shown that it possessed an exceptionally powerful muscle for opening the bill.[25] A similar feature is shown by starlings, for whom it is an adaptation associated with their habit of thrusting their beak into the ground and then opening it to create a hole from which insects are extracted. The similarity between Huia and starling skulls led to the assumption that the two birds were closely related, but it is now thought that this is an example of convergent evolution.[26]

A number of influences have been blamed for the extinction of the Huia and it is probable that it was a combination of these factors that brought about its destruction.[27] Some authorities have suggested that hunting by the Maoris was primarily responsible, but this does not take into account the attitude of the Maoris to the Huia. Before the arrival of the Europeans, the Maoris had certainly hunted the Huia for generations, their white-tipped tail feathers being highly prized as a mark of mourning and as a badge of high status.[28] However, this hunting was not indiscriminate but was controlled by the local Tohunga or priest, who apparently kept a careful check on the numbers of all the bird species that were hunted for food or for their plumage. If any bird became scarce in a particular area, that area and the bird concerned were put under 'Tapu', that is, its capture was forbidden under threat of divine retribution. Thus, through the spiritual authority of their priests, the Maoris achieved a biological equilibrium with at least some of the birds around them. This situation changed with the arrival of the

Europeans, who corrupted the Maoris with financial inducements. Around the turn of this century the Duke of York (later George V) visited New Zealand and was presented with a Huia feather by a Maori chief. He put the feather in his hat and the Maoris were so impressed by the obviously elevated status of their visitor that there was a suddenly renewed fashion for Huia feathers; their value went up and birds were hunted to supply the increased demand.[29]

A large part of the Huia's already limited range was destroyed by deforestation by European settlers and this must have been a major influence in its decline. However, even today large areas of natural forest still remain in the higher mountains and it seems that other factors must have contributed to the Huia's extinction. Introduced predators also probably took their toll of a species that spent so much of its time on or near the ground, but it seems that the primary cause of the Huia's demise was direct hunting by or on behalf of Europeans.

With the European settlers came a number of hunters who supplied a home market of apparently insatiable curio collectors, as well as men with serious ornithological intentions like Buller. These men recruited the Maoris with their wealth of knowledge of the wildlife to help them find specimens. Such were the rewards of the curio trade with its demand for stuffed birds for English drawing rooms and for the Maori headdresses made out of Huia tail feathers as anthropological specimens, that the Maoris were persuaded to abandon their ancient customs of careful husbandry to supply the new trade. Buller recorded that in one month eleven Maoris collected the skins of no less than 646 Huias. In a vain attempt to protect the Huia the government imposed heavy penalties for hunting it, but meanwhile pursued a policy of encouraging deforestation.

Buller's account of his travels in search of the Huia provides a most evocative and graphic description of the New Zealand forest scene in the late 1860s. To the modern ornithologist his records make curious reading with their eloquent descriptions of the beauty of the birds in their natural surroundings ending invariably with an account of his attempts to shoot them. In later years Buller's eagerness to collect specimens in quantity was severely criticized and was cited as a significant factor in the extinction of birds like the Huia. In his defence it has been suggested that Buller foresaw their extinction, and that his enormous collections were made in the belief that it was the ornithologist's duty to collect as many specimens as possible while it was still possible to do so.[30]

A striking feature that is apparent in Buller's writings is the great tameness shown by Huias towards man. Their distinctive whistling call, was imitated by native hunters to lure the birds to their traps. The pair that Buller kept alive had been attracted in this way until they were so close that a noose could be slipped over their heads. Buller also described how Huias were usually encountered in pairs and male and female showed such a degree of attachment that, should one of a pair be captured or shot, its mate would search for it rather than fly away. By such behaviour Huias must have contributed to their own destruction.

One of the Huia skins collected by Buller in 1883 was examined forty years later and under one of the facial wattles were found five bird ticks.[31] These ticks belonged to two species that are not endemic to New Zealand but are of Oriental and African origin. Both species are found naturally on Mynah birds in their native haunts. The Mynah bird was one of several species imported into New Zealand by man and it rapidly became established following its introduction in 1875. It is possible that it passed its natural parasites, together with the diseases they transmit, to endemic species such as the Huia, which would have had no natural immunity to alien infections. There is no direct evidence that bird diseases were imported in this way, but it is possible that they may have contributed to the demise of the Huia.

The scientific interest of the Huia lies in the disparity in form of the male and female beaks.[32] Differences in the appearance of the two sexes, called sexual dimorphism, are widespread among birds, but are usually associated with features such as colouration or plumage which play an important part in courtship displays. Such differences reflect the different roles played by the two sexes in courtship. Very commonly the male, whose sexual role is to attract and stimulate the female, is very much more vividly coloured than she. The structure of a bird's beak is adapted primarily for handling food items with maximum efficiency and in most species male and female have similar beaks and eat the same food. As we have seen, however, male and female Huias were adapted to feed in different ways and were thus able to extract grubs from wood of different textures. This meant that, as a pair, Huias were able to obtain food from a wider range of wood types than if they had had similar beaks. From Buller's field notes it is clear that Huias were almost invariably seen in pairs, as one would expect if male and female depended on mutual co-operation to find food; and although his claim that the two partners actually fed each other on the prey they had obtained by their different methods is probably pure whimsy, taken together the good anatomical evidence and the rather sketchy behavioural observations do suggest that the Huia possessed a feeding technique quite unlike that of any living bird.

Were it alive today, there is little doubt that the Huia would be the subject of intense scrutiny by sociobiologists. Sociobiology is a recently-developed discipline which examines the relationship between social behaviour, ecology and other aspects of animal life such as anatomy. It is probably wrong to suppose that the adaptive advantage of the disparity in bill shape between male and female Huias was that they could assist each other in feeding. The more likely explanation is that it meant male and female did not compete with one another for the same food items. A less extreme disparity in bill length is shown by the Hispaniolan Woodpecker, though in this species the male has the longer bill.[33] Significantly, this woodpecker is an island species and the difference in bill size is much greater than that of its close relative on the mainland, the Golden-fronted Woodpecker. It is argued that in the island environment, where there is less intense competition from birds with similar diet, the sexes have diverged in their feeding habits, exploiting food supplies which on the mainland would be the preserve of other species. If each sex eats different food, or, as in the case of the Huia, the same food but in different circumstances, they do not, as a pair, have to defend as large a feeding territory as they would if they had similar diets. Thus a disparity of feeding habits allows for the more efficient use of space.

The last accredited report of a living Huia was made in 1907. Its close relative, the Kokako, survives to this day, though it has become extremely rare.[34] Also called the Wattled Crow and the Organ Bird, the latter because of its deep, melodious calls, the Kokako was once

20. *The Kokako*

represented by two distinct races. The extinct South Island race had blue wattles, while the North Island race has orange ones which are blue at the base. Like the Huia, the Kokako is a weak flier and it moves about mostly by means of its long, powerful legs, hopping along the ground, leaping from branch to branch and occasionally gliding from one tree to another. Kokakos build large, untidy nests among branches of trees some distance from the ground. The bond between male and female is maintained throughout the year and it seems that larger social gatherings may be a characteristic of this species. Buller reports an observation of more than twenty Kokakos hopping through the forest in single file. The South Island race was last reported in 1962 but the North Island race survives in small and declining numbers in a few isolated localities. Less severely hunted than the Huia, the Kokako has probably declined as a result of the general deterioration of its habitat. As yet, there is no specific project designed to ensure its survival.

The Saddleback is the smallest member of the wattlebird family.[35] About the size of a European starling, its plumage is entirely black except for the large chestnut-orange patch on its back which gives it

21. The Saddleback

its name. The wattles at the base of its bill are also orange. Capable of flying for only a few yards at a time, the Saddleback inhabits low undergrowth and shrubbery, where it forages for insects and fruits. It builds its nest low down in the dense undergrowth and around this it defends a territory, whose possession it loudly proclaims by singing. Buller described how Saddlebacks often followed flocks of Yellowheads, or Bush Canaries; they may well have been picking up insects disturbed by the passing flock. There are distinct North and South Island races of the Saddleback which differ slightly in colouration. There is a more marked difference between the juveniles of the two races, that of the North Island race looking like its parents while that of the South Island race is entirely cocoa-brown in colour. This led Buller to describe the juvenile South Island Saddleback as a separate species, called the Jack Bird.

The Maoris called the Saddleback the Tieke, probably in an onomatopoeic reference to one of its calls. It was said that the great god Maui once ordered the Saddleback to bring him water. When it failed to do so he grasped it in his fiery hand and cast it away, leaving the orange scorch-mark on its back. Saddlebacks were also used as auguries of success or failure in war. If a war party heard their call to the right, victory was at hand, but when heard to the left it meant defeat. Curiously, Romans had a similar belief, and used the appearance of eagles to the left or to the right as an omen of their fortunes in battle.

The Saddleback was a common forest bird when the European colonists began to arrive but its decline was rapid in areas close to human settlements. In the first edition of his book Buller described it as a common bird but in his second edition, published in 1888, he commented on a marked deterioration in its numbers. Its principal enemies appear to be cats and rats. More than once in recent years it has been clear that the arrival on an offshore island of either of these animals has coincided with a rapid decrease in the Saddleback population. In one such affected population there was found a distorted sex ratio of three males to every female, suggesting that females are more susceptible to predation. This is probably because they alone incubate the eggs and are thus confined for long periods to the nest, which is built in a vulnerable position near the ground. Saddlebacks had become virtually extinct on the main islands by 1900 and have since been confined to small offshore islands which they, alone among the wattlebirds, have long inhabited.

The earliest attempt to increase the range of the Saddleback by transporting birds to offshore islands where they had not previously lived was made in 1925.[36] This failed, as did some later attempts, because alien predators were not cleared from the islands first. In recent years Dr D. V. Merton and other members of the New Zealand Wildlife Service have perfected the technique of Saddleback transfer. Birds are lured to a trap by a recording of a Saddleback call and are then quickly transferred to the island where they are to be liberated. This has previously been carefully surveyed to ensure that it provides a suitable habitat and that all predators have been eliminated. Both North and South Island races have been successfully transferred from islands where they occurred naturally to several others where they did not, so that there now exist several viable breeding populations. There was considerable urgency about the transfer of South Island Saddlebacks,

which in 1964 had to be rescued from three islands that had become
infested by rats. They were transferred to two rat-free islands and have
since been introduced to a further three islands. It was estimated in 1975
that the population of the North Island race numbered about 1000
birds, that of the South Island race about 200. The introduction of
Saddlebacks to new islands has provided a unique opportunity for the
study of their habits. A study made by Dr Peter Jenkins of Saddlebacks
introduced to Cuvier Island off the east coast of North Island has shown
how individual idiosyncracies in song are passed by imitation from
father to son and from one bird to his immediate neighbour.[37] This
provides a most elegant example of cultural transmission in animals and
it was made possible because, as the Saddleback population expanded
to fill the island, so the distinctive songs of the few original immigrants
were passed from one male to another.

New Zealand contains so many rare species, many with interesting
habits, that it is impossible to discuss them all in as much detail as one
would wish. For the rest of this chapter I shall deal rather briefly with
just a few of these species, selected for their ornithological importance
or because they illustrate a particularly interesting point relating to the
general themes of this book.

The other two families descended from early immigrants to New
Zealand, the 'wrens' and the 'thrushes', have fared even worse than
the wattlebirds. The New Zealand Wrens are thought to be descended
from a family of Asian birds called Pittas and bear only a superficial
resemblance to the true wrens, most of which live in the Americas.
Small, ground-nesting birds with short wings and virtually no tail, they
have very limited powers of flight and spend most of their time hopping
and darting about on the ground.[38] The Bush Wren, now almost
certainly extinct, was a bird of the forests and was once common
throughout New Zealand, with distinct North and South Island races.
The Rock Wren inhabits open rocky screes and, though it is rarely
seen, is not thought to be in imminent danger of extinction. A third
species, slightly larger than the other two, was the Stephens Island Wren,
whose fate I mentioned earlier. It lived only on one tiny island off the
northern coast of South Island and was never seen alive by an ornithologist. It is known only from corpses brought home by the light-

22. The New Zealand Bush Wren

house keeper's cat in 1894. According to the lighthouse keeper it ran about like a mouse and did not fly at all. There is little doubt that the decline of these tiny birds has been due to their vulnerability to introduced predators.

Like the wrens, the New Zealand Thrushes got their name from their similarity to familiar Old World birds. They resemble the European thrushes both in appearance and in the richness of their songs.[39] Also known by a Maori name, Piopios, they are thought to be descended from birds of Asian origin rather similar to the ancestors of the wattlebirds. They were very common when the Europeans arrived but declined rapidly in the face of agricultural and urban development. Piopios were renowned for the musical quality of their songs and, as with so many of New Zealand's birds, their Maori name describes the commonest of their calls. Buller wrote that in the morning they continued to sing long after other species had finished their dawn chorus. He kept one in a cage for over a year and found it a most companionable pet until its curiosity proved its undoing when, peering into the next-

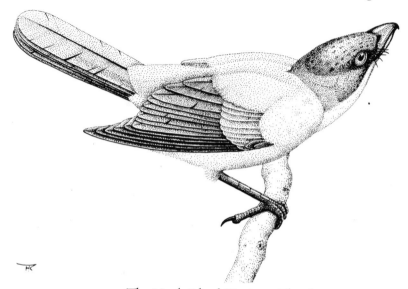

23. The North Island Piopio or Thrush

door cage, it had its head bitten off by a Sparrowhawk. Extremely tame
and inquisitive birds, Piopios gathered in large numbers in the camps
of the early explorers, where they were readily snapped up by dogs.
Once again it seems that introduced predators were primarily responsible for the elimination of these ground-feeding birds. So rapid
was their decline in the late nineteenth century that Buller predicted
that they would soon become extinct. The last confirmed observations
of Piopios were made in 1948 in South Island and in 1955 in North
Island.

Among the more recently-evolved of New Zealand's birds that have
become extinct is the Laughing Owl, called the Whekau by the
Maoris.[40] The largest indigenous owl, standing about fifteen inches tall,
it had long, powerful legs and spent most of its time on the ground,
building its nest in deep crevices between rocks. Among a variety of
sounds attributed to it was an eerie, low chuckle. It was declining in
Buller's time and he attributed this to the replacement by European
rats of the Maori rat or Kiore, on which he believed Laughing Owls
primarily fed. It is more likely that, as with many other ground-
nesting birds, its decline was due to predation by alien mammals.

24. The Laughing Owl

The Kea is a most unusual parrot which lives high in the mountains around the border between the forests and more open alpine vegetation.[41] It feeds mostly on fruits, leaves and insects but was for many years ruthlessly hunted by farmers because of its reputation as a killer of sheep. Hunters received a bounty for every Kea that they shot. There is no doubt that, like crows and ravens, they will attack sheep that are dying or sick, pecking through the back with their long hooked bills and eating the fat beneath the skin. However, there is no evidence that they ever attack healthy sheep and attempts are now being made to change the attitude of farmers to this unusual bird which, though rare, is not regarded as an endangered species.

Some of New Zealand's endemic waterfowl have suffered severely at the hands of both Maoris and Europeans, principally through hunting but also in more indirect ways.[41] The Auckland Island Merganser was once found throughout South Island and some of its smaller neighbouring islands where it lived in sheltered inlets and streams, feeding on small fish.[43] It was apparently exterminated on the larger islands

25. The Auckland Island Merganser

by the Maoris and its remains have been found in their kitchen middens. Its last refuge was in the Auckland Islands, which were probably at the edge of its range and therefore did not provide an ideal habitat. The introduction to the Auckland Islands of pigs, sheep and a variety of predators brought about the species' extinction, which was hastened by the shooting of large numbers by sportsmen in 1901 and 1902. The Blue Duck is a very rare species which is unusual among dabbling ducks in being fiercely territorial.[44] It has an unusual bill with fleshy lateral flaps with which it feeds on aquatic insects. Its decline has been attributed to the introduction by Europeans of trout and other freshwater fish which probably compete with it for the same food. The New Zealand Brown Teal is an endangered species of nocturnal habits which has declined as the result of the draining of many areas of wetlands and the filling-in of the small ponds which are an essential part of its habitat. A very different kind of threat faces the New Zealand Grey Duck as the result of the introduction of the Mallard. The two species are closely related but, being naturally widely separated from each other, have never evolved the differences in courtship behaviour which commonly prevent closely-related species mating with one another. In New Zealand Grey Ducks and Mallards have frequently hybridized.[45]

Hybridization is detrimental to the species because often the progeny of hybrid matings do not survive and, if they do, they are less able to reproduce than their parents so that valuable reproductive potential is lost from the population. If the hybrids are able to reproduce they may mate with members of the parental species and eventually the 'pure' species will be replaced by a motley collection of intermediate birds rather like many populations of domestic ducks.

The present position of some of New Zealand's birds could not be more precarious. The entire population of the Chatham Island Black Robin numbered fourteen birds in 1975 but it has survived in roughly those numbers for the last seventy years.[46] They live in about ten acres of scrub land on Little Mangere Island, the only island in the Chatham group which has not been infested by cats. There is concern at the present time because the population shows very low reproductive output; this is probably due to a deterioration of the trees through the activities of a dense population of Muttonbirds also living on the island. It is hoped that it may be possible to set up a second population on another island, following the successes achieved with the Saddleback.

Most of the rare and endangered birds of New Zealand were common and widespread in the days of the early white settlers. A species which has long been rare and which has actually become more well known with the passing years is the Takahe, which for a long time was thought to be extinct.[47] This large, flightless rail was first described in 1848 by Sir Richard Owen of the British Museum from bones discovered among moa remains at Waingongoro and Wanganui in North Island by Walter Mantell. By the end of the nineteenth century living Takahes had been seen only four times, first in 1849, when one was run down and captured by seal hunters in Dusky Bay, South Island. Further living specimens were collected in 1851, 1879 and 1898 but then none were seen for fifty years and it was thought that these four sightings were of the very last members of a vanished species. In 1948 the Takahe was rediscovered by G. B. Orbell in the Lake District of South Island, where he estimated there were about seven pairs. It has since been found that there is in fact a population of a few hundred Takahes which had remained undiscovered because of the remoteness of their mountain refuge.

The Takahe is a most colourful bird with iridescent indigo, peacock-blue, green and white plumage, a massive red bill and heavy red legs and feet (Plate XI). Standing about two feet tall, it is larger than most rails and is quite incapable of flight. Male and female are identical in appearance; they pair for life and together defend a territory of anything between 5 and 140 acres which they hold throughout the year. They feed on the young shoots of alpine tussock-grasses and when this is covered by winter snow they resort to the beech forests to eat the stalks and rhizomes of ferns. In pre-European times they were widespread throughout New Zealand and were known by the Maoris who hunted them for food as Takahes in South Island and as Mohos in North Island. They are now confined to a few valleys in the Murchison and Kepler Mountains in South Island's Lake District. These valleys, all at altitudes between 2400 and 4000 feet, are contained in a 700-square-mile nature reserve where measures are taken to control the numbers of stoats, which are thought to pose a serious threat to Takahe eggs and chicks.

In 1966 the Takahe population was estimated to be rather less than 500 birds.[48] A census in 1969 recorded about 200 pairs. Between 1964 and 1974 there was a steady decline in their numbers, but a survey carried out in 1972 suggested that this was principally due to a sharp fall in just one area. In other areas the population appeared to be stable. The declining population, in Takahe Valley, showed a very low reproductive output and low adult survival rate, apparently caused by the poor quality of the grass. Takahe Valley may be an area of sub-optimal habitat that provides a home for birds unable to acquire territories in more favourable neighbouring valleys. There is some evidence that Takahes suffer through competition with deer, which browse on the same grasses and, more critically, share the same winter food.[49]

The Takahe is one New Zealand bird for whose decline man is not held primarily responsible. The fact that it had become rare before Europeans arrived and that it has continued to decline despite very careful protection suggests that it may be under the influence of natural changes in its habitat brought about by climatic variations. Plans for its conservation include the continued protection of its mountain refuge, including control measures against deer. An attempt has also been made to breed Takahes in captivity at Mount Bruce Native Bird Reserve.[50] Despite many problems they have eventually been induced to lay fertile eggs and, in 1973, to hatch living young, though these soon died from congenital defects. In the immediate future the prospects for the Takahe look good. Its long-term survival depends on whether the wild population continues to decline and, if it does, whether captive-bred birds can be successfully introduced to sustain it or to establish further populations elsewhere.

The adjective 'unique' is one that is liberally used in most accounts of New Zealand's birds. If any species deserves such a description it is the Kakapo, or Owl Parrot, whose many peculiarities amply justify the assertion by the great nineteenth-century ornithologist John Gould that it is 'one of the most wonderful, perhaps, of all living birds'.[51] The largest of all the world's parrots, it is set apart in a sub-family of its own. It is the only flightless parrot and possesses a very small breast-bone, reflecting the poor development of its flight muscles. It has been discovered recently that it mates at a lek, the only parrot and the only New Zealand species to do so.[52] It nests in crevices at ground level but, unlike most ground-nesting species, whose chicks are able to run about and find much of their own food very soon after hatching, its young are quite helpless. This is quite the opposite of the situation found in the kiwis, whose habits are in some respects rather similar.

Male and female Kakapos are similar in appearance with green plumage, barred with yellow and brown, and a heavy bill whose serrated edges are adapted for grinding their plant food (Plate X). They have an owl-like disc of stiff feathers around each eye, and the similarity to owls extends to their nocturnal habits. Kakapos have sensory hair-like feathers around their bill which serve as whiskers for locating objects in the dark. They are incapable of true flight but can travel very fast along the ground, especially downhill, by a combination of running, jumping and gliding with their large rounded wings outstretched. They live mostly at high altitudes, emerging from the forests to feed on the alpine vegetation above the tree line. They eat berries, leaves and shoots, grinding them in their mill-like bills. They also chew grass, which they masticate and suck dry while it is still on the plant, leaving behind characteristic balls of compressed leaves which, together with their well-worn tracks, are a sure sign of the presence of these secretive birds.

In the breeding season, in January and February, the males advertise themselves by their 'booming', a sound rather like that made by blowing over the neck of a bottle. Each male booms about a thousand times an hour and for six or seven hours each night. On calm, damp nights, when the sound travels particularly well, they are especially vociferous. As they produce the sound the males puff themselves up by filling air sacs within their bodies until they become virtually spherical. They boom from the edge of a hollow excavated in the ground. These 'bowls' were previously thought to be dust baths. It is now known that they are carefully positioned and shaped by the males so that they reflect the booming sound as far and as wide as possible over the surrounding countryside.[53] A number of bowls belonging to different males are clustered together and are joined by clearly-marked tracks. Males respond to each other's sounds by booming in reply and the complex of bowls and paths forms a lek to which females are attracted by their combined sound. Between bouts of booming the males perform a 'butterfly' wing display, apparently designed to attract females visually. Booming males are in a state of high sexual excitement and have been known to attempt copulation with the feet of ornithologists. Mating does not seem to occur every year and may be related to food supply, being suspended in years when there are few berries and fruits. The nests are made in natural crevices which may be further excavated by the female, who alone incubates the eggs and looks after the young.

The Kakapo was once distributed throughout both large islands and perhaps Stewart Island and the Chatham Islands also. Its range was already much reduced by the time the Europeans arrived and it has since contracted further. It is now extinct on North Island and occurs only in the Fiordland region of South Island. The primary cause of its decline seems to have been introduced predators, particularly the Maori rat or Kiore and, more recently, European rats. The Kakapo breeds rather late, presumably so that the young can be raised when berries and fruits are most available. The Kiore population tends to reach a peak at this time, following its breeding season, and the helpless young Kakapos are probably very vulnerable to their attacks. Deforestation has eliminated much of the Kakapos' natural habitat and their remaining haunts are thought to be rather less than ideal for them.

The Kakapo is in the strange position that, though a number of individuals are still alive, the species may be effectively extinct. In 1975 the total known population consisted of twelve birds, all of which were probably males. Not one female was known to exist at that time. Females may be more vulnerable to predation because of the time they spend at the nest. Nevertheless steps are now being taken to conserve the Kakapo. Management of the remaining natural habitat is impracticable because of the size and inaccessibility of the area concerned, and captive breeding is ruled out by their lek system, which would be difficult to sustain in captivity. Following the success of other transfer schemes, Maud Island in the Marlborough Sounds was identified as being suitable for Kakapos and was cleared of predators.[54] By 1975 three birds, two of them definitely male, the third of unknown sex, had been transferred there and, judging by the fact that booming was heard, have settled in well. The future of this remarkable bird now depends on whether or not ornithologists can somehow find some females.[55]

In this chapter we have seen how the separation of New Zealand from the major continents at an early date in the earth's history has profoundly influenced the evolution of its bird life. As human technology developed so New Zealand became more accessible and the isolation so crucial to the survival of its birds was lost. The human history of New Zealand is a sad story of the rape of a unique community of plants and animals, not only by man himself but, perhaps more seriously, also by the animals he has taken with him. The only real prospect for the survival of several of New Zealand's birds is provided by small remote islands. In this respect New Zealand points the way for the future of the whole world. As the human population of the earth increases and man's influence on nature spreads, natural habitats and the animals they support will become increasingly confined to tiny islands, either in the literal sense or in the form of nature reserves surrounded by urban or agricultural environments hostile to the survival of all but a few species.

6

Birds on Islands

———⋇⋇⋇⋇⋇⋇⋇⋇⋇———

THE great majority of birds that either have become extinct in recent years or are now considered to be endangered inhabit oceanic islands. Of the 217 species or races that have disappeared in the last 400 years 200 were insular birds. I do not propose in this chapter to present a catalogue of such birds; to do so would make repetitive and depressing reading. The chain of events which led to the extinction of the Dodos and Solitaires of the Mascarene Islands and which destroyed many of New Zealand's birds has been repeated many times on innumerable islands throughout the world. Man arrives, bringing with him a variety of predators and herbivores. While he destroys the indigenous vegetation to make way for crops and grazing land his camp-followers destroy the largely defenceless endemic birds. A unique community of plants and animals, many of which are found nowhere else, is replaced by what is essentially a replica of the colonists' home environment in which alien introduced birds fare much better than the native birds. I intend in this chapter to attempt to answer a general question that arises from this so-often repeated process: why are island species apparently so much more vulnerable than continental species? This question has importance far beyond the immediate field of bird conservation. Islands provide living laboratories; their small confined communities are microcosms of larger, continental ecosystems and, ultimately, of the world itself.

The study of the changes that take place in island communities has greatly increased our understanding of the way the evolutionary process works in the broader context of the global environment. The special significance of islands in the development of evolutionary theory began with the work of Charles Darwin and Alfred Russel Wallace. Their attempts to explain the many peculiarities of island animals that so deeply impressed them during their travels led them independently to formulate similar theories about how the characteristics of animals evolved. Darwin, largely inspired by the birds of the Galapagos Islands, published his theory in 1859 in *The Origin of Species*, which remains to this day the basis of evolutionary theory. In the last decade islands have again come to the forefront of biological thought in the theory of Island Biogeography.[1] This development, initiated in 1963 by Robert MacArthur and Edward Wilson, began as an essentially theoretical attempt to explain the patterns of island communities.[2] Island Biogeography is, however, much more than an academic, theoretical exercise. Not only does it deepen our understanding of how species interact with one another, it also has practical importance in conservation. Nature reserves are essentially islands of favourable habitat and the theory of Island Biogeography can make a vital contribution in their design. I shall discuss this aspect more fully in the final chapter.

Any comprehensive theory that attempts to explain the evolution of island communities must account for three common features of insular animals. First, islands contain fewer species than areas of comparable size on the mainland. Second, island species frequently show characteristics of anatomy, colouration or behaviour quite unlike those of equivalent species on the mainland and many islands are inhabited by species that are found nowhere else, some of them of bizarre appearance. Third, island species are clearly more likely to become extinct than species living on continents.

The question of how many species are found on a particular island provided the starting point for MacArthur and Wilson's theory. They began with two well-established facts; islands remote from the mainland contain fewer species than those near a coast and small islands contain fewer species than larger ones. The first relationship is explained by the argument that the more remote an island, the less likely is it that a group of animals large enough to found a breeding population will find its way there. The area effect arises from the fact that small islands can provide support only for small populations, which are more likely than large populations to become extinct through random climatic events such as storms, or as a result of the detrimental effects of inbreeding. Thus distant islands contain few species because they are colonized at a low rate, and small islands because the populations that settle in them suffer a high extinction rate. MacArthur and Wilson suggested that the number of species found on any given island represents a balance between the rate of colonization by new immigrant species and the rate of extinction of established species, these two rates varying with the island's size and remoteness from a large land mass. Their theory sees island communities, not as associations of species that remain stable over many years, but as a continually changing group of species in which those that become extinct are quickly replaced by new colonists.

This theory is well supported by two kinds of evidence. Some islands, called continental or land-bridge islands, are formed when part of a continent is flooded by the sea. The British Isles, for example, were once part of the European mainland before melting of the polar ice cap caused the sea to rise. Studies of islands in the Caribbean and to the east of New Guinea, which have been cut off in the last 10,000 years by the rising sea level, have shown that they contained many more species when they were part of the mainland than they do now. Thus, as the area of a piece of land decreases, so does the number of species that it supports. Even better evidence of this effect is provided by the island of Barro Colorado in Panama, which became cut off in about 1914 when Lake Gatun was formed by the damming of the Chagres River. Although the island was declared a nature reserve in 1923, about fifteen species that had inhabited this one-time forested hilltop disappeared between 1920 and 1970. On purely theoretical grounds the MacArthur-Wilson theory would have predicted that sixteen species would be eliminated. Other islands, called oceanic islands, are formed from the sea-bed, either by volcanic action or by the build-up of coral. Such islands contain no species at all when they are formed but must acquire them through colonization. On oceanic islands historical evidence suggests that numbers have increased with time towards the expected equilibrium value. Perhaps the best demonstration of this effect was provided by Krakatau, an island between Java and Sumatra which was all but destroyed by a volcanic explosion in August 1883, following three months of continuous eruptions. Half the island vanished and what was left, together with the neighbouring islands of Verlaten and Lang, was buried beneath hot pumice and ash 100 to 200 feet thick. Though every plant and animal was destroyed there has since been a remarkable recolonization of the island. Thirteen species of land birds had gained a hold by 1908 and between then and 1921 there was a rapid increase in the number of species. By 1934 the bird fauna seems to have stabilized with about twenty-eight resident land or fresh-water species, a figure very close to that expected for an island of its size and distance from the mainland. Five of the species that had been collected in 1921 had vanished by 1934 and had apparently been replaced by five similar species, supporting the idea that there is a rapid turnover of species on islands.

This dynamic equilibrium theory has been criticized by, among others, the late David Lack.[3] He did not agree that there is a rapid turnover of species on islands once they have reached ecological stability, though he accepted that there would be during the process of colonization, as there has been on Krakatau. He pointed out that every instance of a species becoming extinct on old, established islands has been shown on investigation to be due to the influence of man.[4] In Lack's view the reason why small and remote islands support so few birds is that they are impoverished in terms of numbers of plant and animal species and therefore provide fewer opportunities for colonists. He showed that two islands of similar size and distance from the mainland can differ considerably in the numbers of species they contain if one is flat and the other is mountainous. Mountains, because climate changes with altitude, support habitats different from those found in lowland areas, so that mountainous islands contain a greater variety of habitats. Lack was also dubious about the theory, particularly in its application to birds, because there is clear evidence that many birds have no difficulty in finding their way even to the most remote islands.

As we saw in the previous chapter many species have repeatedly made the crossing to New Zealand. The problem for birds is not to reach islands but to establish a successful breeding population there and, in Lack's view, many species arrive but few settle because of the ecological poverty of island habitats.

It would be misleading to suggest that the two views I have outlined above are diametrically opposed or incompatible. They simply emphasize different aspects of a complex problem and can both be assimilated in a general theory of island biology. The dynamic equilibrium concept of MacArthur and Wilson seems best for explaining the colonization of islands by plants and small animals like insects whose dispersal to islands over large expanses of sea must be essentially fortuitous. Birds are rather different because of their much greater powers of dispersal and their successful colonization of an island depends less on the vagaries of chance during the crossing and more on the richness and variety of the habitat they find when they get there.

This essentially theoretical approach helps us to understand one aspect of island communities, namely why they consist of so few species. It also suggests that island animals may naturally be more likely to become extinct, though it cannot account for the very high rate of extinction of the last few hundred years, which has been primarily due to human influence. I shall next consider those species that successfully colonize islands and the rather special ways they adapt to their insular habitats, so as to answer the question of why island species are so vulnerable to human invasion.

When a group of birds reaches an island there must be a reasonable number of them if they are to found a successful breeding population, though it is conceivable that one female carrying fertilized eggs could do so. The smaller the colonizing group, the less representative will it be of the population from which it came. Just as a small group of human colonists would not possess all the skills and trades practised by people at home, so a small sample of birds does not contain all the inheritable genetic characteristics found in its parent population. This 'founder effect' means that the new population is inherently less variable, so that its capacity to adapt to its new environment is restricted. Many colonizing groups, perhaps most of them, will die out since they lack characteristics that are suited to their new habitat. However, should there be individuals among the colonists with suitable characteristics they will be favoured by natural selection and will multiply rapidly. The result of the founder effect, combined with isolation from the mainland, is that the colonist population will rapidly become distinctly different from the ancestral population in its appearance and habits.

Let us consider a small population of birds that has survived and become established on a small, remote island. It is very likely that they will find themselves in a largely empty environment, many of the species with whom they had to compete for food and space on the mainland being absent. These are the conditions for the process of 'ecological release' whereby a colonist population evolves characteristics that enable its members to exploit vacant aspects of their habitat.[5] They may, for example, take to feeding on a much greater variety of food items. The supply of their ancestral food may be limited on a small island and individuals with the ability to find alternative food will be favoured by natural selection since they will face less competition from their fellows for the limited resource. Many island birds have longer beaks than their parent species, enabling them to feed on a greater variety of food types.[6] Such birds will live in a wider range of habitats than their mainland ancestors. The Blue Chaffinch of the Canary Islands had evolved a longer beak than its mainland ancestor, the European Common Chaffinch.[7] However, competition from a second invasion by the mainland form has forced it to live only in pine forests. Another feature of many insular species is that they have evolved greater variability between individuals in, for example, beak size or length of leg than their mainland counterparts.[8] This means that each individual is adapted slightly differently from its fellows and is thus likely to compete with them. All these changes come about because of the slackening on islands of the competitive pressure from similar species that exists on the mainland. In the previous chapter we saw how ecological release may have contributed to the evolution of different-shaped bills in the Huia.

As a species broadens its habits by the process of ecological release it becomes more of a generalist and less a specialist. Many island birds are generalists and in the West Indies Lack found islands on which one such species has apparently occupied the niches which, on the mainland and on larger islands, would normally be filled by two or more specialists.[9] Some generalists have also evolved the characteristics of r-strategists, in particular well-developed powers of dispersal and high reproductive potential. Such species, which have been referred to as 'tramps', may invade islands and displace more sedentary and slower-breeding specialists.[10] An example of such a species is Mackinlay's Cuckoo Dove, which is found in many of the smaller islands in the Bismarck Archipelago near New Guinea. The trend towards the evolution of generalists, able to utilize a broad habitat, contributes to the reduction in the number of species that can colonize an island. It will be particularly apparent on smaller islands, where there are fewer opportunities for specialists to maintain large populations. Mackinlay's Cuckoo Dove does not occur on the larger islands in the Bismark group because they contain a number of abundant specialist species.

By no means all island species are generalists, however. Islands, with their availability of vacant habitats, offer unique opportunities to specialists, provided a particular habitat is extensive enough to support a substantial population.[11] The classic examples of adaptive radiation, like Darwin's Finches on the Galapagos and the honeycreepers on Hawaii, involved the adaptation of colonist populations to different specific habitats on different islands.[12] In both these families of birds the original colonist group became divided into isolated populations which each evolved specialized feeding habits. Specialist birds are very much more vulnerable to extinction than generalists. Dependent on a very specific habitat, they are unable to utilize alternative habitats if theirs is destroyed. Also, they tend to be sedentary, lacking the ability of generalist 'tramps' to disperse to other islands. One of Darwin's Finches, the Large-billed Ground Finch, a bird with an especially powerful beak adapted for crushing tough seeds, is now probably extinct. Rather more specialized in its feeding habits than other species, it also had reduced powers of flight.

A common feature of small and remote islands is that they are not inhabited by any birds of prey. Predators are characteristically fewer in numbers than their prey and on small islands there is not sufficient space

26. Darwin's Large-billed Ground Finch

to support a viable population of a predatory species. The same argument would apply to mammalian predators, but these hardly ever colonize islands anyway because of their inability to cross the sea. As we have seen in previous chapters, the absence of predators on islands has led to the reduction or loss of the power of flight in many island birds and to a tendency for them to be less wary and shy than mainland birds. The absence of predators has also led to the adoption of ground-nesting habits by many island birds.

From the foregoing discussion we can summarize the various ways in which island birds are especially prone to extinction. The limited size of islands means that the population of any one species is likely to be small and therefore more likely to be totally wiped out by a natural catastrophe such as severe weather or a volcanic eruption. Because of their small size and of the founder effect, island populations lack the genetic variability that might enable them to adapt to changing circumstances. Colonist populations that become adapted to the special local

conditions that exist on islands become very different from their mainland ancestors and so, should their numbers fall, they cannot be re-
inforced by a further invasion from the parent population. Highly
specialized island species are very vulnerable to any changes in their
habitat, brought about either by natural causes or by human invasion.
Only those species that have evolved generalist habits are likely to
survive radical changes in an island ecosystem. Specialists are also
likely to be adversely affected by the arrival of generalists, whether they
invade of their own accord or are introduced by man. Finally, many
island species have lost those adaptations which protected their mainland ancestors against predators. Apart from these biological factors
that make island birds vulnerable, there is the purely practical fact that
islands, especially small ones, can very easily be totally overrun by
man and the many species that accompany him. Unlike continents,
islands do not provide any refuges in which beleaguered species can be
safe from human activity.

The classic example of an extinct island bird is the Dodo, which I
discussed at some length in Chapter 3. Both the Dodo and its relative,
the Solitaire, were flightless ground-nesters, totally unafraid of intruders; both were exterminated by the same combination of factors
that has destroyed so many island birds, hunting by man, destruction of
their habitat by both men and introduced herbivores, and predation,
particularly of the eggs and young by alien predators. The Dodo and
the Solitaire lived on the islands of Mauritius, Réunion and Rodriguez
which comprise the Mascarene group, and were by no means the only
birds inhabiting those islands to become extinct. Indeed, the Mascarenes can probably claim the dubious distinction of having suffered
the highest extinction rate in the world. There were some twenty-
eight species of land and freshwater birds living on the islands before
man arrived. Of these twenty-eight species, twenty-four are certainly
extinct and another, the Ring-necked Parakeet, has probably also
died out. Among the birds that have vanished were a large, flightless
rail (*Aphanapteryx*) which was said to have reddish-brown, hair-
like plumage, three species of semi-flightless heron, four parrots, two
owls and two kinds of starling.[13] There are also about fourteen species
of 'hypothetical' birds for whose existence there is only the flimsiest

27. Aphanapteryx, *an extinct red rail from Mauritius*

evidence, either single bones or travellers' tales. If any of these did indeed exist the picture of extinction on the Mascarenes becomes even more depressing.

The *Red Data Book*, a list of endangered species published by the International Union for Conservation of Nature and Natural Resources (IUCN), lists thirteen Mascarene birds that are rare or under threat of extinction. Among these is the Mauritius Kestrel, a small falcon which now ranks as one of the rarest birds in the world (Plate XII). At the present time there are just nine kestrels on Mauritius, two of them in captivity where it is hoped they will breed. The Mauritius Kestrel was common about a hundred years ago and was still widespread in the 1920s. Its decline may be partly due to the destruction of its natural habitat, but the principal cause has been direct hunting by man. Its French name is *mangeur-de-poules* (eater of chicken) and it is apparently this reputation that has caused it to be shot by the islanders.

The Hawaiian islands have an extinction record almost as bad as that of the Mascarenes.[14] This chain of more than thirty large and small islands, 1600 miles long, was formed from the Pacific seabed by volcanic activity. The older, eastern islands, such as Laysan and Midway,

are low and flat as the result of millions of years of erosion. The younger
western islands, like Kauai, Maui and Hawaii itself, are still steep and
mountainous. They are 2000 miles from America's west coast and
their remoteness is reflected by the complete absence of truly freshwater fish, amphibians, reptiles and, except for one species of bat,
mammals. Their sixty-eight species of native land birds are thought to
be descended from only fifteen colonizations by ancestral birds. Before the advent of man most of the islands were covered by dense,
luxuriant forests, watered by the heaviest rainfall in the world. Like
New Zealand, the Hawaiian islands have been invaded successively by
Polynesians and Europeans, and once again the most dramatic manifestations of man's impact has been the destruction of the natural
forests. (Deforestation has been primarily the responsibility of Europeans; the Polynesian settlers were much less destructive of the vegetation and wildlife than they were in New Zealand.) The island of
Kauai, for example, is now almost entirely covered by pineapple
groves. Man has brought with him herbivores such as cattle, pigs,
goats and deer that have helped to destroy the natural vegetation, both
by grazing the plants and by compacting the ground around their
delicate roots. Imported cats have helped to eradicate birds at the lower
altitudes but more serious predators have been rats, introduced in the
nineteenth century. Rats have a prodigious reproductive potential; a
single pair can theoretically give rise to around 800 descendants in a
single year. On Hawaii, as on many islands, they have adopted arboreal
habits so that tree-nesting as well as ground-nesting birds are vulnerable to their depredations.

The Hawaiian islands provide the best-authenticated example of the
adverse effects on island birds of introduced diseases.[15] When Hawaii
was visited by Captain Cook in 1778 the native birds inhabited all
parts of the islands from the shoreline to the mountain summits. In
1826 the Night Mosquito was accidentally introduced on the island of
Maui. As it spread rapidly through the lowland forests it carried with it
bird pox, bird malaria and other diseases, passing them on to the native
birds that had never evolved immunity to them. Several birds became
extinct and those that did not were confined to areas at altitudes
greater than about 2000 feet where the mosquito could not survive. If

28. The Crested Honeycreeper

native birds like honeycreepers are caught and brought down to lower altitudes they die within days of one of the insect-borne diseases. Introduced species, which have evolved resistance to these infections, are able to survive at low altitudes, occupying the habitats vacated by the indigenous birds. It has been suggested that immunity might be introduced into the native bird populations, perhaps by inoculation, but as yet this is not a practical proposition.

It has been estimated that the Hawaiian islands once contained sixty-eight species and subspecies of endemic land birds, of which forty-one are now extinct or critically rare. The most severely reduced group of birds are the Hawaiian honeycreepers. Over half the extinct birds belong to this family, whose evolution provides a classic example of adaptive radiation.[16] The original colonist, an American honey-creeper, gave rise to twenty-two distinct species which have exploited a variety of food sources including nectar, fruit, seeds, nuts and insects. Most have become highly specialized, their habitats centred on the flowering trees that are so distinctive a feature of Hawaii's forests. The honeycreepers have been particularly affected by introduced diseases and by deforestation, which has destroyed much of their habitat.

One of the rarest birds of the Hawaiian islands is the Kauai Oo (pronounced 'oh-oh'), the only surviving species of a family called the honeyeaters that once consisted of five or six species (Plate XIII). These were also the product of an adaptive radiation, in this instance from an ancestor of Australian origin that gave rise to distinct forms living on four or five different islands. They were noted for the beauty of their plumage, which was glossy brown and black with bright yellow plumes much prized by the Polynesians for making spectacular cloaks, reminiscent of those of the New Zealand Maoris. Oos made deep, sonorous calls that travelled great distances through the damp forests where they fed on nectar and insects. Though the Polynesians must have killed them in large numbers to make their cloaks, they were still abundant when white men arrived. Their decline was primarily due to trapping by collectors and to the destruction of the flowering trees on which they depended.

Laysan, towards the eastern end of the Hawaiian chain, is an island of just over 700 acres, consisting mostly of low sand dunes surrounding a lagoon of brackish water. Once a steep volcanic peak, it now contains no land higher than forty feet and its vegetation consists of low scrub and grass. Despite its impoverished habitat the island supported five endemic species when Europeans arrived late in the nineteenth century. The first human inhabitants were guano-diggers who excavated deposits of seabird dung from Laysan and neighbouring islands. To make themselves more self-sufficient the diggers introduced rabbits in 1903. These underwent a spectacular population explosion which brought about the destruction of much of the natural vegetation, with serious consequences for the native birds.

Two of Laysan's indigenous birds were products of the adaptive radiation of the Hawaiian honeycreepers. The Laysan Finch, unlike most members of this family, has evolved generalist habits and its catholic diet may well account for the fact that this species has survived where others have died out. The Laysan Honeycreeper, another member of the same group, was not so fortunate. It was so reduced in numbers by the deterioration of its habitat that in 1903 the entire

29. The Laysan Duck

population was swept away in a storm, another illustration of the
vulnerability of very small insular populations to natural catastrophes.[17]
Fearing that the same fate might befall the Laysan Finch, conservationists have transferred some finches to islands around nearby Midway
Island.[18] This exercise has been a qualified success; the finches have
successfully established themselves in their new homes but have done
so at the expense of some of the resident birds, whose eggs they eat.

The Laysan Duck is a close relative of the Mallard and shows many
adaptations typical of island birds.[19] It is a non-migratory duck,
somewhat laboured in flight, that spends most of its time in the undergrowth around pools and near the shore. It is very tame and is largely
nocturnal in its habits, feeding mostly on insects. It shows physiological
adaptations to the habitat on Laysan, which contains no fresh water.
The species has never been resident outside Laysan and neighbouring
Lisiansky but has been successfully bred in captivity in Britain and
America and is frequently seen in wildfowl collections. The guano-
diggers shot the ducks in large numbers for sport and food and they
were already decimated by the time the rabbits arrived in 1903. The
birds on Lisiansky were totally wiped out, probably by shooting, by
1895. By 1909 the Laysan population was reduced by the combined

effects of men and rabbits to less than twenty-five birds. There followed a critical period, between 1911 and 1924, when the Laysan Duck teetered on the brink of extinction, its population fluctuating between just seven and twelve birds. It has been reported that in 1930 the population fell to only one bird, a female carrying fertile eggs, though one can never be certain that others were not alive at that time.[20] In 1924 conservationists began to cull the rabbits, already reduced in numbers through the destruction of much of their own food supply. The vegetation began to recover and as a result the ducks multiplied. By 1957 there were between 400 and 600 Laysan Ducks, rising to nearly 700 by 1961. In the 1960s and 1970s the population has fluctuated violently, perhaps as a result of mortality due to storms. It has also been suggested that a recent general decline leading to a population of only 200 in 1975 may be the result of inbreeding.[21]

The Laysan Duck is not the only species of wildfowl endemic to the Hawaiian islands that has recovered from the brink of extinction. A more famous bird is the Hawaiian Goose or Néné (Plate XIV) which provides the classic example of the value of captive breeding in the conservation of endangered species.[22] The natural haunts of the Néné are the open sparsely-vegetated larva flows that cover a large part of the mountain slopes of Hawaii and Maui. The water supply in such areas consists of sporadically filled pools and Nénés are able to survive for long periods without water. Once common at all altitudes on the two islands, they were hunted by the Polynesians, particularly when they congregated in the volcanic craters in order to moult. (During moulting they drop all their wing feathers at once and are thus unable to fly.) This hunting had little effect on their population, however, and they were common at the beginning of the eighteenth century, when they numbered about 25,000. By 1850 they were found only in remote refuges at high altitudes and in 1900 they had vanished from Maui. In 1949 the total population stood at less than fifty birds and only about thirty-five of these were living in the wild.

As in so many instances, their decline was brought about by a combination of many factors. Very tame birds, they were easily shot, and they are unusual in having their breeding season late in the year, between September and March, coinciding with the European and

American settlers' shooting season. Large numbers were killed and salted down to provision the Pacific whaling ships that called at Hawaii. Most of their lowland habitat was destroyed by man and converted to plantations or grazing land and introduced herbivores such as feral goats competed with them for their remaining plant food. Predators such as mongooses, rats and cats took their chicks and they may also have been affected by introduced diseases.

The Néné has been rescued from extinction by the vision of individuals, notably Peter Scott in Britain and Herbert Shipman in Hawaii, and by the preparedness of the Hawaiian authorities to back their efforts. It has also been saved by its own propensity to breed in captivity. This may be due to the fact that it is very tame and unafraid of man, a characteristic which, in the wild, has contributed to its decline. In 1911 hunting of wild Nénés was prohibited and in 1918 Herbert Shipman established a captive colony on Hawaii. Five years later a number were shipped to Britain, to Lord Derby's wildfowl collection, where they bred. However, this group became dispersed and eventually died out. In 1949 a captive breeding programme was set up at Pohakuloa in Hawaii and three years later a group at Slimbridge in Britain, set up with birds from Shipman's collection, produced chicks for the first time. Female Nénés are remarkably fecund and, if their eggs are removed, will lay two or three replacement clutches; those eggs which the parents do not rear themselves can be hatched in incubators. However, many eggs proved to be infertile as the result of repeated inbreeding. In 1955 there were more Nénés in captivity than in the wild and a third of them lived in Britain. The fertility rate was doubled by the introduction into the captive population of new wild-caught birds and by a policy of breeding only from birds that produced a high proportion of fertile eggs.

However successful the captive breeding programme, it was not really solving the basic problem. The aim of conservation should be to maintain animals in their natural environment and there was a real danger that the Néné was fast becoming yet another domesticated species, totally dependent on man for its continued survival. Accordingly, the emphasis of the Néné project switched in the 1960s to the task of returning captive-reared birds to their natural habitat. In 1960 birds reared at Pohakuloa were released on Hawaii and in 1962 and 1963 Slimbridge birds were liberated on Maui. The technique used was called 'gentle release'; their wings were clipped and they were put into pens which excluded predators. The time it took for their wing feathers to re-grow gave them the chance to become accustomed to their new surroundings so that when they eventually flew off they were not totally disoriented. While there is evidence that some of these birds did breed in the wild the results were not as good as had been hoped. Recently a different method of release has been tried. This uses a large fenced area called a 'Néné park', into which are released birds whose wings are pinioned so that they will never fly. However, their young are not so impaired and, having had less contact with man than their parents, are less oriented towards him, and more towards fellow geese, by the time they are old enough to fly away. In 1962 the world Néné population stood at over 400 birds. By 1975 there were more than 1000, of which at least 600 were living wild. The production of captive-reared birds is greater than the total world mortality and, if the wild population can be effectively protected from predation, the prospects for the Néné look excellent.

Many of the world's islands were colonized by man at a very early date in human history and it is often difficult to tell what the indigenous birds were like before man's arrival or how he affected them. Thus a number of birds that may once have inhabited the Mascarenes can now only be classed as hypothetical species. An island which was colonized comparatively recently and whose ornithological history is therefore fairly complete is Lord Howe Island, situated between Australia and New Zealand.[23] A small island, less than eight miles long and two miles wide, it possesses two mountain peaks that rise to nearly 3000 feet. These are usually shrouded in cloud and much of the island is covered by rich, mossy forest that thrives in such damp conditions. There are a number of smaller islands and rocky stacks around the coast which provide breeding sites for a variety of seabirds. Despite the fact that the human population has never been large and that the greater part of the natural forest still remains, the birds of Lord Howe Island have been seriously depleted. Of twelve endemic species and subspecies, eight are extinct and two are now extremely rare.

Lord Howe Island was discovered in 1788 and the first account of its wildlife was written by a surgeon, Arthur Bowes, who was so impressed by the luxurious vegetation and abundant wildlife that he compared his visit to a return to the 'golden age of Ovid'. It appears that, if the Polynesians ever visited Lord Howe Island, they never settled there. When the Europeans arrived the island contained numerous unusual birds, notably a large white Gallinule, but no mammals. Until 1834, when human settlement of the island began, it was only sporadically visited. The extinction of its endemic birds took place in two distinct phases. The first, brought about by the direct impact of man, saw the elimination of the White Gallinule and a pigeon, both hunted for food, and of a parakeet, persecuted because of the damage it did in gardens and fields. The second phase began in 1918 when rats escaped on to the island from a supply ship. Between then and 1925 five endemic birds were wiped out, all of them small, tree-nesting birds vulnerable to rats with their arboreal habits. Today Lord Howe Island has a permanent settlement of around 200 people and most of the bird populations are fairly stable. It has been suggested that the island should be 'developed'. Hopefully the Australian government will heed the lessons of the past and will see to it that the destruction of the island's unique fauna is not taken any further.

Nearly 300 species of birds have been listed as having appeared on Lord Howe Island. Over 100 of these are vagrants that do not breed, a fact providing strong support for Lack's contention that birds frequently visit, but rarely settle on remote islands. Only twenty-seven species breed there regularly and a number of these are introduced birds, including the European Starling, that occupy the man-made habitats on the island. Of the dozen original endemic species and subspecies, four survive, two of them being common, the others very rare. The first species to become extinct was the White Gallinule, which was much reduced in numbers by the time settlement of the island began in 1834. This was probably a local race or subspecies of the Purple Gallinule, whose enormous range includes the Mediterranean, East Africa, Persia, India, south-east Asia, Australia, New Zealand and many of the Pacific islands. There is some suggestion from early accounts that not all the Lord Howe Gallinules were white. They

30. The Lord Howe Island Wood Rail

may have been albino individuals belonging to a typically blue or purple race. The rarest of the surviving endemic birds is the Wood Rail or Woodhen, a flightless, brown bird standing about fifteen inches tall. It is very tame and was clubbed to death by the early settlers, who suspected that it took the eggs from their chickens. Common in 1788, it now has a population of about twenty-six birds which are confined to the summits of the two mountains, where they survive despite the presence of the ubiquitous rats. Lord Howe Island has twice been colonized by Silvereyes from Australia, 700 miles to the west. These sparrow-like birds seem to be ideal colonists with their excellent powers of flight and their habit of going around in flocks. The Robust Silvereye is extinct, exterminated by rats between 1918 and 1925, but the Lord Howe Island Silvereye is still abundant.

The history of Lord Howe Island and of its birds is instructive because it shows that even on an island where man's impact is superficially

31. The Abbott's Booby with young (after a photograph by J. B. Nelson)

slight, a majority of the endemic birds can be wiped out. On this island, as on so many others, the chief culprits have been introduced mammals. The vagaries of the earth's geological and geographical history have created innumerable islands on which birds have evolved in isolation from mammals. Man has disturbed the natural distribution pattern of many species, bringing them together in entirely new combinations. It is this redistribution of animals, particularly of mammals, that has been the principal cause of the extinction of so many island birds.

Before leaving this discussion of islands I shall mention briefly a few pelagic species that spend most of their time out at sea but gather on remote islands to breed. The dense colonies formed by these often large birds are a tempting target for human hunters of eggs and meat and the Great Auk provides a classic example of such a species becoming extinct as a result of human predation. Christmas Island, an Australian territory in the western Indian Ocean, is the only breeding place of Abbott's Booby, a member of the gannet family.[24] This species is unusual among gannets in that it nests, not on the ground, but at least seventy feet up in tall trees. It is much less aggressive towards its fellows than most gannets and this is seen as an adaptation to its precarious nest-site. A bird that engaged in a fight might fall to the ground, and, unable to take off among the undergrowth below, would be doomed. The reproductive rate of this species is very slow, each pair laying only one egg in a year. It takes over twenty-four weeks for the young to fledge and then there is a further period of three to four months before it becomes independent of its parents. In 1971 there were between four and five thousand pairs of Abbott's Boobies nesting on Christmas Island but their breeding habitat is threatened by phosphate mining. This highly lucrative business completely destroys the natural habitat, leaving a lunar landscape of bare limestone pinnacles and gulleys. Even if trees are planted in areas that have been mined it will take many years for them to grow to a height at which they are suitable for the Boobies. By 1975 a large part of the nesting areas had been destroyed and the fate of this species now depends on whether effective steps are taken to control the phosphate mining.

The island of Torishima, southernmost of the seven islands of Izu which stretch nearly 400 miles south of Japan, is an active volcano. This tiny island provides the last certain breeding place of Steller's or the Short-tailed Albatross which, even with a wingspan of seven feet, is one of the smaller members of this family of magnificent wandering birds.[25] Formerly common in the northern Pacific, Steller's Albatross was at one time assumed to be extinct and is now thought to number less than 200 birds. In 1887 when the first human settlement was established on Torishima there were at least 100,000 albatrosses breeding there. The Japanese settlers set up a trade in their feathers and in seventeen years killed an estimated five million birds. Although all the feather hunters were killed by an eruption in 1903, others took their place. Laws were enacted in 1906 and 1933, banning the slaughter of albatrosses, but these proved ineffective and by 1939 there were only about forty birds left. Further eruptions caused the island to be evacuated and, except for the presence of a military garrison during the war, it remained uninhabited for many years. A survey in 1949 found no albatross nests and the species was presumed extinct. However, the following year nests were discovered and in 1956, when there were

32. Steller's Albatross

twelve known pairs nesting there, Torishima was declared a national monument. Since then the population has steadily increased and there were fifty-two pairs nesting in 1973. The recovery has been slow because, like the California Condor, albatrosses are long-lived, slow-breeding birds that do not begin to breed until they are quite old and then do so only in alternate years. A breeding population of less than 200 birds would cause concern at the best of times but when its home is an active volcano its future is precarious indeed. There is some evidence that Steller's Albatross may be breeding on some neighbouring islands and it is hoped that this can be encouraged to provide insurance against a major disaster befalling the Torishima population.

A remarkable story of effective conservation is provided by the history of the Cahow, a pelagic petrel that nests in Bermuda.[26] The Cahow once formed huge breeding colonies but these were quickly destroyed by the early British colonists and by the pigs that they brought with

33. Cahows

them. The Cahow is more commonly heard than seen; it spends most of its life far out at sea and comes ashore only in the breeding season and then only at night. It gets its name from its call, which early sailors, hearing it as it flew overhead at night, described as the cry of the devil. With greyish-black plumage above and white below, the Cahow's thirty-five-inch wingspan makes it a powerful flier, well equipped to spend many months at sea. The early settlers quickly wiped out the Cahows on the main island of Bermuda and in 1609, when a plague of introduced rats caused a famine, the islanders turned to the Cahows for food and hunted them in their refuges on the smaller islands. Fearing that they would be totally wiped out the Governor of Bermuda issued proclamations in 1616 and 1621 to stop 'the spoyle and havock of the Cahowes'. These were not effective and no trace of the Cahow was seen for 300 years, though for a long time fishermen have known of a 'Christmas bird' whose cries could be heard at night during the winter. In 1906 a dead Cahow was found but it was not identified as such until 1916. In 1935 a newly-fledged specimen was collected and in 1951 a few

34. The White-tailed Tropic Bird, or Long-tail

nests were located on tiny, wind-swept islands off the Bermudan coast.

The Cahow nests in a hole in the ground where it leaves its single chick during the day while it searches for food at sea. On its original breeding grounds on the larger islands it probably dug its own burrows in the soft ground. On the rocky islands where it has been forced to breed by human persecution it cannot dig in the hard ground but is forced to use natural holes. This brings it into competition with another pelagic bird, the slightly larger White-tailed Tropic Bird, or Long-tail, which builds its nests in natural rock crevices. The habits of the two birds dovetail in time in a remarkable way. Whereas the Cahows are at their nests during the night, the Long-tails are at theirs during the day. Cahows begin to breed in January, the Long-tails not until March. Thus as the Long-tails arrive to breed they find burrows vacated for the day by their Cahow owners and containing a defenceless chick which they quickly destroy. The Cahows return in the evening to find their devastated nest occupied by a more powerful Long-tail. When Cahow nests were rediscovered in 1951 there were only eighteen of them, a measure of the severity of this competition for nest sites. The solution to this problem is a most ingenious device, invented by David Wingate, Bermuda's conservation officer. He has built baffles, placed in front of the nest holes, which leave a gap large enough for a Cahow to squeeze through, but not a Long-tail. He has also built a number of artificial burrows in an attempt to relieve the pressure for nest sites. These measures brought about an increase in the number of breeding pairs of Cahows, but then a new threat to their survival became apparent. Despite the fact that more pairs were breeding, the number of young birds joining the population was not as large as expected. The cause appeared to be pesticide poisoning. Levels of DDT and its derivatives as high as those found in some land birds were detected in Cahow eggs.[27] In the early 1970s there was some evidence that the reproductive rate was beginning to rise again, perhaps reflecting the fact that DDT and similar compounds are being used less now than they were in the immediate post-war years.

The finding of pesticide residues in the eggs of Cahows, a species that feeds on the open seas, illustrates the much greater scale on which man affects nature now as compared with the past. The global distribution of pesticides by rivers and ocean currents underlines the fact that conservation can no longer only be approached at the local level; it has become a worldwide problem. Just as DDT has found its way into every corner of the world, so has the destructive influence of modern Western man. No longer do the world's many oceanic islands provide a safe haven on which the evolutionary process can produce new and unique varieties of animals and plants.

7

Endangered Birds of Europe

EUROPE has been the centre from which Western culture has spread throughout the world. As we have seen in previous chapters, the arrival of Europeans in America, New Zealand and many small islands has brought about environmental changes that have been responsible for the extinction of many species of birds. It is paradoxical, therefore, to find that no European bird has become extinct in historical times except for the Great Auk, and that was a pelagic species found throughout the North Atlantic. The reason why European birds have been less depleted by the same agricultural and industrial practices that have been so destructive elsewhere is probably that Europe constitutes only a small part of a huge and diverse land mass that also includes the whole of Asia. Human development has generally been localized in particular areas so that birds are adversely affected over only a small part of their ranges, which may extend to cover other, unspoiled areas. By contrast, the European colonization of North America swept from the east coast to the west in less than 200 years and many changes in the environment, such as deforestation, were carried out over very large areas.

Europe represents a small part of the vast Palaearctic faunal region which stretches from Portugal in the west to Manchuria and Khabarovsk in the east.[1] Some biogeographers have combined the Palaearctic with the Nearctic region that includes North America in a single northern region called the Holarctic, but there are sufficient differences between their faunas to justify regarding them as distinct regions. The Palaearctic is the largest of the six faunal regions and, despite its ecological diversity, several species of birds are found in both extreme western and eastern localities such as Britain and Japan. European birds vary markedly in the extent of their ranges. Some, like the Long-eared Owl, are found throughout Europe, Asia and America and thus have a Holarctic distribution. The Lesser Spotted Woodpecker has a Palaearctic range, stretching right across Europe and Asia. The Kestrel is described as an Old World species, occurring not only in Europe and Asia but also in a large part of the Ethiopian region that encompasses Africa. The familiar Robin has a European distribution, its range extending only a short distance eastwards into Asia. Finally, some species, such as the Dartford Warbler which lives only in western areas from North Africa to Southern Britain, have a very limited distribution. These different distribution patterns are important in the context of conservation. Whether the decline of a particular species in one area should be a cause for serious concern depends on whether that area represents a large or a small part of its total range and on whether the local decline is occurring elsewhere. Considerable effort is being expended, some might say wasted, on protecting species in one part of their range where they are declining, for example in Britain, while their position elsewhere is quite healthy.[2]

A major influence in the evolution of Palaearctic birds has been the series of ice ages, alternating with milder interglacial periods, which began about two million years ago. The environmental changes resulting from these climatic fluctuations have meant that the ranges of several species have been compressed and then able to expand again. They have also had the effect that, as the sea level rose and fell with the melting and reforming of the ice sheets, several areas of land have been alternately parts of the mainland and offshore islands. Areas of subtropical forest in the southern parts of the Palaearctic were extensive in the interglacial periods but were reduced to discontinuous remnants during the ice ages. This cycle of habitat reduction followed by the opening up of new areas provided favourable conditions for the recent evolution of several new species. For example, the Carrion and Hooded Crows are thought to be descended from a single species whose range was bisected during the last ice age. Separated by the ice sheet, the two populations evolved independently and became distinct, though some regard them as subspecies rather than full species since they form hybrids where their ranges now overlap in central Europe. At present Europe is in an interglacial period and in response to the milder prevailing climate several species that were confined to the south and east by the last ice age are now expanding their ranges northwards and westwards. In recent years the Fieldfare has been colonizing Greenland and the Collared Dove Great Britain. Again, conservation programmes should be planned with these demographic changes in mind. It is a waste of effort and resources to try to conserve a species in an area where its numbers are decreasing when that decline may be a natural process balanced by an expansion of its range elsewhere. We should not expect the bird fauna of, say, Britain to remain constant for thousands of years but should anticipate that a number of species will increase or decline for quite natural reasons.

Many European birds are migratory, taking advantage of seasonal climatic changes to spend different parts of the year in widely separated localities. Some species move between northern parts of Europe where they breed and more southerly areas where they spend the winter. Others. like swallows, travel further afield to Africa. Many species of wildfowl that nest in arctic latitudes come south to winter in northern parts of Europe, particularly around the coast of Britain. During their migration birds are vulnerable to hunting by man and there is considerable disquiet about the number of songbirds that are slaughtered every year in southern Europe as they pass through on their way from their northern breeding areas to Africa. This killing is particularly severe in northern Italy, where the Alps force birds to congregate in dense flocks that follow narrow flight lines through the mountain passes.[3] The Italians shoot, trap or net virtually anything that moves, be it mammal or bird, and it is estimated that 170 million animals are killed every year during the hunting season from late August to March, over half of them birds. Remarkably, there is no evidence that this appalling carnage depletes the breeding populations of northern Europe, though it has greatly reduced the number of birds breeding in Italy itself. Rather less intense hunting of migratory birds is carried out in Belgium, France, Spain, Portugal, Cyprus and Malta.

The only bird, apart from the Great Auk, that is extinct within Europe is the Waldrapp, a species that still survives in very small numbers in North Africa and Turkey.[4] This cliff-nesting bird, which once bred in the valleys of the upper Rhine, Rhône and Danube and in the Italian and Swiss Alps, has been extinct in Europe for some 300 years. Also called the Bald or Red-cheeked Ibis or the Hermit (and this in spite of its very social habits) the Waldrapp is a large bird, about about thirty inches long, with black iridescent plumage, a totally bald head whose skin is red and grey, a shaggy ruff of black feathers around the neck and a long, downward-curving red bill (Plate XV). It was depicted among the hieroglyphics of the ancient Egyptians. The Waldrapp is related to, and may be a subspecies of, the very similar Bald Ibis of southern Africa.

Unlike other species in the ibis family which frequent wetland habitats, the Waldrapp lives in dry, arid country. It feeds on animals such as lizards and insects and is migratory, though where it spends half the year is not altogether certain. The North African and Turkish populations may be entirely isolated from one another, and they differ slightly in size.[5] Waldrapps sighted during the winter in Mauritania are probably birds heading south-east towards the heart of Africa. Birds from the Turkish population migrate to the mountains of Eritrea. Waldrapps gather at their breeding colonies in February or March and disappear again in July or August. The normal clutch is of about three eggs, though in Morocco they may lay only one egg, or none at all in some years, suggesting that the habitat there is not very suitable for them.

The North African population now probably consists of fewer than one hundred pairs, shared between about twenty small colonies in the mountains of Morocco. The largest and most well-known breeding colony is in eastern Turkey, in the town of Birecik on the upper reaches of the River Euphrates.

In 1953 there were 530 pairs in the Birecik colony but this has declined steadily to only twenty-six pairs in 1972, a rate of loss of

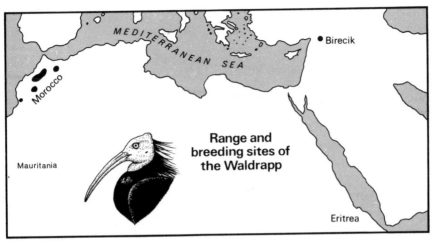

Range and breeding sites of the Waldrapp

twenty-six pairs per year. Part of this decline was due to poisoning by DDT, which was applied to nearby crops between 1958 and 1960. In 1959 and 1960 over a hundred Waldrapps were found dead or dying in the vicinity. A bird that was taken to England in 1972 for analysis was found to contain quite normal levels of pesticide residues, suggesting that the recent continued decline has been due to other factors.[6] As the town of Birecik has expanded, houses have been built closer and closer to the cliffs where the Bald Ibises nest and it seems that these rather shy birds have declined as a result of increasing human disturbance. The World Wildlife Fund has set up a conservation programme which involves widening nest ledges to eliminate egg losses, demolishing the closer houses and re-housing their occupants, controlling the local use of pesticides and generally educating the inhabitants of the town. There is a breeding population of about fifty Waldrapps at Basle Zoo in Switzerland, and there seems no reason why this curious bird should not be saved from extinction and perhaps eventually restored to some of its old haunts in Europe.

The Waldrapp is only one of many bird species that have been adversely affected by man's use of chemical pesticides. The classic case history that established the link between DDT and reproductive failure in birds was that of the Peregrine Falcon in Britain, studied primarily by D. A. Ratcliffe. The Peregrine is the epitome of a swift, deadly predator.[7] One of the most beautiful of all birds of prey with its black, slate-grey and white plumage, it is renowned for its aerobatic prowess (Plate I). In the breeding season pairs tumble and twist through the air in a remarkable courtship ritual. When a Peregrine dives, or 'stoops' on its flying prey, mostly pigeons and game birds such as grouse, it can reach a speed of 250 miles per hour.

Peregrines are found virtually throughout the world, mostly in open rather desolate moorland or tundra habitat. They nest on cliff ledges and rocky crags and are frequently found in coastal areas where they feed extensively on seabirds. The nest or eyrie is often simply a bare ledge, or the appropriated nest of another bird. Three or four eggs are usually laid; incubation takes about a month and the young fledge when they are around forty days old.

During the Second World War Peregrines were systematically shot and their eyries destroyed by government order. Pilots of military aircraft were equipped with homing pigeons which they could release carrying information about their position, if they were forced to ditch their aircraft in the sea. It was feared that Peregrines would take these pigeons, particularly as they crossed the coast, hence the efforts to control their numbers. Immediately after the war, when this practice ceased, the Peregrine population, as expected, began to increase, but as early as 1947 it was clear that something was going wrong and that the Peregrine was not going to regain its former abundance. The story of how the observation that eggs were being broken in the nest led in the 1960s to the discovery of the relationship between DDT and other chemicals and a disturbance of the Peregrine's reproductive physiology was outlined in Chapter 2. In high doses pesticides kill birds by affecting their nervous systems; in low doses they cause the death of embryos and the formation of eggshells so thin that they are crushed by the weight of the incubating parent.

The British Peregrine population has been carefully monitored in a series of surveys carried out since the war.[8] There was a steady decline in numbers until 1963, when the population stabilized at about 40 per cent of its pre-war size It has since remained at roughly the same level, with the average breeding success being only about 15 per cent of what healthy birds can achieve. The decline in numbers and in breeding success has been less marked in southern Scotland and in

Northern Ireland, where pesticides have been less extensively used. A survey published in 1967 showed a stable population of Peregrines and contamination levels in their eggs similar to those found four years earlier, suggesting that an equilibrium has been established between the birds and their polluted environment. However, by 1971 there were signs of an increase among inland birds, though not among those nesting near the coast. It appears that controls of pesticide use on the land are beginning to have an effect but that at sea pollution levels remain high. The seabirds that fall prey to coastal Peregrines also contain high levels of polychlorinated biphenyls (PCBs), poisonous by-products of many industrial processes. While DDT is now virtually never used in Britain, Dieldrin is and continues to threaten the Peregrine population.[9]

In recent years the much-reduced population of Peregrines in Britain has been subjected to a new threat, the collecting of eggs and chicks by and on behalf of falconers. In the summer of 1976 at least thirty-six eyries were raided.[10] The problem arises from the fact that falconers are prepared to pay high prices for this most beautiful and skilful of birds. The Royal Society for the Protection of Birds is doing all it can to apply the law against nest raiders to protect the British population which, unlike those in other parts of Europe and in America, appears to be maintaining itself.

A decline in the numbers of one species, such as the Peregrine, may lead to changes in the relationships between other species in the ecological community. The Peregrine is a predator and, as it disappears from an area, the species that it preys on will tend to increase in numbers so that their impact on the community will become greater. As I mentioned in Chapter 2, it has long been known that the Red-breasted Goose builds its nests near Peregrine eyries, apparently to gain protection from foxes, gulls and skuas which are deterred from taking their eggs by the presence of the falcons. In the last twenty years Red-breasted Geese have declined in numbers and, though there is no direct evidence, it may be that this has been due to increased predation on their now less well-protected nests.

The Red-breasted Goose is one of the smaller geese and also one of the most beautiful with its black and russet plumage picked out in white.[11] It is to be seen in most captive wildfowl collections but its natural habits are somewhat obscure because of the remoteness of its haunts. It visits south-east Europe in the winter, which it spends around the Caspian and Black Seas. It breeds beyond the Arctic Circle, particularly on the Taimyr Peninsula in Siberia, an area of desolate tundra that is free of ice and snow for only a few months each year. The Red-breasted Geese arrive at their breeding grounds in June, immediately after the spring thaw, and often lay their eggs within a few days. They nest on higher ground, though never far from water, usually in groups of four to six nests quite close together. By September, when the tundra begins to freeze up again, the geese and their fledged young have departed for the south. The total population appears to have declined from an estimated 50,000 in 1957 to a present level of around 30,000. This may be due to increased predation at the breeding grounds, or to human interference both in Siberia and in their wintering areas. The frequency with which they are caught for zoos and other captive collections has probably not helped their situation.

The levels and effects of chemical pollutants are carefully monitored in many parts of Europe and in some countries their use is now controlled.[12] In Sweden, as in other countries, seed dressings containing alkyl mercury have been used to combat crop losses caused by fungal diseases.[13] These compounds cause mortality among grain-eating birds like pheasants and pigeons and their predators such as Peregrines and Goshawks. In 1966 these chemicals were banned in Sweden and were replaced by other mercury compounds that do not accumulate in animal tissues but which are just as effective from the agricultural point of view. Mercury compounds are also extensively used in the conversion of wood pulp to paper and have built up in fishes, causing mortality among such birds as Great Crested Grebes and Ospreys. The Swedish government banned their use when it was found that levels of mercury in fish were so high as to threaten human health. DDT was banned in Sweden in 1970 and PCBs in 1971. Recent analysis of pollutant levels in Swedish birds shows that those, such as Robins and Pied Flycatchers, that spend the winter in Mediterranean countries like Spain and Morocco contain higher levels than do resident birds, since DDT and similar insecticides continue to be heavily used in southern European countries. As we have seen, the birds most severely affected by pesticide poisoning are the larger predators and Sweden's White-tailed Eagles that live around the heavily polluted Baltic Sea show high mortality and almost total reproductive failure.

The White-tailed Eagle, also called the Sea Eagle, inhabits coastal areas and larger inland lakes, feeding on birds, especially nestlings, fish, small mammals and carrion.[14] It is found over a huge area stretching from Greenland and Iceland in the west, through Scandinavia and eastern Europe to the Pacific coast of Asia and southwards to the Middle East. A very large bird, it is a typical K-strategist, living for up to thirty years in the wild and breeding for the first time at five or six years old. It is declining in numbers over most of its range and became extinct in Ireland in 1910, Scotland in 1916, Denmark in 1961 and Austria in 1969. White-tailed Eagles survive in the greatest density in Norway, though even there their numbers are dwindling. The main cause of their decline in western Europe was persecution by man who has long regarded them as a threat to livestock. Though they are officially protected in eastern Europe, they continue to be shot and poisoned there by farmers. Since the Second World War chemical pollution, especially in the Baltic, has provided an additional hazard to their survival.

None of Europe's six or seven resident species of eagles can really be considered to be in a healthy position. Their size and rarity make them obvious targets for hunters and collectors and their position at the top of the food chain exposes them to chemical poisoning. The Imperial Eagle, found throughout eastern Europe and Asia, has a distinct Spanish race which is now seriously endangered.[15] Distinguished from the typical form by large white patches on its shoulders, the Spanish Imperial Eagle now numbers only about one hundred birds. The Coto Doñana, where it can most effectively be protected, supports only seven pairs. It is a rather slow-moving predator and feeds mostly on carrion and mammalian prey, such as rabbits, not on birds. It has been the subject of an ingenious conservation technique whose potential value in the protection of eagles and similar species has already been demonstrated with the Lesser Spotted Eagle in Czechoslovakia.

35. The Spanish Imperial Eagle with young

Like many birds, Lesser Spotted Eagles lay more eggs then they eventually succeed in rearing to the point of fledging. The young show 'Cain and Abel' behaviour or, to be more technical, sibling rivalry, in which younger chicks are so ill-treated by their elders that they die.[16] The mother lays two or three eggs at intervals of a few days and starts incubating as soon as the first is laid. Many birds do not start to incubate until they have finished laying, with the result that all the eggs hatch at around the same time. The eagle's behaviour means that the eggs hatch at intervals similar to those at which they were laid so that the first chick is a vigorous nestling by the time the second is hatched. If there is a third chick it will be similarly younger and less robust than its siblings. When they are about a week old the older chicks become aggressive, rarely physically attacking the others but establishing a position of dominance over their younger brethren, denying them access to food and driving them to the edge of the nest where they may starve, become chilled or fall off. Sometimes the nestlings that die in this way are picked up by the parents and fed to the older chicks. This competition between siblings appears to be more severe when the interval between successive hatchings is short. Chicks that are much older than their brothers and sisters are so much more expert at getting to the food brought to the nest by the parents that they apparently do not need to assert themselves aggressively.

It is not easy to see how this seemingly wasteful behaviour could have evolved. Why do eagles go to the effort of producing second and third chicks whose chances of survival are apparently so small? The answer probably relates to a problem that has intrigued ornithologists for many years; what controls the number of young that a pair of birds produces in any one breeding season? There is abundant evidence that many birds adjust the size of their clutch according to the quality of the environment at the time, laying many eggs when food is plentiful, few or none at all when it is scarce. The optimal strategy for any bird is to lay exactly as many eggs as it will be able to rear fully healthy young. To lay fewer would be to waste reproductive potential; to lay more might mean that it overreached its capacity to provide for the young, which would then grow up small, weak and less likely to survive. The solving of the problem seems to require an ability to predict at the time of laying how good the environment will be at the time of rearing the young. For small birds with short breeding seasons, such as the Great Tit, the quality of the habitat apparently does not change much over the course of a breeding cycle and they vary their clutch size according to conditions. For large birds like the eagles, which have to care for their young for many weeks, it is quite possible that conditions will change dramatically and unpredictably between the time of laying the eggs and that of feeding the chicks. For them the problem of how to raise the best number of young has apparently been solved, not by varying their clutch size, but by laying and hatching the eggs at intervals so that, in effect, the behaviour of the young decides how many of them will survive. One would suppose that, in good years when food is abundant, the chicks should compete less with one another so that all will survive. In bad years the eldest chick will fight success-fully for what food is available and its siblings will die. This ensures for the parents that the young they rear, be there one, two or three, are always fully fed and healthy. An equitable sharing of an inadequate food supply would only produce two or three equally ill-nourished chicks. This explanation is not entirely satisfactory, however, because young Lesser Spotted Eagles have been observed to die as the result of sibling competition even when the parents have brought them an excess of food.

Whatever its biological explanation, this natural wastage of young eagles can be exploited by the conservationist. The aggression shown by older chicks to their younger siblings ceases when they are about two months old. If one of the chicks is removed and reared in captivity it can then be returned to the nest after two months and there will be no aggression between the young. The parents are apparently fully prepared to accept extra chicks at this late stage. This has been done in Czechoslovakia, both by removing the older chick so that the younger one can grow unmolested and, alternatively, by fostering the younger chick, returning it when it will no longer elicit the hostility of its older brother or sister. In this way the number of young fledged at any one eyrie can be effectively doubled. In Spain, where there is good evidence that the food supply of Imperial Eagles is insufficient for the rearing of many chicks, conservationists have taken the youngest chicks from three-chick broods and put them in the nests of birds who have none.[17] These transferred nestlings have been successfully reared by their foster-parents, so that reproductive potential that would have been wasted is restored to the population.

Owls are birds of prey that mostly hunt at night and as such are vulnerable to much the same environmental pressures as the hawks, falcons and eagles. The largest of Europe's owls, the Eagle Owl, is also the most endangered, primarily as the result of years of human persecution.[18] It has long been regarded as vermin in many parts of Europe and in Norway the government paid a bounty for every Eagle Owl killed in the early years of this century. It has been particularly detested by gamekeepers, probably because its catholic diet means that all kinds of game are likely to fall prey to it. The Eagle Owl catches mammals of all sizes from voles and rats to young deer, birds, fish, and other creatures like snakes and beetles. Once found in most parts of Europe and Asia, it is now extinct in Belgium, Luxembourg and much

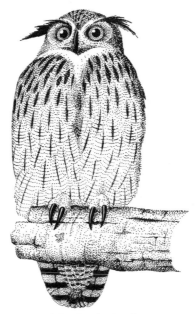

36. The Eagle Owl

of France and is declining in Italy and Finland. In some areas, such as
Norway and parts of south-east Europe, its numbers appear to be
stable. As well as persecution by man, the reduction in the numbers of
rabbits caused by myxomatosis, and general human encroachment
into the remote, desolate areas that it prefers have contributed to
the decline of this magnificent bird. Eagle Owls have been very
successfully bred in captivity in Sweden, suggesting that there is a
good chance that they may eventually be re-introduced to areas where
they have become extinct.[19] Unfortunately, over three-quarters of
these captive-reared birds have died of other than natural causes
after their release, either hitting overhead power-lines and cables or
being run over on roads. Owls are peculiarly susceptible to these
hazards because they are nocturnal and low flying and take their prey
from the ground.

At northerly, arctic latitudes the ecological role played by the Eagle
Owl is taken over by the equally massive and spectacular Snowy Owl,
which has become well known in Britain since it recently began to

breed regularly on Fetlar in Shetland.[20] Well-adapted to snowy conditions with its dense white plumage and heavily-feathered legs, the
Snowy Owl feeds largely on lemmings, small arctic mammals
whose numbers show dramatic four-year cycles of abundance and
sudden decline. It is distributed around a complete circle that covers
the arctic regions of both Asia and North America. It appears to be
declining throughout its range, though why is not clear.

Closely related to the eagles are the vultures, huge birds whose long
wings enable them to remain airborne for long periods with little
effort as they scour the countryside for their carrion food. Four species
live in southern areas of Europe such as Spain, Corsica and Sardinia,
Greece and the Balkan countries. They are the Bearded Vulture or
Lammergeir, the Egyptian Vulture, the Black Vulture and the Griffon
Vulture, all of which are found elsewhere, either in Asia or in Africa.
All four species are declining within Europe, principally because there
are no longer enough corpses of farm or wild animals for them to eat.
In Spain Griffon and Egyptian Vultures and Lammergeirs are being
given human support in the form of animal corpses that are left out in
the open at remote 'vulture restaurants'.[21] It has been suggested that this
may actually be a more hygienic way to dispose of animal carcasses
than burial in the ground. Harmful bacteria, which might find their
way into domestic water supplies from buried corpses, are destroyed
by the digestive juices in the vultures' guts.

The rocky coasts and many offshore islands of Europe support a
rich variety of seabirds including auks, gulls, terns, petrels, shearwaters,
gannets and cormorants. Audouin's Gull is a Mediterranean species that
is in some danger of extinction.[22] Slightly smaller than a Herring Gull,
it has the typical gull's white, grey and black plumage, but is distinguished by dark green legs and a red bill with a black band across it
and a yellow tip. It breeds in a number of scattered colonies on small
islands off Morocco, Cyprus, Corsica and in the Aegean. The total
population numbers about 1250 birds and three-quarters of these breed
on the Charafinas Islands off Morocco's northern coast in much the
largest breeding colony. Here the eggs of Audouin's Gull have long
been collected for making pastry and it appears that direct human
destruction has been the main cause of its decline throughout the

37. Audouin's Gull

Mediterranean. It has been suggested, without clear evidence, that it may also have suffered through predation by Herring Gulls, whose numbers have increased dramatically in recent years.

While Herring Gulls, fulmars and gannets have become more common around Europe's coasts, many other species have declined as the result of pollution and other manifestations of human activity. The crowded shipping lanes around north-west Europe bring the threat of oil slicks which are lethal to any birds that come into contact with them. The wreck of the *Torrey Canyon* off south-west Britain in 1967 and the subsequent mortality among seabirds drew widespread attention to the environmental threat from oil pollution. However, devastating though they may be, such major disasters are probably less damaging in the long term than innumerable smaller spillages that are happening all the time. The birds that are most at risk from oil are those that spend much of their time swimming on the surface of the sea such as auks and divers. The divers are a family of birds whose origins date far back into the

38. The Great Northern Diver

evolutionary history of birds; the huge fossil *Hesperornis* from the
Cretaceous period was very similar to living divers. Largest and rarest
of those that breed in Europe is the Great Northern Diver, a magnificent
bird with an intricately patterned black and white plumage.[23] Primarily
a New World species, its breeding range extends eastwards to Iceland
and Bear Island. The birds that spend the winter around Britain, north-
west Europe and Scandinavia may breed as far west as Greenland. They
are now widely protected on their breeding grounds, for example in
Iceland, where they were once persecuted, and oil pollution in their
more southerly wintering areas appears to be the major threat to their
survival.

The sea around north-west Europe supports huge quantities of fish
which attract innumerable fishing boats from Britain and other
European countries, Iceland and Russia. It is difficult to estimate how
many birds are killed by being inadvertently caught in fishing nets,
but it is clear that fishing poses a serious threat to many marine species.
It has been estimated that fishermen from Denmark who catch salmon

off the western coast of Greenland annually kill about half a million Thick-billed Murres, birds closely related to guillemots.[24]

On the European mainland a number of birds that are dependent on water for all or part of their lives are threatened by the widespread destruction of wetland habitats like marshes, fens and estuaries. The large flocks of wildfowl and other birds that gather in such habitats have for many years attracted hunters. Usually located along the lower reaches and at the mouths of rivers, wetlands are often heavily polluted by chemicals carried downstream from industrial plants inland. The most serious threat to wetlands comes from land reclamation schemes by which they are drained or filled in to create land for other purposes. For example, in Holland, the most densely populated country in Europe, there have been frequent suggestions that the Waddensea, a haven for innumerable waterfowl, gulls and waders, should be re-claimed for industrial and urban development.[25] A number of water birds that inhabit wetlands in south-east Europe, particularly around the lower Danube and along the shores of the Black Sea, have become very rare.[26] They include the White and Dalmatian Pelicans, the Great White Egret, the Pygmy Cormorant and the Glossy Ibis. The Greater Flamingo lives in scattered populations around the Mediterranean, most notably in the Camargue in southern France. Two of Europe's rarest wetland species are birds that live principally in other parts of the world, Europe being the extreme limit of their ranges. The Purple Gallinule, which breeds in Spain and Sardinia, is the same species that is found on many islands in the Pacific; the secretive Crested Coot, which breeds in Spain, is an African bird. A number of wetland birds that became extinct in Britain have become re-established there, largely as a result of the conservation efforts of the Royal Society for the Protection of Birds. They include the Avocet, the Black-tailed Godwit, the Bittern and Savi's Warbler.

One of Europe's largest and most spectacular species is the Great Bustard, of which the male is the world's heaviest flying bird. (Plate XVI).[27] Originally found in Britain, throughout continental Europe and across Asia, the Great Bustard now has a fragmented range from Portugal to Manchuria and is declining in many areas. It last bred in Britain in 1832 and became extinct in France in the 1860s. Its present

39. The Purple Gallinule (left) and the Crested Coot

status in Russia is uncertain; it is said to be declining in the Ukraine but to be on the increase further east where forests have been cleared. Great Bustards are birds of open, treeless plains. Powerful fliers, they are usually seen in small flocks, walking slowly in search of their predominantly plant food. The name 'bustard' means 'slow goose' but, though their size and habits are reminiscent of geese, they are related, not to geese, but to the cranes. They are powerfully built birds, able to run very fast if they are alarmed. They are very rarely seen at close quarters; frequenting only the most open country where there is no cover, they are extremely vigilant and difficult to approach undetected. Males are very much larger than females; indeed, the disparity in size between the sexes is the most extreme of any living bird. Females weigh up to about ten pounds, becoming sexually mature at three years of age. Males weigh as much as forty pounds and mature correspondingly later at about six years old. They may live for over thirty years

40. A male Great Bustard in courtship display

and groups of birds, referred to as 'droves' in Norfolk in England, tend to remain in the same area for many years.

The disparity in size between male and female Great Bustards appears to be related to their sexual behaviour, which is based on a lek system, similar to that of grouse, ruffs and a number of other birds. The males compete with one another for territories from which they advertise for mates, behaviour for which large size is an advantage. The females incubate the eggs and care for the young, activities for which small size and inconspicuousness are more suitable. The leks are traditional sites at which Great Bustards gather each year between February and April. The males generally maintain a distance between one another of between 500 yards and one mile. They strut about and repeatedly contort themselves in one of the most spectacular advertisement displays to be seen among birds. They literally appear to turn themselves inside out, cocking their tails forward and turning their wings back and over to display a billowing mass of pure white feathers so that they look like 'a pile of snow on legs'. At the same time they inflate an air-sac in the neck which blows up to the size of a football and hides the head. This display, which can be seen from several miles away as a succession of white flashes, is conducted in complete silence. Great Bustards are virtually mute and it seems that, since sound does not carry far over open, windswept plains, they have evolved a visual rather than an auditory display for attracting females.

In common with the males of most lekking species, the male Great Bustard does not play any part in the care and protection of the young. After mating, the female moves away from the lek and lays up to four eggs in a simple nest on the ground. The chicks, which are able to run about soon after hatching, are fed primarily on insects in the early months of life. After the breeding season the females and their young join up with the males to roam the plains in small bands.

Great Bustards have long been hunted throughout Europe and Asia. They are said to make excellent eating, and their wariness and open habitat have provided a keen challenge to the hunter. A widely-used technique was to approach them using a 'stalking horse', since they are apparently attracted towards horses. While shooting obviously posed a severe threat to their survival, notably in East Anglia where at least one gamekeeper shot large numbers with a kind of blunderbuss, it was probably not the principal cause of their decline.[28] Great Bustards have simply been driven away from many of their original haunts by changes in the way the land is cultivated and used. They will not inhabit areas that have been broken up into fields by hedges and fences and where trees have been planted as windbreaks to provide shelter for livestock. Their decline in many areas coincided with the introduction of mechanical hoes and harrows which destroy their eggs and chicks.

At present the Great Bustard survives in Europe in three widely-separated populations.[29] There are about 1200 in the Iberian peninsula, between 300 and 400 of them in Portugal. In Poland and East Germany, where they have been protected since the 1950s, there are around 1500. The largest population inhabits an area stretching eastwards from Austria across Hungary, Czechoslovakia and Romania. In Britain, where they once roamed the downlands of Yorkshire, Lincolnshire, Berkshire, Sussex, East Anglia and Wiltshire, a captive colony was set up in the early 1970s.[30] This group, living in a fenced area on Porton Down in Wiltshire and made up of about ten birds imported from Portugal, is intended to be the basis of a breeding population from which birds may eventually be reintroduced to some of their original British breeding areas.

The threats to the survival of several species that live in Europe are similar to those that have brought about the decline or extinction of many birds in other parts of the world. As we have seen, the two most endangered categories of birds are the birds of prey and those species that depend on wetland habitats. In general, large birds are more seriously threatened than smaller ones because they require greater areas of unspoiled habitat and many migratory species have to run the gauntlet of gun-happy hunters. Nevertheless there are good grounds for optimism about the future of some of Europe's rarer species. There are many vigorous and effective conservation organisations and pressure groups at work, particularly in northern Europe, that have achieved some notable successes such as the re-establishment of the Avocet in Britain.

There are those who question the way conservation effort and re-sources are being used in Europe.[31] Would the money and skill used to provide a sanctuary in Britain for the Avocet, a species which is in a healthy position elsewhere, not be better deployed protecting the Mauritius Kestrel, a bird on the brink of extinction? A consideration that arises in this context is that people are more prepared to give money for the protection of a species that they will have an opportunity to see for themselves than one in some remote corner of the world where they are never likely to go. Local conservation efforts are important, even if they do not make an appreciable contribution to the preservation of any one species. Conservation on the global scale will only become possible when people fully understand the issues involved and a local project, even if it is only directed towards conserving a hedge or a small copse, is valuable, because it helps to foster a general awareness about environmental problems. In addition, local schemes are important because they allow for the development in economically and socially favourable conditions of techniques and practices which can eventually be applied in the less developed parts of the world. The Wildfowl Trust at Slimbridge in Britain has been a pioneer in the science of captive breeding, which provides one of the main hopes for saving a number of endangered species throughout the world.

Europe gave the world the Industrial Revolution and European culture was largely responsible for the development of deep-seated attitudes that allow a callous disregard for the fate of other species. The spread of European social, industrial and agricultural practices throughout the world has contributed more than anything else towards the destruction of the world's wildlife. We must hope that in the future Europe will again lead the way, this time in the attempt to restore the balance between man and his environment.

8

Extinct and Endangered Birds of Australia

AUSTRALIA has a special importance in zoology, primarily because it is the principal home of the Marsupials, a unique group of mammals that includes the kangaroo and the Koala Bear. It is perhaps significant that Australia's national emblem is the kangaroo while that of its near neighbour, New Zealand, is a bird, the Kiwi. While the Marsupials have attracted the greater share of biological interest, Australian birds include a number of species that are as unusual and remarkable as any in the world, for Australia's geological, climatic and human histories have combined to mould a cóllection of bird species that are of great ornithological interest. A number of these are now considered to be endangered.[1]

In common with other parts of the world, Australia and its native animals have felt the destructive impact of colonization by Europeans. However, Australian birds have suffered less severely than those of North America or New Zealand in that no species has become extinct since the advent of Europeans. Two distinct birds have become extinct but these, local races of the Emu that lived on offshore islands, are considered to have been subspecies and the surviving subspecies of Emu that lives on the mainland is quite common. However, it is possible that there are full species that are extinct; there are, for example, some species of Australian parrots that have not been reliably recorded for more than thirty years. A number of other species are critically rare, some of them so rare that for many years they were considered to be extinct until they were 'rediscovered' in the course of the last twenty years.

Australia has been referred to as the 'island continent', a phrase that makes reference to two important factors in the evolution of Australian animals.[2] Australia's insularity is reflected in the fact that it has been colonized by some groups of animals that live elsewhere in the world and not by others. As we saw in Chapter 6, groups that do colonize islands are able to adapt to their new environment in new ways because of the absence of those animals that have failed to make the sea crossing. It is Australia's isolation from the rest of the world for more than sixty million years that has enabled the Marsupials to flourish and diversify there while they have declined and largely disappeared elsewhere in the world.[3] The second important factor in the evolution of Australia's animals is its size, which justifies our calling it a continent; Australia has an area of more than two and a half million square miles. So large an island contains a far richer variety of habitats than do the small islands discussed in Chapter 6, with the result that animals that successfully colonized Australia early in its history have given rise to a much greater diversity of forms than one would find on small offshore islands. Australia stretches from the hot, semi-tropical zone in the north to the cool, temperate climates of the southern latitudes and supports some 700 species of birds. Again, the Marsupials, with their many and varied species, provide the classic example of this effect, called adaptive radiation.

Australia's ornithological history, like that of New Zealand, began when it was a part of the great southern supercontinent, Gondwanaland.[4] Before the process of continental drift brought about their separation some sixty-four million years ago, Australia, Africa, South America, Antarctica and New Zealand were all joined together and the birds that existed at that time moved easily between them. At that time Antarctica, like the other incipient continents, supported a rich community of plants and animals that was totally destroyed by its drift towards the south pole. Among the inhabitants of Gondwanaland were the ancestors of the modern Ratite birds, of which Australia's representative is the Emu. Other Australian birds which probably had ancestors living in Gondwanaland include the megapodes or mound-birds, the lyrebirds, the scrub-birds and the remarkable Pied Goose, so distinct from other geese after millions of years of evolution in isolation that it is placed in a sub-family of its own. As the portion of Gondwana-land destined to become Australia drifted away eastwards it became increasingly isolated from other large areas of land and thus less and less likely to be colonized by new groups of birds. After millions of years of drifting it began to approach the Asian land mass which was drifting southwards as the result of the break-up of the northern super-continent, Laurasia. Thus, while Australia's most ancient families almost certainly had their origins in the southern hemisphere, more recently evolved families are more likely to be descended from colonists that came from the Oriental and Palaearctic regions to the north.

Recent research into the phenomenon of continental drift has led to a re-assessment of the date at which the ancient supercontinents became fragmented. It was previously believed that the break-up occurred more than 200 million years ago, that is, before the earliest birds had evolved. Now that the date has been brought forward to about sixty-four million years ago it is clear that continental drift must have profoundly influenced the course of bird evolution. In the context of Australian birds it means that the older colonizing families, derived from southern hemisphere ancestors, evolved in isolation for millions of years before coming into contact with a quite different set of immi-grants arriving from the north.

Australia's isolation throughout much of its ornithological history is reflected in the absence of a number of bird families that are wide-spread in the rest of the world. These include the vultures, the pheasants, the woodpeckers and the finches. It is clear from fossil evidence that flamingoes once lived in Australia but that they have since disappeared. This is probably due to the profound changes in climate that have taken place during Australia's history.

While it remained a part of Gondwanaland, Australia's climate was equable and temperate; there were extensive deciduous forests and many lakes. As it drifted away the climate became more tropical. Most of the continent became covered by dense rain forest, humidity was high and crocodiles, which are now only found in the extreme north of the continent, were widespread. Flamingoes, and probably other birds that have since disappeared, prospered at this time. In the Miocene period, which began about twenty-six million years ago, this tropical climate gave way to one in which there were marked seasonal changes. The continent as a whole became cooler and drier and, as a result, the deciduous trees of the tropical forests were replaced by the Eucalyptus and Acacia trees that dominate Australia's vegetation today. In the Pleistocene period, beginning about two million years ago, there came the succession of ice ages which so radically altered the course of evolution in both the southern and northern hemispheres. Australia never came within range of the southern ice sheets that built up from the south pole but as the ice came close and then receded it created alternating cycles of dry and wet climate which led to the creation of the deserts and semi-arid areas that cover most of present-day Australia. Indeed, Australia is now the driest continent on earth, apart from Antarctica, which, though covered in ice, receives very little of its water by precipitation.

As the great dry area in the heartland of Australia grew, the more verdant habitats that had once covered most of the continent became more and more confined to coastal areas. While this meant that many of the birds that had previously been widespread had to drastically reduce their range, the expansion of the arid zone opened up new opportunities for birds that could adapt to the dry climate and sparse vegetation of Australia's vast interior. The Emu, one of the most ancient of Australia's birds, has, as we shall see, very successfully colonized the arid heartland.

So slight and sporadic is the rainfall on Australia's huge central plateau that it is insufficient to create or maintain a system of streams and rivers draining into the sea.[5] Such rain as does fall mostly drains inwards into large, shallow salt lakes that dry up in periods of drought. The largest of these lakes is Lake Eyre in South Australia. During a rain storm the water runs off some areas of the land and collects in others, causing floods if the rain is very heavy. The areas where rain tends to

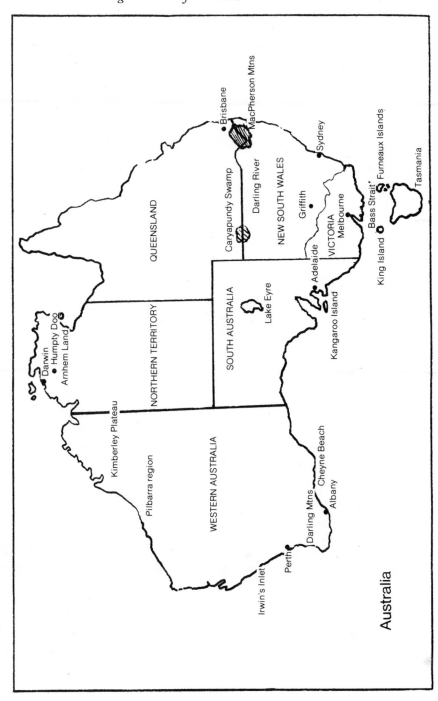

Australia

Brisbane
MacPherson Mtns
Sydney
Furneaux Islands
Tasmania
Caryapundy Swamp
Darling River
NEW SOUTH WALES
Griffith
Bass Strait
QUEENSLAND
VICTORIA
Melbourne
King Island
Adelaide
SOUTH AUSTRALIA
Lake Eyre
Kangaroo Island
Darwin
Humpty Doo
Arnhem Land
NORTHERN TERRITORY
Kimberley Plateau
Pilbarra region
WESTERN AUSTRALIA
Cheyne Beach
Albany
Darling Mtns
Perth
Irwin's Inlet

collect are called 'run-on' areas and are critically important to the animals that live in arid areas.[6] It is on run-on areas that the only permanent vegetation can be found. After rain these areas undergo a dramatic transformation. The dry, · dusty plants almost overnight become a mass of green foliage and brilliantly coloured flowers. At the same time millions of insects and other small creatures emerge from their dormancy and there is a period of feeding-up and breeding which gradually declines as the water disappears and the drier conditions return.

The larger animals, like mammals and birds, that cannot become dormant during periods of drought have got to be adapted to an environment in which food and water supplies are only sporadically available if they are to survive in the arid zone. There are, broadly speaking, three strategies which animals may adopt in the face of such conditions. They may avoid them altogether, they may become permanent residents, or they may become nomadic, moving from one area where rain has recently fallen to another. Some mammals have evolved a remarkable array of anatomical and physiological adaptations that enable them to survive the intense heat of desert areas for long periods without having to drink at all, and they are thus able to live in one locality, essentially surviving from one rainy period to the next. The Red Kangaroo uses its remarkable method of locomotion to be nomadic. For birds, with their powers of flight, the nomadic strategy seems the more obvious one to adopt and many of the birds of Australia's heartland travel huge distances in the quest for hospitable habitat. Even the flightless Emu is nomadic, moving across the dry countryside on its long powerful legs, but, unable to fly far afield when conditions deteriorate, it has evolved the physiological capacity to survive periods of great heat and lack of water for longer than most birds.

As we saw in Chapter 1, environments in which food supply and other vital resources occur sporadically and unpredictably favour the evolution of animals that are able to disperse quickly and effectively and which can breed rapidly; such animals are called r-strategists. One of the best examples of an r-strategist among birds is the Budgerigar, an inhabitant of Australia's outback and a popular cage bird throughout the world.[7] In the wild, Budgerigars form huge itinerant flocks that darken the sky and assail the ears with the sound of countless whirring wings in a manner reminiscent of the Passenger Pigeon in North America. Their numbers within any given area fluctuate wildly as their food supply of seeds and foliage flourishes and declines. Their capacity to breed is remarkable. A male Budgerigar is fully mature and fertile within sixty days of fledging, one of the shortest periods of 'adolescence' known among birds. In captivity pairs of Budgerigars can produce several broods of young in quick succession; most birds need a period of some months after breeding before they become fertile again.

Another bird with spectacular powers of dispersal is Australia's Grey Teal.[8] Whenever an inland area becomes flooded after heavy rain large numbers of Grey Teal will congregate there and start to breed. Their response to wetter conditions is remarkably rapid and they will start to breed within days of the local water level beginning to rise. The huge numbers of Grey Teal that gather in flooded areas have long provided an attractive target for hunters. As the water drains away or evaporates and the breeding area dries up again the Grey Teal vanish, dispersing in all directions. They appear to fly in random directions, each individual setting off on its own path and apparently flying in a straight line. It seems that when they reach the coast they carry on flying over the sea and Grey Teal have been known to reach New Guinea to the north and New Zealand to the south-east. Presumably many that fail to reach land must perish far out to sea. They are very powerful flyers; birds marked in Humpty Doo near Darwin in northern Australia have been recovered thirteen and nineteen days later in the Pilbarra region of Western Australia, over 1200 miles away. The Grey Teal pays a high price for its migratory habits. It has been found that, compared with its more sedentary close relative, the Black Duck, it suffers a higher rate of mortality and has a lower life expectancy.[9] The fact that it remains a common species throughout Australia suggests that it must possess some counteracting adaptation, perhaps an ability to breed at an early age or to breed more often than once a year.

Another resident of the Australian interior that gathers in large numbers is the Flock Pigeon.[10] This fairly small pigeon has a short tail and large wings that enable it to sustain a powerful flapping flight over long distances. Pigeon flocks are nomadic, moving about in search of their food which consists mostly of seeds. They appear not to breed at any specific time of year but after a period of rain when food becomes abundant. Since the arrival of Europeans they have been a favourite target for hunters and before that they were hunted by Aborigines, particularly when they came in to drink at a water hole in the evening. It is said that Flock Pigeons alight on water at the precise moment that the sun dips below the horizon. The method used by Aborigines to hunt Flock Pigeons involved the building of artificial bushes along the edge of a likely drinking pool. This caused the birds at the front of the incoming flock to check their flight, creating a confused mêlée behind them into which the Aborigines threw their boomerangs. It has been suggested that the apparently hesitant behaviour shown by Flock Pigeons as they repeatedly circle a water hole before coming down to drink has evolved as a response to this Aboriginal hunting technique. The Flock Pigeon is found throughout a huge part of northern and central Australia. For a bird with so large a range and whose numbers in any one locality can fluctuate between spectacular abundance and virtually total absence, it is difficult to assess the overall population size. Recent books on Australian birds describe its status as 'uncertain' and there are those, no doubt with the example of the Passenger Pigeon in mind, who fear for its continued survival.

The Aborigines, who hunted the Flock Pigeon and many other species of birds, were the original human inhabitants of Australia. It is not certain how severe or extensive their impact on the environment was, but in view of their rather small numbers in relation to Australia's huge area, such changes as they brought about can only have been local and are unlikely to have seriously threatened any of the indigenous birds. Their influence seems to have been minimal compared to that of the Maoris in New Zealand. The same cannot be said of the European colonizers of Australia who, as in so many parts of the world, have altered the natural environment to a degree and at a speed out of all proportion to the changes brought about by the original human inhabitants.

The ways in which Europeans have altered the natural face of Australia form a pattern all too familiar to those who have read the earlier chapters of this book.[11] The energies of the early colonists were directed primarily towards the creation of a vigorous agricultural economy. Forests and scrubland were cleared to make way for fields and pastures, wetlands were drained and arid areas irrigated. Large open spaces were broken up into smaller units by fences. The farming communities supplemented their diet by hunting native animals like the kangaroo and birds such as the Australian Bustard. While many of the indigenous birds were forced to retreat before the expanding human population, others were able to exploit new opportunities created for them in the new farmland and were regarded as pests by the colonists. Wildfowl fed in the rice fields, crows and eagles took lambs, cockatoos attacked the wheat fields and parrots and parakeets the orchards. As a result such birds were severely persecuted, though whenever research has been carried out into the effects of bird pests, their impact has usually been found to be less severe than it appears at first sight.

Paradoxically, the species most damaging to Australian agriculture is one which man has introduced himself, the European rabbit.[12] Some twelve pairs of rabbits were introduced on to a ranch in Victoria in 1859, presumably to provide sport. They spread and increased in numbers so rapidly that by 1865 it was possible for 20,000 to be killed in the course of one hunt. By 1900 the rabbit had spread throughout most of Australia. In the absence of any species with comparable powers of reproduction among the endemic Marsupial mammals, the rabbit's impact on the native vegetation was catastrophic. Huge areas were denuded of grass, the soil was loosened and began to be swept away by erosion. The principal victims of this devastation were sheep, which formed so important a part of the agricultural economy of the colonists. All attempts to control the rabbits by shooting, poisoning and fencing proved to be futile and it was not until a biological method of control, in the form of the disease myxomatosis, was tried that numbers began to be reduced. The myxoma virus is indigenous to South America, where rabbits suffer from the disease, which takes the form of a fibrous cancer of the skin, but do not usually die from it. European rabbits have evolved no immunity to the disease and, when they were first infected with it, usually died. The first successful introduction of myxoma virus was made in 1950 in Victoria. Carried by mosquitoes from one rabbit to another, it spread rapidly and the first myxomatosis epidemic killed 998 out of every 1000 rabbits. The second epidemic killed 90 per cent of the rabbits that survived but the third epidemic killed only about 50 per cent of the next generation. Clearly, the disease was losing its efficacy as a means of controlling the rabbit population. This was because of the effect of natural selection acting both on the rabbit population and on the myxoma virus. Rabbits that had immunity to the disease survived and bred so that their numbers increased in the population, while strains of the virus that killed their hosts quickly left fewer of their own progeny than less virulent strains whose hosts survived for longer. The combination of the spread of less susceptible rabbits and of less virulent strains of the virus was largely responsible for the rapid decline in the impact of the disease on the rabbit population. In addition, infected rabbits that survived the disease were effectively inoculated against it and thus survived subsequent outbreaks. After the initial success of myxomatosis introduction to Australia, the rabbits have steadily increased in numbers and are once again posing a serious threat to the agricultural economy.

The devastation wrought on Australia's vegetation by introduced rabbits must have posed a severe threat to some of the indigenous birds. Those that fed on grass seeds would have had their food supply drastically reduced and those that nested on the ground or relied on low vegetation as cover for their nests would also have been adversely affected. However, since so little is known about Australia's birds before the advent of Europeans it is not possible to assess how severe the effect of rabbits on their numbers was.

European man has been responsible for the introduction of several other alien species to Australia. Other herbivores which competed with the endemic mammals and which have profoundly changed the vegetation include sheep, cattle and goats. Man has also imported a number of carnivores such as cats, rats and foxes which have preyed upon the indigenous birds. Some introduced birds have competed with the native birds, both for food and, as in the case of the European Starling, for holes in trees which both they and native birds such as parrots use as nest sites. In general Australia's birds have suffered less severely from the changes brought about by man than the endemic

Marsupial mammals, a number of which have become extinct since Europeans arrived.

One way in which some birds have proved to be a serious pest to man, not only in Australia but throughout the world, is by gathering in large numbers on or near airports.[13] Birds being sucked into jet engines have not only caused severe damage to aircraft but have led to fatal accidents. Around Sydney Airport the culprits were Silver Gulls which gathered in large numbers around the runways to rest when they were not feeding on nearby rubbish tips and to drink and bathe in the large shallow rain-pools that formed on the flat ground. It has been a widespread experience that attempts to kill birds around airports have proved to be ineffective.[14] So also have techniques designed to scare them away, such as periodic detonations or the broadcasting of alarm calls, since birds rapidly habituate to them, realizing that there is no real threat. The only effective solution is to make the airport environment less attractive to birds. At Sydney this was done by closing many of the nearby rubbish tips, by burning much of the rubbish rather than dumping it, by handling rubbish at night rather than during the day and by draining the pools of water on the airport itself.

As described earlier in this chapter, climatic changes during the last few million years have created an area of desert and arid scrubland that now covers the greater part of the Australian continent. Rainfall is low and is inconsistent both in its timing and its quantity, a condition favouring bird species with the capacity for breeding quickly and dispersing far afield. It is often implied that a breeding season that coincides with periods of vegetation and food abundance following sporadic rain, rather than one linked to a particular time of the year, is a characteristic of birds that live in arid environments. In fact, there are many birds for which this is not true. When it is monitored carefully the rainfall in the dry Australian heartlands is in fact found to be more regular than it appears to be to the casual observer, who is most impressed by the irregular heavy downpours that occur from time to time. In many parts of the arid scrubland rain falls regularly at certain times of year, often only in small quantities, but sufficient to support the vegetation that grows on the run-on areas that are so crucial to the resident birds. One such bird is the Emu, which does breed regularly at the same time each year.

Like its Ratite relative from Africa, the Ostrich, the Emu is a large, flightless bird with long, powerful legs, small wings and a long thin neck.[15] The Emu is rather smaller than the Ostrich and weighs about ninety pounds. There has been an interesting example of convergent evolution among birds and mammals that run about on open plains whereby the number of their toes has become reduced. The antelopes and the Ostrich have only two toes; the Emu, bustards and quail have three. The Emu's long legs enable it to run at speeds of up to 30 miles per hour for a distance of a mile or more. It feeds on flowers, fruits and seeds and also on insects; it has not evolved the capacity to digest the dry, tough leaves and stems of the plants that grow in the arid scrubland.

41. Emus

Emus form pairs in December or January and remain together for some five months, wandering about their extensive home range before starting to breed in May or June. The female lays anything between five and twenty eggs, each weighing just over a pound. After this enormous effort she retires exhausted into the bush, leaving the male to incubate the eggs. He is a most conscientious father, rarely leaving the nest, even to feed, and by the time the eggs hatch in June or July he has lost a good deal of weight. After hatching the chicks are quickly on their feet and follow their father into the scrub in search of food. They hatch at a time that coincides with the annual rainy period so that, provided there has been a reasonable amount of rain, there is plenty of plant and insect food for them. In years when there is very little rain there is high mortality among the chicks.

Emus travel widely in search of food, often in large groups. These wanderings have brought them into contention with man where they have moved into wheat fields in search of food. So seriously was the Emu regarded as an agricultural pest that in 1923 the legal protection from hunting which it had previously enjoyed was lifted and a bounty was paid for every Emu shot. This bounty was still being paid in 1948 and possibly more recently than that. In 1934 there occurred the 'Emu war' in which the army was called in to cope with them and large numbers were machine-gunned to death. Many Emus died when they were unable to move out of unfavourable areas because of fences that had been put up in an attempt to control rabbits. As a result of man's persecution the Emu population steadily declined. Recently their numbers seem to have stabilized and in some ways man has contributed to their present healthy position. In some of the drier areas of the out-back wells have been drilled to provide water for crops and stock and Emus have benefited from the increased vegetation that has resulted. Grazing by sheep and rabbits has created a turf of short grass which provides suitable food for the Emus.

Around Australia's coasts there are a number of islands, the largest of which is Tasmania. The isolation afforded by such islands has created conditions in which populations of birds which have dispersed outwards from the mainland have evolved distinctive characteristics so that they have become separate subspecies and, eventually, new species. At one time there were at least two subspecies of the Emu living on offshore islands, one on Tasmania, the other on Kangaroo Island off the coast of South Australia. These populations probably became isolated from their mainland counterparts when the melting of the ice sheets caused the oceans to rise, cutting off what had previously been part of the mainland.

The Tasmanian Emu differed from the mainland race in lacking any black colouration on its neck. Only three specimens of this bird are known; two are in the British Museum, the other is in Frankfurt. It was almost certainly extinct by the early nineteenth century and its demise seems to have been due to hunting by the early European inhabitants of Tasmania. The Kangaroo Island Emu was abundant when Flinders discovered the island in 1802. For some years the island was virtually untouched by man but, by the time intensive colonization began in 1836, the Kangaroo Island Emu was extinct. The island is some ninety miles long and thirty-five miles wide and it is unlikely that the few people who lived on the island during the thirty years following its discovery could have wiped out all the Emus by hunting them. It has been suggested that the entire population was wiped out by a forest fire sweeping across the island sometime during that period. The Kangaroo Island Emu, of which there exists only one specimen, collected in 1803 and now in Paris, was smaller than the mainland Emu.

The evolutionary history of the Emus is a long one and in prehistoric times it appears that there were yet more distinct forms. The fossil remains of a small Emu-like bird have been found in deposits from the Pleistocene period on King Island, in the Bass Strait between Tasmania and Victoria. On the mainland fossilized remains of at least three distinct Ratite birds have been found in Pleistocene rocks. These are all large birds and in many ways resemble the moas of New Zealand. Two of them were more heavily built than the living Emus, with massive heads. As the Australian representative of the living Ratites, the Emu is one of a handful of survivors of one of the most ancient of all families of birds which during its long history has given rise to a rich variety of species throughout the world.

Up until about twenty years ago it seemed that the two island races of the Emu were not the only Australian birds that had become extinct. At least three species which had not been seen for many years were rediscovered during the 1960s. One of these species is the Noisy Scrub-bird, now found only in a very restricted area in the south-western coastal region.[16] The Noisy Scrub-bird lives in dense, tangled undergrowth in the wetter parts of the coastal forest. A small bird, about eight and a half inches long, it has short wings and rarely, if ever, flies, preferring to scuttle through the tangled vegetation near the forest floor, Its movements have been described as more like those of a rat than a bird. The Noisy Scrub-bird gets its name from the rich variety of loud, piercing whistles and trills, many of them mimicking other species, that it makes as it moves about. The richness of its vocabulary appears to have evolved as an adaptive response to the denseness of its habitat, in which communication by means of visual displays would be relatively ineffective.

Noisy Scrub-birds eat insects and seeds. They are territorial, the male defending an area of about fifty square yards, proclaiming his presence to other males by means of one of his calls. The nest is a domed structure made of reeds and grass and lined with a 'plaster' formed from masticated plant material. The female, who lays one or two eggs in September or October, incubates the eggs on her own while the male is defending the territory.

The decline of the Noisy Scrub-bird to its present extreme rarity has taken place in two stages, the first due to natural causes, the second due to man. The scrub-birds, of which there are two living species, the Noisy and the Rufous, are one of Australia's most ancient families, almost certainly descended from an ancestral stock that lived in Gondwanaland before it broke up. With their dependence on dense vegetation they no doubt prospered in the early days of Australia's separation from the rest of the world when most of the continent was covered in forest. With the more recent development of the arid zone, forested areas have become more and more restricted to coastal areas and the once widespread scrub-birds have been split up into isolated populations of which only two remain, the Noisy Scrub-bird in the south-west and the Rufous Scrub-bird in a restricted area of forest in the north-east corner of New South Wales. The amount of forest habitat suitable for scrub-birds has been further reduced by man, who has deforested extensive areas in order to create agricultural land. Man has frequently been the deliberate or inadvertent instigator of forest fires, which not only destroy the undergrowth but which are lethal to species like scrub-birds with their limited capacity for flight. Other factors that have probably contributed to the decline of the Noisy Scrub-bird include a series of droughts that led to a general deterioration of the south-western forests in the late nineteenth century and the introduction by Europeans of cats.

The Noisy Scrub-bird was discovered in 1842 by John Gilbert, who saw it in the Darling Mountain Range of Western Australia. Over the next fifty years its numbers declined rapidly and from 1889 until its rediscovery more than fifty years later it was not reliably recorded at all. In 1962 H. O. Webster found the Noisy Scrub-bird in Two Peoples Bay, just to the east of Albany, Western Australia. The area is now subject to strict conservation regulations and the scrub-bird population is carefully watched. It is difficult to count a bird that is so elusive in its habits but an assessment of the population size can be made by listening for the calls of territorial males. It seems that the population in Two Peoples Bay has remained fairly stable at about forty-four territorial males for at least the last ten years. A population as small as this is always at risk from a natural or man-made disaster like a storm or a forest fire. Apart from this danger, the Noisy Scrub-bird seems to be safe, at least for the immediate future, under the watchful eyes of the Australian conservation authorities.

The Rufous Scrub-bird is not as rare as its close relative but it is much less common and is found in a much more restricted area than when Europeans first arrived in Australia.[17] A bird of very similar habits and habitat requirements to the Noisy Scrub-bird, it is now found principally in the forested MacPherson Mountains in an area contained within the Lamington National Forest. Previously it was found over a wide area but deforestation by man has severely restricted the amount of suitable habitat available to it.

Two other species of Australian birds which have been rediscovered belong to a group called the Grasswrens, of which there are eight species in all.[18] Grasswrens are small birds with long tails which they keep cocked as they flit about with quick, jerky movements on or near the ground. In general they run more than they fly; they are rather furtive in their habits, being for the most part silent and rarely emerging from cover during the day. Most of the Grasswrens live in arid areas, feeding on seeds and insects and hiding among rocks. The Eyrean

Grasswren is coloured cinnamon-brown above and white below. It lives in an area of bleak desert around the Macuba River just north of Lake Eyre in South Australia. First discovered and described in 1874, no specimens were collected between 1875 and its rediscovery in 1961 at Christmas Water Hole. The Black Grasswren is generally darker in colour and inhabits rocky gorges in a restricted area in the northern part of Western Australia called the Kimberley Plateau. After many years during which it was not known whether it still survived, the Black Grasswren was collected at Manny Creek near Kimberley in 1968.[19] A third species, the Grey Grasswren, is as rare as the other two. Unlike them, it lives in swampy habitat and is found only in the Caryapundy Swamp on the border between Queensland and New South Wales. It is not clear why these tiny birds have become so rare. It may well be that their habits of nesting and feeding on or near the ground have made them particularly vulnerable to predators such as rats and cats that have been introduced by man.

One of the most remarkable of Australia's birds, and one of its most ancient inhabitants, is the Mallee Fowl.[20] This is a member of a family of birds that incubate their eggs, not in a nest and by means of their own body heat, but in a large mound which they fill with plant material that rots, generating the heat necessary for the eggs to develop. They are called mound-birds because of this habit or, alternatively, megapodes because of their large feet which they use for excavating and moving the soil. The megapodes are found not only in Australia but also in the tropical islands to the north. While most members of the family live in dense tropical forests and rely almost entirely on heat from decaying plant material, the Mallee Fowl lives in the more arid environment of Australia's Mallee scrub, and also relies on the sun to heat its egg mound. Mallee scrub consists of low Eucalyptus trees and grows in areas that receive less than seventeen inches of rain in a year. The Mallee Fowl has been studied in great detail by H. J. Frith, who has analysed the way in which a pair meticulously control the temperature at which their eggs are kept.

The amount of time and sheer physical effort that a pair of Mallee Fowl invest in the production and care of their eggs is impressive. A female lays an average of nineteen eggs each year and may lay as many as thirty-three. The eggs are very large, each one weighing a tenth of the female's own body weight, and it takes her between five and ten days to produce each one. The average female takes nearly four months to lay her full clutch, which represents a production equivalent to more than twice her weight. The male is responsible for the maintenance of the mound in which the eggs are laid. He visits it every day for five and a half months to check its temperature, and, if necessary, digs out sand or replaces it in order to keep the temperature at exactly the right level. It takes a good deal of practice for the male to acquire the skills of maintaining a mound and an inexperienced pair usually have three or four relatively unsuccessful breeding seasons before they achieve a reasonable hatching rate. Mallee Fowl generally pair for life but lead an essentially solitary existence, male and female meeting only at the

42. A Mallee Fowl at its nest

mound when the female comes to lay an egg. They feed and roost on their own.

The large size of the Mallee Fowl's egg is related to the fact that the chicks have to fend for themselves as soon as they hatch and thus have to be at an advanced stage of development when they do so. Their first task is to tunnel their way up from the depths of the egg-mound to the surface. This may take them anything from two to fifteen hours and it has been found that newly-hatched Mallee chicks can survive for up to twenty-two hours buried under the sand. When they reach the surface they stagger off into the scrub, rarely if ever seeing their parents. By their first night they are able to roost among the branches and by their second day they can fly. During the first few days they are very vulnerable to predators like the endemic Dingo and the introduced fox and mortality among young birds is very high.

The breeding cycle begins in April or May when a pair begins to excavate a pit, sometimes a new one but usually an old pit from which they remove all decayed plant material. Responding to showers of rain the pair dig sporadically until they have excavated a pit ten feet wide and three feet deep. During the late winter months of June and July they gather plant litter from a wide area and rake it into the pit. In August the early spring rains stimulate them to create an egg chamber in the middle of their compost heap. The rain moistens the heap which begins to decompose and heat up and the pair rake sand into a pile up to three feet thick that covers the plant material, keeping it moist. Females differ in the extent to which they assist the male during these early phases of mound building, but once they start to lay eggs they leave the work at the mound almost entirely to the males. Throughout the spring the female comes to the mound when she has an egg ready for laying. The male opens up the mound for her and rakes back the sand as soon as she has finished. The effort of laying the large egg may take her up to three hours. During the spring the eggs are heated primarily by the fermenting compost; each morning the male opens the mound to let excess heat escape and then quickly closes it again.

By the early summer fermentation in the mound is slowing down and the mound largely looks after itself, the male only occasionally having to open it up and cool the eggs. During December, the height of the summer, more heat is provided by the sun than by the decaying vegetation in the mound. The male now rakes more sand on to the heap to provide a thicker layer to insulate the eggs. Each morning he spreads out the sand to dispel any heat that has remained in the mound from the previous day; he then rebuilds the mound with the cooled sand. The female is still producing eggs at this stage but, if she comes to the mound during a cool spell of weather, the male will keep her away so as not to risk the eggs becoming chilled while the mound is open. In the autumnal months heat from the sun is declining and fermentation within the mound has virtually ceased. The male now completely opens the mound each day so that the eggs can be directly heated in the sunshine. Late in the day he carefully collects sand that has been warmed by the sun so that the mound remains warm through the night. By April all the eggs have hatched and the mound is abandoned.

Sadly, this remarkable bird has steadily declined in numbers since the arrival in Australia of Europeans. Their mounds have long been raided and their eggs taken by Dingoes and Aborigines and this predation has been intensified by Europeans and introduced predators such as foxes. Introduced herbivores such as sheep have competed with the Mallee Fowl for its plant food. However, the most important factor in their decline has been the destruction of large areas of Mallee scrub to make way for pasture and cultivation. Some of the remaining areas of Mallee scrub are now being conserved, including Pulletop Fauna Reserve near the town of Griffith in New South Wales where H. J. Frith made his study of the Mallee Fowl.

Perhaps the most numerous, varied and colourful family of Australian birds are the parrots and parakeets. This very successful group of birds seems to have had its origins in Gondwanaland and now has representatives in most parts of the world. As we have seen, the Budgerigar has adapted very successfully to the arid conditions of Australia's heartland and is one of the most numerous species in the world. Other members of the family have not fared so well and are very rare; at least one may be extinct. Two closely related species, the Ground Parrot and the Night Parrot, share a number of features with the

Kakapo of New Zealand.[21] They are both green in colour with dark brown and yellow markings, making them very well camouflaged among the grass where they live. The Ground Parrot is distinguished by a red forehead and the Night Parrot by yellow cheeks. Both species feed and nest on the ground and are nocturnal in their habits.

The Ground Parrot is a shy, elusive bird that is extremely difficult to observe and much of what has been written about it in the past may be inaccurate.[22] For example, it has often been said that it is a weak flyer. In their movements Ground Parrots are rather like quail; they are usually seen as they break cover when they are disturbed. They rise a few feet into the air and, alternately beating their wings and gliding, fly rapidly for about thirty yards before settling again. On the ground they can move very fast and their legs are rather longer than those of most members of the parrot family. They feed by night, eating fresh shoots and seeds, and give distinctive high-pitched calls at dawn and dusk. Their nests are shallow hollows in the ground made in the centre of dense grass thickets. Ground Parrots are birds of the coastal wetlands and it is the draining and clearing of their habitat that has been the primary cause of their decline. A hundred years ago they were common in coastal areas and on offshore islands from south-east Queensland to South Australia, in southern Western Australia and on Tasmania. There are three distinct geographical races which have all declined, but to varying degrees.

The Tasmanian race is in the healthiest position and is regularly recorded from the west coast of the island. The eastern race, which was previously found from Brisbane to Adelaide, is now extinct in Queensland and is found only in a few restricted sites in New South Wales, South Australia and on some islands off the coast of Victoria and in the Bass Strait. The western race is in danger of extinction. Once common from Perth to Albany, it was thought to be extinct in the early part of this century. It was recorded at Cheyne Beach in the 1940s and in 1962 and 1963, and at Irwin's Inlet in 1952.

The Ground Parrot has declined rapidly wherever the relentless advance of human civilization has intruded on its range. Apart from the loss of much of its wetland habitat, it has suffered severely from introduced predators like cats and rats to which it falls easy prey through its ground-living habits. It is now protected by law but this in itself probably contributes little to its conservation. The Ground Parrot's habitat requires careful management. This species seems to be dependent on coastal scrubland that is at a particular stage in its growth. Areas that are not grazed or occasionally burned are unsuitable, as are those that are excessively grazed or frequently burned. Effective conservation of the Ground Parrot requires the careful maintenance of a balance between these two extremes.

The Night Parrot may already be extinct.[23] In contrast to the Ground Parrot, it lives in dry desert areas, feeding mainly on the seeds of porcupine and spinifex grass. Grass tussocks provide it with the cover that it needs while it is resting during the day and for its nest which is made at the end of a grassy tunnel. It was long thought that the first specimen of the Night Parrot to be obtained was one found in Western Australia in 1854, but recently a specimen collected in 1845 was found in the Merseyside County Museum, Liverpool.[24] This had been misidentified by the great nineteenth-century ornithologist John Gould. The only unquestionable sightings of living birds were made between 1912 and 1935 and an intensive search for Night Parrots made in 1959 failed to reveal any. Unconfirmed sightings were made in Western Australia in 1960 and 1971 and in South Australia in 1970. The species was given legal protection in 1937, probably too late to do any good. Since the Night Parrot is known to have disappeared from very remote localities far from any human activity, it is possible that its decline may not be due to man, but to natural long-term changes in its habitat.

Some of Australia's rarest parrots belong to two closely-related groups called the Grass Parrots and the Grass Parakeets.[25] These are all brilliantly coloured birds, variously patterned in green, yellow, red and blue, of which some species are prospering while others are in danger of extinction. In addition to being reduced by the general habitat changes brought about by man that have adversely affected many other species, these birds have been heavily collected to supply the world's cage-bird trade. Furthermore, some of them have suffered through competition for their nest holes with introduced species like the European Starling.

The Turquoise Grass Parakeet, once found in Queensland, New South Wales, Victoria and South Australia, was reported to be extinct early in this century. Up until the 1880s it was much sought after as a cage bird and it may also have declined as a result of changes in its habitat caused by sheep and cattle grazing. Since trapping of this and other species was made illegal it may have increased in numbers, though sightings are rare and widely scattered. The Orange-bellied or Orange-chested Grass Parakeet is a native of south-east Australia. Two geographical races have been distinguished, one living on Tasmania, the other in Victoria and South Australia. The Tasmanian race, which is barely distinguishable from the very common Blue-winged Grass Parakeet, has not been seen since 1956. The mainland race has not been seen in Victoria this century and in South Australia since the late 1920s. The Splendid or Scarlet-chested Grass Parakeet, once a great favourite of the cage-bird trade, comes from Western Australia and South Australia. Reported to be extinct in 1917, it has been sighted occasionally since 1948.

There are three endangered species of grass parrot which all differ from the other two quite common species in their genus in that they build their nests in holes in termite hills rather than in trees. It is possible that termite holes are more accessible to introduced predators such as rats than are tree holes. The Beautiful or Paradise Parrot, previously found in south-east Queensland and central New South Wales, was rediscovered in the 1920s, having previously been thought to be extinct. It is now thought that there are less than 150 members of this species, confined to an area around the upper reaches of the Darling River. The Hooded Parrot is an extremely rare inhabitant of Arnhem Land in Western Australia. The Golden-shouldered Parrot, though not as beautifully coloured as other species, has long been highly prized throughout the world as a cage bird.[26] Less than 250 of them now survive in Queensland. Like other rare species, they are protected by law and a collector was successfully prosecuted for trapping them in 1964. Some of these parrots have been successfully bred in captivity, not only in Australia, but also in Europe and America. For example, the Paradise Parrot has been bred in Australia in artificial termite mounds.

The draining of wetlands in Australia, as in many parts of the world, has seriously depleted a number of species of wildfowl. As we have seen, a species like the Grey Teal, with its capacity to disperse widely and to breed in flooded areas, has remained numerous. Wildfowl that are more sedentary and conservative in their habits have not fared so well; one such species is the Freckled Duck.[27] Found principally in Western Australia and over a wide area in the south-eastern part of the continent, the Freckled Duck is endemic to Australia and is declining in numbers. A dark brown bird, speckled with white, it lives in dense vegetation near fresh water. It feeds mostly at night, either in shallow water or on land, where it displays a liking for rice fields. By day it either roosts in thick cover or rests far out on open water. A shy and retiring bird, it breeds only in permanent swamps, building its nest close to the water. Many of its remaining breeding areas are threatened by land drainage and reclamation schemes.

43. The Freckled Duck and the Cape Barren Goose

A species of wildfowl that has been the object of an intensive and successful conservation effort is the Cape Barren Goose.[28] With its plump body, long neck, strong legs and short bill the Cape Barren Goose looks very like other geese, but is generally considered to be a duck, showing strong affinities to the shelducks. It has been suggested that, with its extinct relative, *Cnemiornis* from New Zealand, it is descended from a primitive group of wildfowl that formed an ancestral link between the ducks and the geese. Cape Barren Geese are found on a number of islands off the south-eastern coast of Australia and in the Bass Strait; occasionally they will visit the mainland coast. The sexes look alike, being ash-grey in colour with a white crown and black markings on the shoulder. They frequent grassland, rarely venturing on to water, and are gregarious except in the breeding season when they become territorial and very aggressive. They usually build a nest on the ground but will sometimes use a tree or a rocky ledge.

Cape Barren Geese have long been persecuted by man. The early human inhabitants of the islands in the Bass Strait shot them for food and also collected their eggs. The geese did not endear themselves to farmers by grazing on the same grass as their sheep. As well as depriving the sheep of some of their food, the geese so fouled the pastures with their droppings that the sheep refused to eat the grass. As a result of man's activities the Cape Barren Goose steadily declined in numbers. Aerial surveys carried out between 1958 and 1960 indicated a decrease in the size of the population over that period and a great effort was made to excite public interest in the species.[29] The success of this campaign can be gauged from a survey conducted in 1967 that revealed a sharp recovery of numbers and a widening of the species' range.[30] This seems to be primarily due to a relaxation in the pressure exerted by hunters and egg collectors. Also, man has probably contributed to the improved status of the Cape Barren Goose by clearing islands previously covered in woodland and scrub, creating new areas of grassland pasture. However, while the geese are quick to exploit a new area of feeding habitat they are more conservative about their breeding sites and seem loath to breed on islands other than those where they have traditionally bred. The greatest concentration of breeding birds is on islands in the Furneax archipelago.

The Bristlebirds are a group of only three species that is unique to Australia.[31] Like the scrub-birds they were once widespread but have been forced by long-term climatic changes into isolated coastal areas on opposite sides of the continent. Their affinities to other birds are obscure, though they are probably related to warblers. They get their name from a set of stiff bristles at the base of the bill. The Eastern Bristlebird is found in scrubland along the coast of New South Wales and the Western Bristlebird in similar habitat in one small area to the east of Albany, though it is known to have ranged as far north as Perth in historical times. Both species are very rare and are considered to be in danger of extinction.

The Honeyeaters are a large family of Australian birds containing no fewer than seventy species.[32] Most of them feed by extracting nectar from the flowers of the many types of Eucalyptus trees. The rarest member of the family was the Helmeted Honeyeater, an inhabitant of woodland in hilly country.[33] Now confined to a small area around Yellingbo, east of Melbourne, the Helmeted Honeyeater has declined in numbers from an estimated 300 in 1963 to 170 in 1967 and to 100 in 1974. This decline has been caused primarily by the clearing of the lower levels of woodland vegetation; where their habitat has been left alone, numbers have remained steady. In 1974 an area of 100 acres adjoining an existing nature reserve was purchased by the Victorian government as a reserve for the Helmeted Honeyeater. As a result of such conservation measures its population, though small, now seems to be fairly stable.

The last species to be discussed in this chapter, the Tasmanian Native Hen, is not in any danger of extinction but has been greatly reduced in numbers by man because it is regarded as an agricultural pest.[34] It is a bird of considerable biological interest because of its curious system of social and sexual relationships. The Tasmanian Native Hen is a flightless relative of the moorhens and gallinules and, though heavily built, it can run at more than 30 miles per hour. It is closely related to the Black-tailed Native Hen, which lives on the mainland and has excellent powers of flight, congregating on recently flooded areas in a similar way to the Grey Teal. The Tasmanian Native Hen thus provides another example of the evolution of flightlessness by birds that have colonized offshore islands.

Native hens are grazing birds, preferring young grass shoots. They thrive when they can associate with other large grazers which create a suitable turf for them. In the past this function was served by the herbivorous Marsupials; since the arrival of Western man native hens have relied more on sheep and rabbits. While grass was plentiful native hens were not regarded as a problem, but during the summer, when green grass is found only near water, they represented serious competition for grazing stock. In the 1950s, when effective control of rabbits was achieved by means of a poison, attention was turned to the native hen. As a result, Dr Michael Ridpath was appointed to study the Tasmanian Native Hen and to assess its importance as an agricultural pest. He concluded that the damage it does to grassland or to crops is slight, that effective control of its numbers can be achieved simply by removing cover near fields and that wholesale slaughter was unjustified.[35]

The Tasmanian Native Hen has a biased sex ratio of six males to four females. It lives in small groups, usually consisting of six or seven individuals, that occupy a territory bordering on a stream. Occasionally the territories are defended by violent fights between individuals or groups, but usually this is done by means of calling. The syrinx that contains the vocal cords is of a different shape in males and females so that the sexes produce calls of different pitch. A male and a female within a group will call antiphonally, producing a characteristic 'see-saw' sound. When they breed adults may form pairs, but, because of the distorted sex ratio, are more usually seen in trios or quartets, each female attended by two or three males and accompanied by their collective young. This social system raises an interesting question for the evolutionary biologist. Why should a male tolerate the presence of another male near his mate and, indeed, assist in the rearing of another male's chicks, presumably to the detriment of his own reproductive success? A female can lay only a certain number of eggs and a male who shares her with another male will have fathered only some of those eggs, whereas he could have fathered them all if he maintained sole possession of the female. This apparently runs counter to the theory of natural selection, which states that animals should be selected to maximize their reproductive output. The problem is resolved by Ridpath's finding that the group of males attending a female are brothers.[36]

Since brothers have genes in common, a male assisting in the rearing of his brother's offspring is contributing to the survival and multiplication of his own genes. This modified form of natural selection is called kin selection, and the Tasmanian Native Hen provides one of the few instances where its effects have been documented in nature.

Australian birds provide an excellent illustration of the way natural changes in the environment and changes attributable to man interact to influence the abundance of a species. For a number of Australian birds a long history of slow decline caused by gradual climatic changes has been followed by an accelerated decline following the arrival of Europeans. A feature of this chapter has been the number of species that, once thought to be extinct, have recently been rediscovered. In some instances this may indicate that the birds in question have become more numerous as man has become aware of the need to conserve his environment. In others it may simply reflect a greater level of interest in birds among the Australian public which has meant that rare birds are more likely to be seen.

9

The Conservation of Endangered Birds

—————⊰※⊱—————

THE purpose of this final chapter is to discuss what we can learn from the histories of birds which have become extinct or which are now very rare that might help us in our efforts to prevent extinctions in the future. In the previous chapters I have discussed a number of case histories in varying detail in an attempt to identify the factors that cause species to decline and become extinct. In most instances it is not possible to identify a single cause. While all the species I have discussed have been severely diminished through the many complex influences of man, I hope that I have convincingly shown that human pressures interact with various aspects of the biology of the birds concerned. In other words some species are biologically more susceptible to human influences than others. I have also described a number of attempts, most of them successful, that are being made to conserve endangered species, and how an intimate understanding of the habits of these birds has been essential in these enterprises. An underlying theme of this book is that to understand the extinction process, and to prevent it, we must first achieve a deep understanding of bird biology. I have discussed two recent developments in biology, the analysis of the parameters of breeding biology that underlie the r- and K-strategist dichotomy and Island Biogeography, that I feel have made an important contribution in this area. Another theme has been that man's destruction of birds cannot be blamed simply on an irresponsible or blood-thirsty minority, but that it reflects a deep-seated human attitude towards the rest of nature that characterizes Western civilization in particular. Later in this chapter I shall argue that effective conservation can only be achieved if this attitude is changed. I shall first deal briefly with the question: why should we conserve birds at all? I shall then go on to discuss some practical ways in which we might go about it.

Does it really matter if a species of bird becomes extinct and, if so, to whom? This question has been discussed many times and the protagonists of conservation have usually based their case on five lines of argument, ethical, aesthetic, economic, scientific and ecological. The ethical argument is simply that we have no moral right to exploit our fellow-creatures either for nourishment or in the pursuit of our own pleasure. Man's 'speciesism', which was mentioned briefly in Chapter 2, can be traced back to the long-held but ill-founded view that man is the supreme being, for whose convenience other creatures were created. The 'animal liberationist' points out that eradicating speciesism would not only put an end to needless suffering by animals but would also have profound material benefits for man. Were man to become vegetarian he could probably solve his food problem, since growing crops is a far less wasteful way to use land that the rearing of livestock. There are signs that basic attitudes to animals are changing; the more contentious and emotive manifestations of human exploitation of other animals such as vivisection and blood sports arouse increasingly strident protest. To be pragmatic, we cannot really hope to reverse deeply-entrenched attitudes, however unsound their basis, in a short time. While many of us might support the abolition of bull-fighting or the importing of leopard skin coats, relatively few people are yet prepared to go without meat. Nor are ethical arguments likely to have much impact in the poorer nations of the third world, where the protein in a wild bird might make a significant contribution to the health and welfare of a family. The moral argument for conservation is likely to have most influence in preventing more frivolous exploitation of birds such as their importation for pets, the use of their feathers and skins for personal adornment and their pursuit for sport.

The aesthetic argument for conserving other animals is that each species is not only a thing of beauty but is a unique and irreplaceable product of the evolutionary process. The argument is essentially the same as that for preserving works of art. As with the ethical argument, there are many people who do not need to be convinced that birds are things of beauty and of considerable interest; ornithological societies in Britain, America and elsewhere have enormous memberships. However, bird-watchers constitute a tiny minority of the world's population and aesthetic considerations are unlikely to carry much weight with those who govern the undeveloped parts of the world. The paintings of Michelangelo and Renoir can be preserved simply by placing them in a modest building; the conservation of animals requires large areas of unspoiled land which represent resources denied to the human population. When decisions are made about the use that is to be made of as yet unexploited land, aesthetic considerations are likely to take second place to more urgent human needs.

The economic argument for conservation is that, properly designed and managed, nature reserves, game parks and zoos can be profitable and can thus be directly equated with other uses to which land might be put. This argument seems to me to be false for two reasons. Firstly, it is essentially pragmatic and does not provide a permanent solution to the question of how the earth's limited resources should be used. It implies that land should be set aside for animals only for so long as it is more profitable to do so. On this basis all nature reserves would eventually disappear as improving agricultural technology made impoverished land more productive. Secondly, this argument is itself an expression of an economic system which underlies man's destruction of the world environment. At present the stability of the world's economy is dependent on continuous economic growth which can only be maintained by using up the earth's natural resources far faster than they are replenished.

To the biologist the extinction of a species represents a tragic loss of potentially invaluable research material. Every species represents the outcome of a unique combination of diverse evolutionary pressures and one cannot predict which species may hold the vital clue to a new scientific discovery. There are a number of extinct species of which we can be sure that, had they survived, they would have been of great interest to biologists. The Huia would have provided insight into the evolution of division of labour between the sexes, comparison of the Great Auk with the penguins might have deepened our understanding of physiological adaptations for diving, and the Passenger Pigeon, with its immense potential for population growth, might have provided ideal material for research into population dynamics. This, the scientific argument for conservation, is a rather tenuous one since the potential benefits that might accrue to mankind from the study of any one species are so imponderable. A cynic might argue that there are so many species that scientists have not yet got around to studying in detail that one or two less will not make much difference.

I have pointed out some of the weaknesses of the ethical, aesthetic, economic and scientific arguments for conservation, not because I think they are invalid, but because I feel that their persuasive power is limited. The problem for conservationists is not to convince one another of the validity of their cause but to convince hard-headed politicians and economists. In a conflict of interests between the needs of a few endangered birds and the provision of food for a starving human population none of these arguments is likely to have much impact. A much more powerful argument, I believe, is the ecological one.

There is more to extinction of a species than the disappearance from the natural scene of a population of unique creatures. Extinction is a symptom of disturbance in the complex interrelationships between plants and animals that form the basis of stable communities. A species may vanish, but the factors that brought about its demise usually do not. There is no better illustration of this point than the impact of pesticides on the world's birds of prey. The DDT and Dieldrin that have decimated so many species of eagles, hawks and falcons accumulates in the bodies of most animals, including our own, and represents the slow poisoning of all forms of animal life.[1] In many parts of the world man has destroyed huge areas of natural forest, seriously depleting many species as a result. Deforestation has ramifications far beyond the destruction of trees and the animals that live among them. It alters the pattern of water drainage off the land, it disrupts the natural cycles by which vital nutrients like nitrogen are retained within a biological community and it has even been suggested that should the vast forests of the Amazon basin be cut down there would be a significant decrease in the world's oxygen supply. Throughout the world there are extensive areas of land, once covered by luxuriant forests, that are now virtually useless, having been stripped of their topsoil by floods and careless over-grazing. In China attempts are being made to restore the forests in such areas which were deforested during the early Chinese dynasties. The essence of the ecological argument is that the extinction of a species is usually the result of a deterioration in its environment which we cannot afford to ignore since that environment is also ours.

The present relationship between man and his environment is rather like that of a colonizing population of animals that has recently arrived on an uninhabited island. The human population is increasing rapidly; it is estimated that in forty years' time it will have doubled. A colonizing animal population increases in a similar manner until the capacity of its environment to support it is reached. We saw in Chapter 6 how rabbits introduced on Laysan Island underwent a population explosion until, having destroyed much of the vegetation, their numbers declined and then stabilized at a lower level. We cannot predict accurately how many people the world might eventually be able to support; we can only be sure that the number is finite. If we go on recklessly destroying our environment we will find that, when it begins to exert a constraint upon our numbers, it will be depleted and unbalanced. It would be absurd to suggest that the survival of such birds as the Peregrine or the Kakapo is in itself vital to the survival of mankind. The lesson that we should learn from the decline of such birds is that at the moment our treatment of our environment is wrong. If mankind is to survive in large numbers without some catastrophic mass disease or famine he has to discover the art of living within the constraints and capacities of the world environment. If we can succeed in preventing further species from becoming extinct it might be a sign that we are beginning to do so.

Turning then to the question of how we might set about conserving endangered species, we must first restate the reasons why species become extinct. A species will decline in numbers as long as its death rate is greater than its reproductive rate. This is obviously a truism, but it helps to differentiate two different approaches to conservation. We may either try to identify and eliminate the factors that have increased mortality, or we may seek to boost the reproductive capacity of a species, or we may try to do both. Reducing mortality may often be a simple matter of legislating against excessive hunting and collecting, or habitat destruction. Increasing the reproductive rate is usually a more complex task requiring considerable biological knowledge and expertise. There are essentially two different approaches to conservation. The first can be characterized as passive and entails the setting up of nature reserves and conservation areas and the prevention of harmful influences by legal and other social means. The second approach is an active one and involves the direct intervention of biologists in an effort to manipulate various elements of a species' biology. David Zimmerman, in his book *To Save a Bird in Peril*, has named this active approach 'clinical ornithology'.[2] The analogy with medicine is an obvious one; we can forestall the extinction of a species either by prevention or by cure.

The most obvious single step that may be taken in the passive conservation of birds is the creation of nature reserves and conservation areas in which human influences are kept to a minimum. The theory of Island Biogeography can make an important contribution to the design of such areas since it can predict what would be their optimum size and shape.[3] The theory has been found to apply not only to real islands surrounded by sea, but also to 'habitat islands' within larger areas of land, such as small areas of woodland or single mountain peaks that are set apart from a larger range.[4] Such areas, like nature reserves, are similar to islands in the sense that they are surrounded by habitat which is hostile to the majority of creatures living within them. They differ from oceanic islands in that immigrants do not necessarily have to arrive from afar but may be living within the surrounding habitat. A problem with many small reserves within urban areas is that they are subject to continuous exploitation by such birds as sparrows, starlings and pigeons that have successfully adapted to urban environments. Parks in the middle of cities, though they are planted with trees typical of the open countryside, rarely contain birds other than these urban species.

The larger a nature reserve is, the more species will be able to live successfully in it. This relationship is well illustrated by the island of Barro Colorado in Panama which, although designated a nature reserve, lost about fifteen species of birds as its size was reduced by the rising lake around it.[5] The species most likely to disappear from small reserves are those in which each individual requires a large area of habitat, since they will be able to maintain only very small populations which are liable to be exterminated by a natural catastrophe. The larger birds of prey have very large territorial requirements and only very big nature reserves can support them in reasonable numbers. Large reserves are thus better than small ones not only because they support more species but also because those that live in them are less likely to become extinct. A number of small reserves, even though their total area may be equivalent to that of one large reserve, will not conserve as many species. Some species, though this rarely applies to birds, will not cross a highway or a firebreak that cuts across a reserve. Such barriers effectively divide a reserve into two smaller islands and the number of species they contain is then determined by their separate areas, not by their combined area. It has been suggested that running a road across a reserve could lead to the extinction of as many as one-sixth of the very sedentary species that would have otherwise survived.[6]

It will often not be possible to set aside one large reserve and conservationists will have to settle for a number of smaller ones. The reduced capacity of such areas to support several species can be increased if they are joined by corridors of favourable habitat that will help to maintain a high immigration rate to the reserves. This provides a sound argument for the protection of birds outside the confines of nature reserves. Many species are able to make a living, albeit in small numbers, in urban and agricultural areas. Peregrine Falcons have been known to nest on tall buildings in the heart of big cities. Protecting such birds wherever they are found means that there is an additional population from which numbers within reserves can be made up should they decline. A number of small reserves may actually be better in some respects than one large one, since it will make it possible to conserve a greater variety of habitats and natural disasters, such as diseases, can be more easily controlled in small areas. However, small reserves, even several of them, will not provide a reliable sanctuary for the larger species that occupy the higher positions in food chains. The theory of Island Biogeography suggests that reserves should be as nearly circular in shape as possible. For a given area, a circle provides the shortest possible circumference and, therefore, the fewest opportunities for species invading from outside.[7]

It would be misleading to suggest that conserving animals in nature reserves is an entirely passive process in which, once the land has been set aside, animals can simply be left to their own devices. It has frequently been the experience of those that manage reserves that they have to intervene actively in the lives of the animals in their charge. In the Serengeti National Park in Tanzania elephants have had to be culled because their increased numbers threatened to destroy too many of the trees. Also reserves are not immune to changes taking place in the areas surrounding them. They may, for example, be invaded by diseases affecting farm animals, a threat which may have to be countered by the inoculation of wild animals within the reserve.

Unnecessary mortality among endangered species can be reduced by legislation against shooting, trapping and the collecting of their eggs. However, while it is a relatively simple matter to pass a law prohibiting such activities it is very difficult to enforce it. In Britain many birds are protected by an Act of Parliament of 1954, but the Royal Society for the Protection of Birds has detected many cases of poisoning, pole-trapping and egg-collecting in recent years.[8] When an Osprey's egg can fetch a price of £100 and a stuffed Golden Eagle £200, the incentives to break such laws are considerable. The long-term prevention of these activities is less likely to be achieved through legislation than through the education of the public. Many game-keepers still trap or poison birds of prey in the mistaken belief that they constitute a serious threat to game. A number of key sites, such as Osprey nests in Scotland, are now protected from egg-collectors and vandals by all the paraphernalia of modern security methods, including electronic devices.

When a species becomes very rare it may not be enough to set aside a reserve for it and to give it legal protection. More radical, active measures have to be adopted. One of these is the control of the birds'

HC

44. The Osprey

natural enemies, their predators, parasites and competitors. The building of elevated platforms on which Ospreys in Connecticut could build their nests eliminated predation of their eggs. The heavy losses in Kirtland's Warbler eggs have been reduced by trapping and killing their brood parasite, the Brown-headed Cowbird. Competition for nest-sites between Cahows and White-tailed Tropic Birds has been prevented by placing baffles over the entrances of burrows. These last two measures have been necessary because of changes in the habitats of Kirtland's Warblers and Cahows for which man is responsible. Previously Cowbirds did not occur in the nesting habitat of Kirtland's Warbler and Cahows were able to find areas where they could dig their own burrows. On New Zealand's offshore islands alien predators have to be eliminated before birds can be released, and on Laysan Island introduced rabbits had to be culled to protect the Laysan Duck and other birds. All these measures are essentially corrective, reversing changes that man has brought about through carelessness or ignorance.

A more complex form of active intervention in the life of a species is the boosting of its reproductive output. Usually this involves finding a way of exploiting the fact that many species have greater reproductive potential than they normally deploy. Many species are capable of laying more eggs than they can rear, an ability that enables them to replace a clutch that is lost by predation or natural disaster. This extra capacity has been used very successfully to boost the reproductive output of Ospreys on America's east coast. Other species lose chicks through sibling rivalry and we saw in the previous chapter how this can be eliminated among Europe's Imperial and Lesser Spotted Eagles. Breeding output is usually limited by food supply and the provision of supplementary food for vultures in California and Spain may succeed in increasing their reproductive rate. A particularly ingenious idea which has yet to be put into practice is to establish pigeon colonies near the eyries of birds of prey such as Peregrines. In these the pigeons would be fed on food uncontaminated by pesticides in the hope that they would be taken by the falcons, whose diet would thus be at least partly 'clean' and whose breeding success would be increased accordingly.[9]

The technique of active conservation that has been used so success-fully by the New Zealand Wildlife Service is the resettlement of endangered species in new, unspoiled localities. The success with which the Saddleback and other species have been transferred to a number of offshore islands is largely due to the fact that those islands are well within the natural range of the birds concerned. It has been proposed that a number of species of South American ducks should be introduced to the south-east United States, presumably to add some variety to the local scene. The moving of birds to new areas far removed from their natural ranges should be approached with great caution for a number of reasons. Introduced species may prey upon resident species, as the Laysan Finch did when it was transferred to other islands. Birds moved from one place to another may carry with them diseases to which birds native to their new homes have no immunity. Introduced birds may readily hybridize with indigenous species, leading to reduced repro-ductive success, as in the example of the Grey Duck of New Zealand which has hybridized with the introduced Mallard. Introduced species may adversely affect resident species through competition. A good example of this effect, though it is not a bird, is the Grey Squirrel, which, since its introduction to Britain, has displaced the indigenous Red Squirrel from much of its former habitat.

A method of active conservation of which much has been expected is the breeding of endangered species in captivity and their subsequent release into the wild.[10] Unless captive breeding programmes are combined with effective attempts to correct the factors in the natural habitat that brought about the decline of the species concerned, they will serve only to delay inevitable extinction or to produce more domesticated species. Captive breeding should be designed to create a 'bank' from which wild populations can be augmented should they become reduced in numbers. Captive breeding has been attempted with a number of birds and, with the Néné, appears to have made a crucial contribution to the survival of a species. Experience gained from the various successful and unsuccessful breeding programmes has revealed a number of problems that have to be overcome.[11]

One of the problems that arises in captive breeding programmes is inbreeding, the repeated mating of closely related individuals which must inevitably be more frequent in a small group of animals. The harmful consequences of inbreeding are well illustrated by the high incidence of haemophilia in the royal houses of Europe in the nineteenth century. Haemophilia is caused by a gene which is 'recessive', meaning that it does not express itself unless it is paired, in the same person, with another similar gene. Repeated marriages between cousins and other relatives, all of whom were likely to be carrying this gene, increased the probability that two such genes would appear in one person, who would thus be a haemophiliac. Inbreeding is harmful because it increases the probability that deleterious or lethal genes will find expression, most commonly in the form of infertility. Most animals, including man, appear to have behavioural mechanisms by which they avoid incestuous matings. In small captive populations animals may have little choice but to mate with their parents, brothers and sisters or cousins. It is clear from the experience with Néné geese that inbreeding was at one time threatening the success of the captive breeding programme.[12] It was averted by the introduction of new, unrelated geese brought in from the wild population. It is not at all clear

45. Hawaiian Geese or Nénés

how large a population must be for inbreeding to cease to be a problem. If there is a 'critical' population size it may well differ from one species to another. Virtually the entire British population of Golden Hamsters is descended from a single pregnant female imported from North Africa, suggesting that, for the hamster at least, the critical population size may be very small. Until more is known about the genetic processes underlying the harmful effects of inbreeding the solution appears to be to maintain as large and as many captive breeding populations as possible and to introduce new stock into them from the wild at frequent intervals.

In a captive breeding population the natural pressures of climate, food supply and predation that affect wild populations are relaxed.

This means that individuals who in the wild might have succumbed to such pressures will survive. There is thus a danger that captive breeding will 'dull the edge' of natural selection with the result that birds may be poorly adapted when they are eventually returned to the wild.[13] Indeed, such is the temptation to breed from birds that 'do well' in captivity that one may actually be selecting for characteristics that are quite different from those that would be advantageous to wild birds. The only solution to this problem is to keep captive populations in conditions as similar as possible to the natural environment and to keep the time between captive breeding and eventual release as short as possible.

Captive-bred birds are liable to become socially attached to their human custodians or to some inanimate feature of their enclosure.[14] This process is called imprinting and most people are familiar with the Greylag Geese that became imprinted on Konrad Lorenz, following him around as if he were their mother and eventually making him the object of their sexual preferences. Birds kept in captivity have to be prevented from becoming too tame and oriented towards man or they will never survive and breed successfully in the wild. For this reason it is best if their contacts with man are kept to a minimum.

While many of the problems involved in actually breeding birds in captivity have been solved for several species, there remains the very difficult question of how such birds are to be successfully returned to the wild. In this respect the earlier releases of captive-bred Nénés and, more recently, of Whooping Cranes in America, have not been very encouraging.[15] What is required is a transition period, like that provided by the 'slow release' method used for Nénés, during which birds can lose habits acquired in captivity, particularly their dependence on man, and learn the skills of food-finding and predator avoidance that they will need in the wild. For captive-reared birds of prey such as Peregrines and Eagle Owls, this transition period takes the form of 'hacking back' by which the bird is trained to find an increasingly large proportion of its food for itself.[16]

Many zoos and wildlife parks have successfully bred a number of species in captivity but their efforts have made little or no contribution to the conservation of those species in the wild. There are those who are severely critical of zoos, pointing out that they create a constant drain on wild populations, the great majority of zoo animals dying without breeding. Gerald Durrell, founder of the Jersey Wildlife Preservation Trust, has described many of the wildlife parks that have recently proliferated in Britain as 'abattoirs in a sylvan setting'.[17] For many species the problem is exacerbated by high mortality in transit between the point of capture and their destination, which means that for every bird that goes on show several others die needlessly. While zoos are essentially places of entertainment, it should be said in their defence that they can serve an educative function. Without them their visitors might be unaware of the existence of many species and they can help foster an interest in the world's wildlife which ultimately can benefit the conservation movement. However, for many people their value does not adequately compensate for the depleting effect they have on wild populations. It would be better if zoos could be more self-sustaining, increasing their breeding facilities so that they could show more captive-bred animals. Zoos are certainly not the best environment for breeding animals destined for reintroduction to the wild. As we have seen there are good biological reasons why captive breeding of birds requires seclusion, the very thing they must of necessity be denied in zoos.

An analysis made in 1970 of the success of captive breeding attempts showed that, of the 340 birds classified as endangered in the IUCN *Red Data Book*, only twenty-four have been bred at all frequently.[18] Only nine species were being bred in such numbers as to exceed or equal their death rate in captivity. Most of these were pheasants, ducks and geese. The survey also concluded that among the world's zoos and similar establishments there were only twenty institutions that were adequately equipped to breed birds in numbers likely to contribute to the survival of endangered species.

It is significant that the best results in this field have been achieved by specialist establishments such as the Wildfowl Trust at Slimbridge and the Pheasant Trust in Norfolk. Since its inception in 1959 the Pheasant Trust has bred several of the sixteen species of pheasant that are in danger of extinction throughout the world.[19] One of them, Swinhoe's Pheasant, has been successfully reintroduced to its natural

46. Swinhoe's Pheasant

habitat in Taiwan. The Jersey Wildlife Preservation Trust has been developed expressly for the purpose of conserving and breeding endangered species and its enclosures and cages are designed with the welfare of their inmates in mind, not for the convenience of human visitors. Captive breeding is a complex task requiring expert knowledge and expertise and the best results are likely to be obtained at purpose-built establishments such as those mentioned above and those at Patuxent in America and at Mount Bruce in New Zealand.

The measures discussed so far are those that have been used to conserve species that have become dangerously rare. In terms of the analogy with medicine, they are essentially curative. If conservation is also to be a preventative exercise, that is, one by which species are not allowed to become critically rare, it will be necessary to first identify those species that are likely to be at risk. From the examples of extinct and endangered birds discussed in the previous chapters, we can identify five categories of birds that are biologically prone to extinction.[20] We can also suggest practical steps that should be taken to prevent the extinction of such species.

The first category of extinction-prone birds are those that occupy an ecological niche at the top of a food chain. They are, of necessity, widely dispersed and thus locally rare and they are usually large birds with a slow breeding rate. Most of the larger birds of prey, including Ospreys, eagles and the California Condor fall into this category, together with such species as the Ivory-billed Woodpecker. They require a very large area over which to hunt and thus nature reserves intended to protect them have to be very extensive. Many birds of prey may be able to survive in agricultural areas and there should be total prohibition on hunting them wherever they are found. Predators are the species most vulnerable to pesticide poisoning, a threat to wildlife which can only be eliminated by international agreement to ban the use of DDT and similar compounds.

On the larger continents another category of birds that are particularly sensitive to changes in their environment are those with very specialized habits. The Everglade Kite, with its dependence for food on just one species of snail, is a good example of such a species. Specialists can only be protected by the conservation of their habitat and for that nature reserves are essential.

Probably the largest category of extinction-prone birds are those species endemic to remote islands. The greatest threats to such birds are invasions by other species, particularly mammalian predators, and the destruction of their habitat. It is to be hoped that those oceanic islands that have not yet been colonized and exploited by man will be left alone. The best-known group of relatively unspoiled islands are the Galapagos Islands, which have been carefully conserved largely because of their significance in the history of biological theory. Such islands provide unique opportunities for studying many biological phenomena and their scientific value as 'natural laboratories' must surely outweigh any benefits that can be gained from their commercial exploitation. The isolation of islands that has brought about their special biological character also makes their conservation a relatively simple matter.

A group of birds that are particularly vulnerable to direct exploitation by man are those that nest in dense colonies. The Great Auk was a species that became extinct primarily because of human destruction on its breeding grounds. On Isla Saoma off Dominica in the West Indies is a colony of the White-crowned Pigeon where the collection of squabs is reminiscent of the destruction wrought in the nesting colonies of its extinct relative, the Passenger Pigeon. The protection of colonial species is fairly easily achieved by legislation which, because of the restricted area involved, is relatively easy to enforce.

The last of these five categories of vulnerable species consists of migratory birds which, compared with some others, are particularly difficult to protect. Birds that spend different parts of the year in widely separated localities not only have to be protected in both parts of their range, but also, ideally, during their migratory journeys in between. Conservation on this scale often requires international cooperation which, because of political differences, may be difficult to achieve. Among a number of very rare migratory birds that breed in North America are the Eskimo Curlew, Kirtland's Warbler and Bachman's Warbler, which spend the winter in South America, the Bahamas and Cuba respectively.

There are a number of conservationists who deplore some of the manipulative techniques discussed in this chapter. Their ideal is the preservation of areas of natural wilderness and some would rather see a species become extinct than have it be dependent on man's support. Such purists regard birds bred in captivity as works of man, not of nature. These views are surely naive; we have to accept the fact that the pressing needs of the expanding human population mean that we must settle for a world diminished in its biological variety and largely dependent on careful management for its stability. To deny an endangered species the chance of survival through captive breeding or some other form of intervention in its biology is like witholding a proven cure from a man dying of a disease. Conservation is like medicine in that, as our understanding of biological processes deepens and new techniques are developed, so our obligation to use our knowledge to save other species increases. Man's view of his place in the natural world is gradually changing from one in which all nature is at his disposal to that of the responsible protector and curator of other forms of life.

The greatly accelerated rate at which birds have become extinct in the last 300 years has naturally alarmed ornithologists. It should be a cause for concern to everyone, whether they are interested in birds or not, because it is symptomatic of man's excessive exploitation of his own environment. The decline in the number of species that the world supports has been parallelled by the reckless depletion of vital biological and mineral resources. Man is currently using up natural reserves of metals and fossil fuels, felling forests and slaughtering marine fish and whales far faster than any of these commodities can be replaced by natural processes. It is inevitable that as long as governments maintain their commitment to economic growth the world's resources will continue to be depleted until many of them run out. Already there have been warning signs; already such minerals as copper have become so scarce that, for many purposes, they have had to be replaced. The British government apparently intends to extract the newly-found oil beneath the North Sea as fast as possible, with no clear idea of what it will do for energy when it is all used up. Conservation, not only of wildlife but of natural resources of all kinds, requires that governments take a long-term view. The larger whales require eight or nine years to reach maturity, forests take hundreds of years to regenerate after they are felled and oil is the product of millions of years of geological changes. Unfortunately, governments are essentially pragmatic in their outlook, thinking more of the next election than of the quality of life two or three generations hence. To persuade governments to formulate policies with long-term considerations in mind is perhaps the greatest challenge facing the conservationist. Until some radical change can be achieved at the highest level the conservation effort has largely to be applied locally in the often-repeated fight between conservationists and commercial interests.

To be really effective conservation must become a worldwide exercise, one to which all governments are committed. There is a growing awareness that the world is small and contains finite resources. The phrase 'global village' eloquently expresses the way in which changes in one part of the world are increasingly affecting life further afield. The rubbish one community throws over its back wall turns up on another's doorstep. One might think that the devastating effect chemical pesticides have had on wildlife would have been heeded as a warning. On the contrary, many governments are intending to develop nuclear power programmes producing waste that is lethal, not for ten or twenty, but for thousands of years. Such developments, whose effects are likely to be felt throughout the world, must be challenged on an international basis and such organizations as the International Union for the Conservation of Nature and Natural Resources (IUCN), the International Council for Bird Preservation (ICBP) and the World Wildlife Fund provide the basis for effective international pressure groups.

The professional biologist has an important part to play in the field of wildlife conservation. Writing in 1970, Guy Mountfort deplored our lack of basic knowledge about the biology of recently extinct and endangered species.[21] He made a plea that academic ornithologists should devote more of their attention and expertise to endangered species to provide those actively engaged in conservation work with the vital information they need to carry out their task. Five years later D. R. Zimmerman wrote that this call has gone largely unheeded and that most professional ornithologists continue to work on the biology of species whose future is healthy.[22] I have tried to show in this book how important a contribution a deeper understanding of bird biology can make to the conservation effort and we can but hope that in the future more scientists will turn their attention to the preservation of endangered species.

In the final analysis the effective conservation of many species of birds depends on setting aside land for nature reserves. Such land is necessarily made unavailable for exploitation by man and, as the human population grows, one can expect an increasingly severe conflict of interests over the use to which as yet unspoiled areas are to be put. Such decisions will not be easy and in many instances human considerations will certainly win. To have conserved the Pink-headed Duck, for example, would have probably meant denying the use of large areas of land to the expanding and starving population of Bangladesh. Man will increasingly have to make a choice between taking more natural resources for himself and sharing the world with a rich and varied wildlife. Material benefits to ourselves are gained at the cost of a diminished environment; to conserve other species in that environment we must limit the share that we take for ourselves. Throughout this book we have seen that the recent extinction of many birds has been the result of man's disturbance of the complex relationships between animals and plants that provide stability in the natural world. Our own survival now depends on our ability to find ways to achieve a new balanced relationship between ourselves and nature.

Notes and Bibliography

———✦———

TO keep the number of bibliographic entries to a minimum I have tried, wherever possible, to give references to my most important sources only once, at the beginning of each chapter or major section. Otherwise references relate to specific points in the text.

General Sources

Greenway, J. C. *Extinct and Vanishing Birds of the World*, 2nd edn, Dover (New York, 1967)
Vincent, J. (ed.) *Red Data Book*, Vol. 2 *Aves*, International Union for the Conservation of Nature and Natural Resources (IUCN) (Morges, Switzerland, 1966)
Fisher, J., Simon. N. and Vincent, J. *The Red Book: Wildlife in Danger*, Collins (London, 1969)

Greenway's book is comprehensive in its detailed coverage of all species that have become extinct during the last 300 years. It also deals with many birds that are rare or endangered, but the best source for information on such species is the *Red Data Book*, a loose-leafed volume written in note-form which is brought up to date regularly. *The Red Book* provides expanded and illustrated accounts of the species contained in the *Red Data Book*.

Chapter 1
1 Principal sources for this chapter:
P. Brodkorb, 'Origin and evolution of birds', in *Avian Biology*, D. S. Farner and J. R. King (eds.), Academic Press (New York, 1971), vol. 1, ch. 2
J. C. Welty, *The Life of Birds*, 2nd edn, Saunders (Philadelphia, 1975), ch. 23

W. E. Swinton, *Fossil Birds*, 2nd edn, British Museum (Natural History) (1965)

2 P. Brodkorb, 'How many species have existed?', *Bull. Florida State Museum*, **5** (1960), 41—53
R. E. Moreau, 'On the estimates of the past numbers and on the average longevity of avian species', *Auk*, **83** (1966), 403–15
Brodkorb, 'Origin and evolution of birds'

3 It has been estimated that the average longevity of a bird species is about 500,000 years. See Brodkorb, 'How many species have existed?'

4 J. H. Ostrom, '*Archeopteryx* and the origin of flight,' *Quarterly Review of Biology*, **49** (1974), 27–47

5 J. H. Ostrom, '*Archeopteryx* and the origin of birds', *Biological Journal of the Linnean Society*, **8** (1976), 91–182

6 R. W. Storer, 'Adaptive radiation in birds', in *Avian Biology*, D. S. Farner and J. R. King (eds.), Academic Press (New York, 1971) vol. 1, ch. 4

7 The trend by which animals evolve towards larger size is referred to as Cope's rule. See:
S. M. Stanley, 'An explanation for Cope's rule', *Evolution*, **27** (1973) 1–26
A. Hallam, 'Evolutionary size increase and longevity in Jurassic bivalves and ammonites', *Nature*, **258** (1975), 493–6

8 D. Lack, *Island Biology Illustrated by the Land Birds of Jamaica*, University of California Press (1976), 203–4

9 D. Lack, *Darwin's Finches*, Cambridge University Press (1947)

10 D. Amadon, 'The Hawaiian Honeycreepers', *Bull. Amer. Mus. Nat. Hist.*, **95** (1950), Article 4

11 Throughout this book I have used the word 'endemic' in the strict biological sense. A species that is endemic to a particular locality is found only there; a species that is indigenous is found there and in other localities.

12 C. B. Cox, I. N. Healey and P. D. Moore, *Biogeography: an ecological and evolutionary approach*, Blackwell Scientific Publications (Oxford, 1976), ch. 6

13 J. Cracraft, 'Continental drift, palaeoclimatology, and the evolution and biogeography of birds', *J. Zool. Lond*, **169** (1973), 455–545; and 'Phylogeny and evolution of the ratite birds', *Ibis*, **116** (1974), 494–521

14 For a most readable account of how thinking of genes as the fundamental unit of natural selection helps our understanding of the evolutionary process see: R. Dawkins, *The Selfish Gene*, Oxford University Press (1976)

15 D. Amadon, 'The evolution of low reproductive rates in birds', *Evolution*, **18** (1964) 105–10
T. R. E. Southwood, 'Bionomic strategies and population parameters', in *Theoretical Ecology: principles and applications*, R. M. May (ed.), Blackwell Scientific Publications, (Oxford, 1976), ch. 3

16 R. F. Johnston and R. K. Selander, 'House Sparrows: rapid evolution of races in North America', *Science*, **144** (1964) 548–50

17 J. Terborgh, 'Preservation of natural diversity: the problem of extinction-prone species', *Bioscience*, **24** (1974), 715–22

Chapter 2

1 Principal sources for this chapter:
  J. Dorst, *The Life of Birds*, Weidenfeld and Nicolson (London, 1974), vol. 2, ch. 23
  J. C. Welty, *The Life of Birds*, 2nd edn, Saunders (Philadelphia, 1975), ch. 24
2 E. G. Turbott, *Buller's Birds of New Zealand*, Whitcombe and Tombs (Wellington, 1967)
3 T. P. Inskipp and G. J. Thomas, *Airborne Birds*, R.S.P.B. (1976)
4 J. R. Jackson, 'Do Keas attack sheep?', *Notornis*, **10** (1962), 33–8
5 D. B. Peakall, 'Pesticides and the reproduction of birds', *Scientific American*, **222** (4) (1970), 72–8
6 D. A. Ratcliffe, 'Broken eggs in Peregrine eyries', *British Birds*, **51** (1958), 23–6
7 D. A. Ratcliffe, 'Decrease in eggshell weight in certain birds of prey', *Nature*, **215** (1967), 208–10.
8 Peakall, 'Pesticides and the reproduction of birds'
9 In America DDT has been detected in human breast milk in quantities that would make it illegal produce if it were cow's milk. See: P. R. and A. H. Ehrlich *Population, Resources, Environment*, 2nd edn, W. H. Freeman (San Francisco, 1972), 160
10 K. Wodzicki, 'The status of some exotic vertebrates in the ecology of New Zealand', in *The Genetics of Colonising Species*, ed. H. G. Baker and G. L. Stebbins, Academic Press (New York, 1965), 425–60
11 J. Kear and P. J. K. Burton, 'The food and feeding apparatus of the Blue Duck, *Hymenolaimus*', *Ibis*, **113** (1971), 483–93
12 R. E. Warner, 'The role of introduced diseases in the extinction of the endemic Hawaiian avifauna', *Condor*, **70** (1968), 101–20
13 J. Fisher, 'Extinct birds', in *A New Dictionary of Birds*, A. Landsborough Thomson (ed.), Nelson (London, 1964), 259–64
14 P. Singer, *Animal Liberation*, Jonathan Cape (London, 1976)
15 The word 'speciesism' was actually coined by Richard Ryder. See: R. D. Ryder, *Speciesism: the ethics of vivisection*, Scottish Society for the Prevention of Vivisection (1974)

Chapter 3

1 H. G. Strickland and A. G. Melville, *The Dodo and its Kindred*, Reeve, Benham and Reeve (London, 1848)
2 H. Friedmann, 'New light on the Dodo and its illustrators', *Smithsonian Report*, 1955 (Washington, 1956), 475–81
3 G. Clark, 'Account of the late discovery of Dodo's remains in the island of Mauritius', *Ibis*, (1866) 141–6
4 E. Newton, 'On the reported discovery of Dodo's bones in a cavern in Mauritius', *Proc. Zool. Soc. Lond.*, (1890) 402–3
5 M. Hachisuka, *The Dodo and Kindred Birds*, Witherby (London, 1953)
6 J. Lüttschwager, 'Die Drontevögel', *Die Neue Brehm-Bücherei* (Wittenberg-Lutherstadt, 1961), 276
7 E. A. Armstrong, 'Territory and birds. A concept which originated from study of an extinct species', *Discovery* (July 1953), 223–4

8 T. Mortensen, 'On the "Solitaire" of the Island of Rodriguez', *Ardea*, **22** (1933), 21–9

9 M. Hachisuka, 'Revisional note on the didine birds of Réunion', *Proc. Biol. Soc. Washington*, **50** (1937), 69–71
M. Hachisuka, *The Dodo and Kindred Birds*

10 R. W. Storer, 'Independent evolution of the Dodo and the Solitaire', *Auk*, **87** (1970), 396–70

11 F. Bruemmer, 'Funk Island', *Natural History* (*J. Amer. Mus. Nat. Hist.*), **80** (1971), 52–7

12 This account of the Great Auk is based primarily on the thorough analysis made by Symington Grieve of all the evidence available in the late nineteenth century:
S. Grieve, *The Great Auk, or Garefowl*, Thomas C. Jack (London, 1885), and 'Recent information about the Great Auk or Garefowl (*Alca impennis*, Linn.)', *Trans. Edinburgh Field Naturalists' and Microscopical Soc.* (1888), Presidential Address, Session 20

13 J. Fisher and R. M. Lockley, *Sea Birds*, Collins (London, 1954), 65

14 Grieve, *The Great Auk*

15 Bruemmer, 'Funk Island'

16 Grieve, 'Recent information'

17 A. Newton, 'Abstract of Mr J. Wolley's researches in Iceland concerning the Garefowl or Great Auk (*Alca impennis* Linn.)', *Ibis*, **2** (1861), 374–99

18 Ibid.

19 Ibid.

20 Many seabirds, both large and small, lay only one or a very few eggs. This is thought to reflect the difficulty of carrying enough food for a large brood when the feeding grounds may be far out to sea and some distance from the nest. See:
N. P. Ashmole, 'Seabird ecology and the marine environment', in *Avian Biology* D. S. Farner and J. R. King (eds.), Academic Press (New York, 1971), vol. 1, ch. 5

21 T. Parkin, 'Sale of a Great Auk's egg', *British Birds*, **6** (1913), 256–7
For an illustrated account of seventy-five Great Auk eggs and of their histories, see:
P. M. L. and J. W. Tomkinson, 'Eggs of the Great Auk,' *Bull. Brit. Mus.* (*Nat. Hist.*), **3** (1966), 97–128

22 R. W. Storer, 'Evolution in the diving birds,' *Proc. 12th Int. Ornith. Congress* (1960), 694–707
R. W. Storer, 'Adaptive radiation in birds', in *Avian Biology*, D. S. Farner and J. R. King (eds.), Academic Press (New York, 1971), vol. 1, ch. 4

23 Fisher and Lockley, *Sea Birds*

24 J. Sparks and T. Soper, *Penguins*, David and Charles (Newton Abbott, 1967)

25 S. Ali, 'The Pink-headed Duck, *Rhodonessa caryophyllacea* (Lathan)', *Wildfowl Trust 11th Ann. Report* (1960), 55–60
A. A. Prestwich, 'The Pink-headed Duck (*Rhodonessa caryophyllacea*) in the wild and in captivity', *Avicult. Mag.*, **80** (1974), 47–52

26 S. Ali and S. D. Ripley, *Handbook of the Birds of India and Pakistan*, Oxford University Press (1968), vol. I, 175–7

E. C. S. Baker, *The Indian Ducks and their Allies*, Bombay Natural History Society (1908), 41

27 F. Finn, *Indian Sporting Birds*, Francis Edwards (London, 1915), 24–6

28 F. B. Simson, 'Notes on the Pink-headed Duck (*Anas caryophyllacea*)', *Ibis* (1884), 271–5

29 J. C. Phillips, *A Natural History of Ducks*, Longmans Green (London, 1923) vol. 1, 90

30 J. Bucknill, 'The disappearance of the Pink-headed Duck (*Rhodonessa caryophyllacea* Lath.)', *Ibis* (1924), 12th series, vol. I, 146–51

31 A. Ezra, 'Arrival of a very rare duck. The Pink-headed Duck (*Rhodonessa caryophyllacea*)', *Avicult. Mag.* Series 4, **3** (1925), 299–300
A. Ezra, 'The Pink-headed Duck (*Rhodonessa caryophyllacea*)', *Avicult. Mag.* Series 4, **4** (1926), 325
A. Ezra, 'Élévages et observations à Foxwarren', *L'Oiseau*, **11** (1930), 501–5

32 Ali, 'The Pink-headed Duck'

33 Ibid.

34 J. Delacour, *The Waterfowl of the World*, Country Life (London, 1954), vol. 2, 197
P. S. Humphrey and S. D. Ripley, 'The affinities of the Pink-headed Duck (*Rhodonessa caryophyllacea*)', *Postilla*, **61** (1962), 1–21

Chapter 4

1 E. Mayr, 'Nearctic region,' in *A New Dictionary of Birds*, A. Landsborough Thomson (ed.), Nelson (London, 1964), 514–16

2 D. C. Peattie, *Green Laurels: the lives and achievements of the great naturalists*, Harrap (London, 1937), ch. 10
A. Ford, *John James Audubon*, University of Oklahoma Press (1964)
E. W. Teale, *Audubon's Wildlife, with Selections from the Writings of John James Audubon*, Thames and Hudson (London, 1965)

3 A. C. Bent, *Life Histories of North American Gallinaceous Birds*, Smithsonian Inst. *U.S. Nat. Mus. Bull. No. 162* (1932; republished 1963 by Dover, New York)
A. W. Schorger, *The Passenger Pigeon*, University of Wisconsin Press (Madison, 1955)
I. L. Brisbin, 'The Passenger Pigeon. A study in the ecology of extinction', *Modern Game Breeding*, **4** (1968), 13–20

4 D. Goodwin, *Pigeons and Doves of the World*, British Museum (Natural History) (1967), 203–5

5 W. Craig, 'The expressions of emotion in the pigeons. III. The Passenger Pigeon (*Ectopistes migratorius*, Linn.)', *Auk*, **28** (1911), 408–27
Bent, *Life Histories of North American Gallinaceous Birds*

6 Goodwin, *Pigeons and Doves of the World*

7 W. B. Barrows, *Michigan Bird Life*, Michigan Agricultural Office (1912), 238–51
Bent, *Life Histories of North American Gallinaceous Birds*

8 W. Brewster, 'The present status of the Wild Pigeon (*Ectopistes migratorius*) as a bird of the United States, with some notes on its habits', *Auk*, **6** (1889) 285–91

9 C. O. Whitman, *The Behaviour of Pigeons*, Carnegie (Washington, 1919)

10 Barrows, *Michigan Bird Life*
11 J. L. Hoogland and P. W. Sherman, 'Advantages and disadvantages of Bank Swallow (*Riparia riparia*) coloniality', *Ecological Monographs*, **46** (1976), 33–48
   E. O. Wilson, *Sociobiology*, Belknap, Harvard University Press (1975), 41
12 Brisbin, 'The Passenger Pigeon'
   L. Griscom, 'The passing of the Passenger Pigeon', *American Scholar* (Autumn 1946), 212–16
13 Brisbin, 'The Passenger Pigeon'
14 J. J. Audubon, *Ornithological Biography*, Adam Black (Edinburgh, 1831), vol. 1, 135–40
   E. M. Hasbrouck, 'The Carolina Paroquet (*Conurus carolinensis*)', *Auk*, **8** (1891), 369–79
   A. W. Butler, 'Notes on the range and habits of the Carolina Parakeet', *Auk*, **9** (1892), 49–56
   A. H. Howell, (1932) *Florida Bird Life*, Coward-McCann (New York, 1932), 283–6
   A. C. Bent, *Life Histories of North American Cuckoos, Goatsuckers, Hummingbirds and Their Allies*, Smithsonian Inst. U.S. Nat. Mus. Bull. No. *176* (1940; republished 1964 by Dover, New York)
   J. M. Forshaw, *Parrots of the World*, Landsdowne (Melbourne, 1973), 414–18
15 W. Brewster, 'Nesting habits of the Parakeet (*Conurus carolinensis*)', *Auk*, **6** (1889), 336–7
   Bent, *Life Histories of North American Cuckoos, Goatsuckers, Hummingbirds and Their Allies*
16 Audubon, *Ornithological Biography*
17 Ibid.
18 H. Kruuk, 'The biological function of gulls' attraction towards predators', *Animal Behaviour*, **24** (1976), 146–53
19 D. McKinley, 'The Carolina Parakeet in pioneer Missouri', *Wilson Bull.*, **72** (1960) 274–87
20 Hasbrouck, 'The Carolina Paroquet'
21 Bent, *Life Histories of North American Gallinaceous Birds*
22 R. J. Robel and W. B. Bullard, 'Lek social organisation and reproductive success in the Greater Prairie Chicken', *American Zoologist*, **14** (1974), 121–8
23 Bent, *Life Histories of North American Gallinaceous Birds*
24 Ibid.
25 P. S. Humphrey, and R. S. Butsch, 'The anatomy of the Labrador Duck, *Camptorhynchus labradorius* (Gmelin)', Smithsonian Misc. Collection: 135, No. 7 (1958)
   J. Delacour, *The Waterfowl of the World*, Country Life (London, 1954), vol. 3, 160–2
26 V. L. Emanuel, 'Texans rediscover the nearly extinct Eskimo Curlew', *Audubon Magazine*, **64** (1962), 162–5
27 Ibid.
28 A. H. Miller, I. I. McMillan and E. McMillan, *The Current Status and Welfare of the California Condor*, National Audubon Society Report No. 6 (1965; summarized in *Audubon Magazine*, **67** (1), 38–41)

29 D. B. Mertz, 'The mathematical demography of the California Condor population', *American Naturalist*, **105** (1971), 437–53
D. R. Zimmerman, *To Save a Bird in Peril*, Coward, McCann and Geoghegan (New York 1975), ch. 7
30 F. S. Todd, 'The tenacious Thunderbird', *Wildlife*, **17** (1) (1975), 8–13
31 J. T. Tanner, *The Ivory-billed Woodpecker*, Dover (New York, 1942)
32 J. J. Hickey (ed.), *Peregrine Falcon Populations: their biology and decline*, University of Wisconsin Press (Madison, 1969)
T. J. Cade and R. Fyfe, 'The North American Peregrine survey 1970', *Canadian Field Naturalist*, **84** (1970), 231–45
33 T. J. Cade, C. M. White, and J. R. Haugh, 'Peregrines and pesticides in Alaska,' *Condor*, **70** (1968), 170–8
J. M. Enderson, and D. D. Berger, 'Chlorinated hydrocarbon residues in Peregrines and their prey species from northern Canada', *Condor*, **70** (1968), 149–53
34 J. M. Enderson, 'A breeding and migration survey of the Peregrine Falcon', *Wilson Bulletin*, **77** (1965), 327–39
35 T. J. Cade, 'Falcon farming', *Animal Kingdom*, **78** (1975), 3–9
Zimmerman, *To Save a Bird in Peril*, ch. 1 and 6
36 W. O. Stieglitz, and R. L. Thompson, *Status and Life History of the Everglade Kite in the United States*, U.S. Dept. of the Interior, Fish and Wildlife Service, Special Scientific Report No. 109 (1967)
P. W. Sykes and W. B. Robertson, 'Kites in the Everglades', *Nature*, **220** (1968), 939–40
37 A. Sprunt, 'Bald Eagles aren't producing enough young', *Audubon Magazine*, **65** (1) (1963), 32–5
38 P. L. Ames, and G. S. Mersereau, 'Some factors in the decline of the Osprey in Connecticut', *Auk*, **81** (1964), 173–85
C. J. Henny, and H. M. Wright, 'An endangered Osprey population: estimates of mortality and production', *Auk*, **86** (1969), 188–98
Zimmerman, *To Save a Bird in Peril*, ch. 2
39 Ames and Mersereau, 'Some factors in the decline of the Osprey in Connecticut'
40 S. N. Wiemeyer *et al.*, 'Effects of environmental pollutants on Connecticut and Maryland Ospreys', *Journal of Wildlife Management*, **39** (1975), 124–39
41 Zimmerman, *To Save a Bird in Peril*, ch. 4
42 R. C. Ericksen, 'Report on Whooping Crane research and management—1974', *12th Bull. I.C.B.P.* (1975), 122–5
43 Zimmerman, *To Save a Bird in Peril*, ch. 8
44 N. F. Leopold, 'The Kirtland's Warbler in its summer home', *Auk*, **41** (1924), 44–58
45 H. Mayfield, 'A census of the Kirtland's Warbler', *Auk*, **70** (1953), 17–20; and '1961 decennial census of the Kirtland's Warbler', *Auk*, **79** (1962), 173–82
46 S. D. Ripley, 'Saving the Wood Duck *Aix sponsa* through captive breeding', *Int. Zoo Yearbook*, **13** (1973), 55–8
R. S. Palmer, (ed.), *Handbook of North American Birds*, Yale University Press (1975), vol. 3, 252–77

Chapter 5

1 C. A. Fleming, 'History of the New Zealand land bird fauna', *Notornis*, **9** (1962),
270–4
R. M. McDowall, 'Extinction and endemism in New Zealand land birds',
Tuatara, **17** (1969), 1–12
G. R. Williams, 'Birds', in *The Natural History of New Zealand: an ecological
survey*, G. R. Williams (ed.), Reed (Wellington, 1973), ch. 13
P. C. Bull and A. H. Whitacker, 'The amphibians, reptiles, birds and mammals',
in *Biogeography and Ecology in New Zealand*, G. Kuschel (ed.), Junk (The Hague,
1975), ch. 5

2 C. A. Fleming, 'New Zealand biogeography. A palaeontologist's approach',
Tuatara, **10** (1962), 53–108
C. A. Fleming, 'The geological history of New Zealand and its biota', in *Bio-
geography and Ecology in New Zealand*, ch. 1

3 J. Cracraft, 'Continental drift, palaeoclimatology, and the evolution and biogeography of birds', *J. Zool. Lond.*, **169** (1973), 455–545; and 'Phylogeny and evolution of the ratite birds', *Ibis*, **116** (1974), 494–521

4 The fish that inhabit New Zealand's rivers and lakes, apart from those introduced
by man, are descended from marine fishes and most have the ability to move between fresh and salt water.

5 There is some dispute about how many species of moa there were. Some would put
the number nearer ten than twenty-five, pointing out that much of the variation in
the fossil material can be attributed to sexual, age and racial differences. See:
R. A. Falla, 'Moa', in *A New Dictionary of Birds*, A. Landsborough Thomson
(ed.), Nelson (London, 1964)

6 Bull and Whitacker in *Biogeography and Ecology in New Zealand*

7 J. T. Salmon, 'The influence of man on the biota', in *Biogeography and Ecology in
New Zealand*, ch. 17

8 R. C. Green, 'Adaptation and change in Maori culture', in *Biogeography and Ecology in New Zealand*, ch. 16

9 C.A. Fleming, 'The extinction of Moas and other animals during the Holocene
period', *Notornis*, **10** (1962), 113–17

10 Green in *Biogeography and Ecology in New Zealand*

11 G. Searle, 'The tragedy of New Zealand's forests', *Ecologist*, **5** (1975), 126–32

12 Salmon in *Biogeography and Ecology in New Zealand*
Searle, 'The tragedy of New Zealand's forests'; and *Rush to Destruction*, Reed
(Wellington, 1975)

13 K. Wodzicki, 'The status of some exotic vertebrates in the ecology of New
Zealand', in *The Genetics of Colonising Species*, M. G. Baker and G. L. Stebbins
(eds.), Academic Press (New York, 1965), 425–60

14 Ibid.

15 McDowall, 'Extinction and endemism in New Zealand land birds'

16 G. R. Williams, 'Extinction and the land and fresh water-inhabiting birds of
New Zealand', *Notornis*, **10** (1962), 15–32

17 B. D. Bell, 'The rare and endangered species of the New Zealand region and the
policies that exist for their management', *12th Bull. I.C.B.P.* (1975), 165–72

18 E. G. Turbott, *Buller's Birds of New Zealand*, Whitcombe and Tombs, (Wellington, 1967); Introduction in *A New Dictionary of Birds*

19 Falla in *A New Dictionary of Birds*
Fleming, 'The extinction of Moas and other animals during the Holocene period'

20 R. A. Falla, R. B. Sibson, and E. G. Turbott, *A Field Guide to the Birds of New Zealand*, 2nd edn, Collins (London, 1970) 17–20
B. Reid and G. R. Williams, 'The Kiwi', in *Biogeography and Ecology in New Zealand*, ch. 7

21 B. M. Wenzel, 'Olfactory prowess of the Kiwi', *Nature*, **220** (1968), 1133–4

22 G. R. Williams, 'The New Zealand Wattlebirds (*Callaeatidae*)', *Proc. 16th Int. Ornith. Congress* (1976), 161–70

23 Turbott, *Buller's Birds of New Zealand*, 7–13

24 Ibid.

25 P. J. K. Burton, 'Anatomy of head and neck in the Huia (*Heteralocha acutirostris*) with comparative notes on other Callaeidae', *Bull. British Museum (Nat. Hist.)*, *Zoology*, **27** (1974), 1–48

26 A. H. Garrod, 'Notes on the anatomy of the Huia bird (*Heteralocha gouldi*)', *Proc. Zool. Soc.* (1872), 643–7
Burton, 'Anatomy of head and neck in the Huia'

27 W. R. B. Oliver, *New Zealand Birds*, 2nd edn, Reed (Wellington, 1955), 512–19

28 J. G. Myers, 'The present status of the endemic birds of New Zealand', *N. Z. Journal of Science and Technology*, **6** (1923), 65–99

29 Oliver, *New Zealand Birds*, 518

30 Myers, 'The present status of the endemic birds of New Zealand'

31 Ibid.

32 R. K. Selander, 'Sexual dimorphism and differential niche utilisation in birds', *Condor*, **68** (1966), 113–51

33 Ibid.

34 Turbott, *Buller's Birds of New Zealand*, 3–7
Falla *et al.*, *A Field Guide to the Birds of New Zealand*, 238–40

35 D. V. Merton, 'A brief history of the North Island Saddleback', *Notornis*, **12** (1965), 208–12
Turbott, *Buller's Birds of New Zealand*, 13–17

36 D. V. Merton, 'Success in re-establishing a threatened species: the Saddleback—its status and conservation', *12th Bull. I.C.P.B.*, (1975), 150–8; and 'The Saddleback: its status and conservation', in *Breeding Endangered Species in Captivity*, R. D. Martin (ed.), Academic Press (London, 1975), 61–74
D. R. Zimmerman, *To Save a Bird in Peril*, Coward, McCann and Geoghegan (New York, 1975), ch. 10

37 P. Jenkins, 'Cultural transmission of song patterns and dialect development in a free-living bird population', *Animal Behaviour*, **26** (1978), 50–78

38 Turbott, *Buller's Birds of New Zealand*, 62–5
Falla, *et al.*, *A Field Guide to the Birds of New Zealand*, 195–6

39 Ibid.

40 Ibid.

41 Falla, *et al.*, *A Field Guide to the Birds of New Zealand*, 195–6

J. R. Jackson, 'Do Keas attack sheep?', *Notornis*, **10** (1962), 33–8

C. M. H. Clarke, 'Observations on population, movements and food of the Kea (*Nestor notabilis*)', *Notornis*, **17** (1970), 105–14

42 G. R. Williams, 'Extinction and the Anatidae of New Zealand', *Wildfowl Trust Report*, **15** (1964) 140–6

43 J. Kear, and R. J. Scarlett, 'The Aukland Islands Merganser', *Wildfowl*, **21** (1970), 78–86

44 J. Kear and P. J. K. Burton, 'The food and feeding apparatus of the Blue Duck, *Hymenolaimus*', *Ibis*, **113** (1971), 483–93

45 M. Williams and G. Roderick, 'The breeding performance of Grey Duck, *Anas superciliosa*, Mallard, *Anas platyrhynchos* and their hybrids in captivity.' *Int. Zoo Yearbook*. **13** (1973), 62–9

46 J. A. D. Flack, 'The Chatham Island Black Robin, extinction or survival?', *12th Bull. I.C.B.P.* (1975), 146–50

47 Turbott, *Buller's Birds of New Zealand*, 162–7

G. R. Williams, 'The Takahe (*Notornis mantelli* Owen, 1848): a general survey'. *Transactions of the Royal Society of New Zealand*, **88** (1960), 235–8

B. Reid, 'Survival status of the Takahe, *Notornis mantelli*, of New Zealand', *Biological Conservation*, **1** (1969), 237–40

48 J. A. Mills, 'Population studies on Takahe, *Notornis mantelli*, in Fiordland, New Zealand', *12th Bull. I.C.B.P.* (1975), 140–6

49 J. A. Mills, 'Takahe and Red Deer', *Wildlife—a Review* (N. Z. Wildlife Service), **6** (1976), 24–30

50 C. D. Roderick, 'Mount Bruce Native Bird Reserve', *Wildlife—a Review* (N. Z. Wildlife Service), **4** (1973), 42–6

51 G. R. Williams, 'The Kakapo (*Strigops habroptilus*, Gray). A review and reappraisal of a near-extinct species', *Notornis*, **7** (1956); 29–56

Falla, *et al.*, *A Field Guide to the Birds of New Zealand*, 172–3

J. M. Forshaw, *Parrots of the World*, Landsdowne (Melbourne, 1973), 269–70

52 D. V. Merton, 'Kakapo', *Wildlife—a Review* (N. Z. Wildlife Service), **6** (1975), 39–51

53 Ibid.

54 D. V. Merton, 'Kakapo on Maud Island', *Wildlife—a Review* (N. Z. Wildlife Service), **7** (1976), 30–5

55 Kakapos have recently been found on Stewart Island by Dr D. V. Merton.

Chapter 6

1 J. M. Diamond and R. M. May, 'Island biogeography and the design of nature reserves', in *Theoretical Ecology: principles and applications*, R. M. May (ed.), Blackwell Scientific Publications (Oxford, 1976), ch. 9

C. B. Cox, I. N. Healey and P. O. Moore, *Biogeography: an ecological and evolutionary approach*, Blackwell Scientific Publications (Oxford, 1976), ch. 5

2 R. H. MacArthur and E. O. Wilson, 'An equilibrium model of insular zoogeography', *Evolution*, **17** (1963), 373–87; and *The Theory of Island Biogeography*, Princeton University Press (1967)

3 D. Lack, 'The numbers of bird species on islands', *Bird Study*, **16** (1969), 193–209; 'The numbers of species of Hummingbirds in the West Indies', *Evolution*, **27** (1973) 326–37; and *Island Biology Illustrated by the Land Birds of Jamaica*, University of California Press (1976)

4 Ibid. See also J. F. Lynch, and N. K. Johnston, 'Turnover and equilibria in insular avifaunas, with special reference to the California Channel Islands', *Condor*, **76** (1974), 370–84

5 A. Keast, 'Ecological opportunities and adaptive evolution on islands, with special reference to evolution in the isolated forest outliers of southern Australia', *Proc. 16th Int. Ornith. Congress* (1976), 573–84

6 P. R. Grant, 'The adaptive significance of some size trends in island birds', *Evolution*, **19** (1965), 355–67

7 The longer bill of the Blue Chaffinch may have evolved because it enables the bird to probe into pine cones for seeds. See: Lack, *Island Biology Illustrated by the Land Birds of Jamaica*

8 P. R. Grant, 'Bill size, body size and the ecological adaptations of bird species to competitive situations on islands', *Systematic Zoology*, **17** (1968), 319–33; and 'Population variation on islands', *Proc. 16th Int. Ornith. Congress* (1976), 503–615

9 Lack, 'The numbers of species of Hummingbirds in the West Indies' and *Island Biology Illustrated by the Land Birds of Jamaica*

10 J. M. Diamond, 'Colonisation of exploded volcanic islands by birds: the supertramp strategy', *Science*, **184** (1974), 803–6; and 'Assembly of species communities', in *Ecology and Evolution of Communities*, M. L. Cody, and J. M. Diamond, (eds.), Belknap, Harvard University Press (1975), ch. 14

11 S. Carlquist, *Island Biology*, Columbia University Press (New York, 1974)

12 D. Lack, *Darwin's Finches*, Cambridge University Press (1974)
    D. Amadon, 'The Hawaiian Honeycreepers', *Bull. Amer. Mus. Nat. Hist.*, **95** (1950), Article 4

13 The scientific names of these rails are *Aphanapteryx bonasia* for the Mauritius species and *Aphanapteryx leguati* for that from Rodriguez.

14 S. Carlquist, *Hawaii: a natural history*, Natural History Press (New York, 1970)
    A. J. Berger, 'Hawaiian birds 1972', *Wilson Bulletin*, **84** (1972), 212–22

15 R. E. Warner, 'The role of introduced diseases in the extinction of the endemic Hawaiian avifauna', *Condor*, **70** (1968), 101–20

16 Amadon, 'The Hawaiian Honeycreepers'

17 D. R. Zimmerman, *To Save a Bird in Peril*, Coward, McCann and Geoghegan (New York, 1975), ch. 10

18 Ibid.

19 R. E. Warner, 'Recent history and ecology of the Laysan Duck', *Condor*, **65** (1963) 3–23

20 Zimmerman, *To Save a Bird in Peril*, ch. 10

21 Ibid.

22 J. Kear, 'Returning the Hawaiian Goose to the wild', in *Breeding Endangered Species in Captivity*, R. D. Martin (ed.), Academic Press (London, 1975), 115–23
    Zimmerman, *To Save a Bird in Peril*, ch. 5

23 H. F. Recher, 'Colonisation and extinction: the birds of Lord Howe Island', *Australian Natural History*, **18** (1974), 64–8
 H. F. Recher and S. T. Clark, 'A biological survey of Lord Howe Island with recommendations for the conservation of the island's wildlife', *Biol. Conservation*, **6** (1974), 263–73
 P. J. Fullager and H. J. de S. Disney, 'The birds of Lord Howe Island: a report on the rare and endangered species', *12th Bull. I.C.B.P.* (1975), 187–202

24 J. B. Nelson, 'The biology of Abbott's Booby, *Sula abbotti*', *Ibis*, **113** (1971), 429–67; and 'Report on the status and prospects of Abbott's Booby (*Sula abbotti*) in relation to phosphate mining on the Australian territory of Christmas Island, August 1974', *12th Bull. I.C.B.P.* (1975), 131–40
 G. F. van Tets, 'A report on the conservation of resident birds on Christmas Island', *12th Bull. I.C.B.P.* (1975), 238–42

25 G. A. Sanger, 'The recent pelagic status of the Short-tailed Albatross (*Diomedea albatrus*)', *Biol. Conservation*, **4** (1972), 189–93
 W. L. N. Tickell, 'Observations on the status of Stellar's Albatross (*Diomedea albatrus*) 1973', *12th Bull. I.C.B.P.* (1975), 125–31

26 R. C. Murphy and L. S. Mowbray, 'New light on the Cahow, *Pterodroma cahow*', *Auk*, **68** (1951), 266–80
 Zimmerman, *To Save a Bird in Peril*, ch. 3

27 C. F. Wurster and D. B. Wingate, 'DDT residues and declining reproduction in the Bermuda Petrel', *Science*, **159** (1968), 979–81

Chapter 7
 1 R. Meinertzhagen and K. H. Voous, 'Palaearctic region', in *A New Dictionary of Birds*, A. Landsborough Thomson (ed.), Nelson (London, 1964), 583–8
 2 J. Gooders, 'Viewpoint: a question of priorities', *British Birds*, **69** (1976), 16–19
 3 Anon., 'The deathly hush', *Birds*, **6** (4) (1976), 34–6. See also editorial comment in the same issue.
 4 R. Hudson, *Threatened Birds of Europe*, Macmillan (London, 1975), 28
 K. D. Smith, 'The Waldrapp, *Geronticus eremita* (L.)', *Bull. British Ornithologists' Club*, **90** (1970), 18–24
 5 W. R. Siegfried, 'Discrete breeding and wintering areas of the Waldrapp, *Geronticus eremita* (L.)', *Bull. British Ornithologists' Club*, **92** (1972), 102–3
 6 J. L. F. Parslow, 'Organochlorine insecticide residues and food remains in a Bald Ibis *Geronticus eremita* from Birecik, Turkey', *Bull. British Ornithologists' Club*, **93** (1973), 163–6
 7 Hudson, *Threatened Birds of Europe*, 80
 8 D. A. Ratcliffe, 'The status of the Peregrine in Great Britain', *Bird Study*, **10** (1963), 56–90; 'The Peregrine situation in Great Britain 1963–64', *Bird Study*, **12** (1965), 66–82; 'The Peregrine situation in Great Britain 1965–66', *Bird Study*, **14** (1967), 238–46; and *The Peregrine in Britain in 1971*, British Trust for Ornithology Report (1972)
 9 J. A. Bogan and J. Mitchell, 'Continuing dangers to Peregrines from Dieldrin', *British Birds*, **66** (1973), 437–9
10 Anon., 'Endangered aristocrats', *Birds*, **6** (4) (1976), 6

11 Hudson, *Threatened Birds of Europe*, 36

12 I. Prestt and D. A. Ratcliffe, 'Effects of organochloride insecticides on European birdlife', *Proc. 15th Int. Ornith. Congress* (1972), 486–513

13 T. Odsjö and C. Edelstam, 'Effects of toxic chemicals on bird life', *12th Bull. I.C.B.P.* (1975), 114–21

14 Hudson, *Threatened Birds of Europe*, 66

15 Ibid, 64

16 B. U. Meyburg, 'Sibling aggression and mortality among nestling eagles', *Ibis*, **116** (1974), 224–8
D. R. Zimmerman, *To Save a Bird in Peril*, Coward, McCann and Geoghegan (New York, 1975) ch. 9

17 B. U. Meyburg and J. G. Heydt, 'Sobre la protección del Aguila imperial (*Aquila heliaca adalberti*) aminorando artificialmente la mortandad juvenil', *Ardeola*, **19** (1973), 107–28

18 Hudson, *Threatened Birds of Europe*, 122

19 P. Wayre, 'Conservation of Eagle Owls and other raptors through captive breeding and return to the wild', in *Breeding Endangered Species in captivity*, R. D. Martin (ed.), Academic Press (London, 1975), 125–31

20 Hudson, *Threatened Birds of Europe*, 120

21 Zimmerman, *To Save a Bird in Peril*, ch. 7

22 Hudson, *Threatened Birds of Europe*, 105

23 Ibid, 10

24 W. B. King, 'Incidental sea-bird kills from salmon gillnet fisheries'. *12th Bull. I.C.B.P.* (1975), 259–60

25 G. Harmsen, 'Review of recent development of the proposal to keep the Waddensea in its present form', *12th Bull. I.C.B.P.* (1975), 226–8

26 S. Cramp, Introduction to Hudson, *Threatened Birds of Europe*

27 Ibid., 92
N. Collar, 'Bringing back the Bustard', *Wildlife*, **18** (6) (1976), 254–7
R. Lütkens and M. Dangel, 'The situation of the Great Bustard (*Otis tarda*, L.) in Austria', *12th Bull. I.C.B.P.* (1975), 212–16

28 D. A. Bannerman, *The Birds of the British Isles*, Oliver and Boyd, (Edinburgh and London, 1962), vol. 11, 38–52

29 R. Lütkens, 'Bustard group: general report', *12th Bull. I.C.B.P.* (1975), 210–12

30 Collar, 'Bringing back the Bustard'

31 J. Gooders, 'Viewpoint: a question of priorities'

Chapter 8

1 Principal sources for this chapter:
J. D. Macdonald, *Birds of Australia*, Witherby (London, 1973)
I. Rowley, *Bird Life*, Collins (Sydney, 1974)
W. R. Wheeler, 'Report on rare and endangered species of birds from the Australian mainland', *12th Bull. I.C.B.P.* (1975), 159–64

2 E. Mayr, 'The challenge of island faunas', *Australian Natural History*, **15** (1967), 369–74

3 The Marsupials differ from other mammals in that their young are born at a

very early stage in their development. Only some species, generally those that lead the most active lives, have an abdominal pouch in which the young develop.

4 J. Cracraft, 'Continental drift and Australian avian biogeography', *The Emu*, **72** (1972), 171–4; and 'Continental drift, paleoclimatology, and the evolution and biogeography of birds', *J. Zool. Lond.*, **169** (1973), 455–545

D. L. Serventy, 'Origin and structure of Australian bird fauna', in *Birds of Australia*

P. V. Rich, 'Changing continental arrangements and the origin of Australia's non-passeriform continental avifauna', *The Emu*, **75** (1974), 97–112

C. B. Cox, I. N. Healey and P. D. Moore, *Biogeography: an ecological and evolutionary approach*, Blackwell Scientific Publications (Oxford, 1976), 369–74

5 Rowley, *Bird Life*, ch. 2

6 S. J. J. F. Davies, 'Land use by Emus and other wildlife species in the arid shrublands of Western Australia', in *Arid Shrublands*, Proc. 3rd Workshop U.S./Australia Rangelands Panel, Tucson, Arizona (1973), 91–8; 'Environmental variables and the biology of Australian arid zone birds', *Proc. 16th Int. Ornith. Congress* (1976), 481–8

7 Rowley, *Bird Life*, 192–3

8 H. J. Frith, 'Movements of the Grey Teal, *Anas gibberifrons* Muller (Anatidae)', *C.S.I.R.O. Wildlife Research*, **7** (1962), 50–70

Rowley, *Bird Life*, 200–2

9 H. J. Frith, 'Movements and mortality rates of the Black Duck and Grey Teal in south-eastern Australia', *C.S.I.R.O. Wildlife Research*, **8** (1963), 119–31

10 D. Goodwin, *Pigeons and Doves of the World*, British Museum (Natural History), (1967), 184–5

11 Rowley, *Bird Life*, ch. 22

12 R. E. Ricklefs, *Ecology*, Nelson (London, 1973), 570–2

13 Rowley, *Bird Life*, 240–1

14 E. N. Wright, 'Modification of the habitat as a means of bird control', in *The Problems of Birds as Pests*, R. K. Murton and E. N. Wright (eds.), Academic Press (London, 1968), 97–105

15 S. J. J. F. Davies, 'Emus', *Aust. Nat. Hist.*, **14** (1963), 225–9; and 'Land use by Emus and other wildlife species in the arid shrublands of Western Australia'

16 Macdonald, *Birds of Australia*, 278–9

G. T. Smith and F. N. Robinson, 'The Noisy Scrub-bird: an interim report', *The Emu*, **76** (1976), 37–42

17 Macdonald, *Birds of Australia*, 278

18 Macdonald, *Birds of Australia*, 315–19

19 B. Campbell, *The Dictionary of Birds in Colour*, Michael Joseph (London, 1974), 229

20 H. J. Frith, *The Mallee Fowl*, Angus and Robertson (Sydney, 1962) Rowley, *Bird Life*, ch. 13

21 J. M. Forshaw, *Parrots of the World*, Landsdowne (Melbourne, 1973), 266–9

22 Forshaw, *Parrots of the World*, 267

J. M. Forshaw, P. J. Fullager and R. H. Groves, quoted in Wheeler, 'Report on rare and endangered species of birds from the Australian mainland'

23 Forshaw, *Parrots of the World*, 267–8

24 J. M. Forshaw, P. J. Fuilager and J. I. Harris, 'Specimens of the Night Parrot in museums around the world', *The Emu*, **76** (1976), 120–6

25 J. Fisher, N. Simon and J. Vincent, *The Red Book: Wildlife in Danger*, Collins (London, 1969), 252–5

26 H. J. Lavery and C. M. Weaver, quoted in Wheeler, 'Report on rare and endangered species of birds from the Australian mainland'

27 J. Delacour, *The Waterfowl of the World*, Country Life (London, 1956), vol. 2, 223–5
  H. J. Frith, 'Ecology of the Freckled Duck, *Stictonetta naevosa* (Gould)', *C.S.I.R.O. Wildlife Research*, **10** (1965), 125–39
  Macdonald, *Birds of Australia*, 90–1
  L. W. Braithwaite, 'Notes on the breeding of the Freckled Duck in the Lachlan River Valley', *The Emu*, **76** (1976), 127–32

28 Delacour, *The Waterfowl of the World*, vol. 1, 199–202
  Macdonald, *Birds of Australia*, 91–2

29 E. R. Guiler, 'The 1958–60 Cape Barren Goose aerial surveys', *The Emu*, **61** (1961), 61–4

30 E. R. Guiler, 'The Cape Barren Goose, its environment, numbers and breeding', *The Emu*, **66** (1967), 211–35

31 Macdonald, *Birds of Australia*, 326–7

32 Ibid., 403–5

33 R. Buckingham, quoted in Wheeler, 'Report on rare and endangered species of birds from the Australian mainland'

34 Rowley, *Bird Life*, ch. 12

35 M. G. Ridpath and G. K. Meldrum, 'Damage to pastures by the Tasmanian Native Hen, *Tribonyx mortierii*', *C.S.I.R.O. Wildlife Research*, **13** (1968), 11–24; and 'Damage to oat crops by the Tasmanian Native Hen, *Tribonyx mortierii*', *C.S.I.R.O. Wildlife Research*, **13** (1968), 25–43

36 J. Maynard Smith and M. G. Ridpath, 'Wife sharing in the Tasmanian Native Hen, *Tribonyx mortierii*: a case of kin selection?', *American Naturalist*, **106** (1972), 447–52

Chapter 9

1 See: Chapter 2, Note 9

2 D. R. Zimmerman, *To Save a Bird in Peril*, Coward, McCann and Geoghegan (New York, 1975)

3 J. M. Diamond, 'The island dilemma: lessons of modern biogeographic studies for the design of natural reserves', *Biol. Conservation*, **7** (1975), 129–46
  J. M. Diamond and R. M. May, 'Island biogeography and the design of nature reserves', in *Theoretical Ecology: principles and applications*, R. M. May (ed.), Blackwell Scientific Publications (Oxford, 1976)

4 N. K. Johnson, 'Controls of number of bird species on montane islands in the Great Basin', *Evolution*, **29** (1975), 545–67

5 E. O. Willis, 'Populations and local extinction of birds on Barro Colorado Island, Panama', *Ecological Monographs*, **44** (1974), 153–69

6 R. M. May, 'Island biogeography and the design of wildlife preserves', *Nature*, **254** (1975), 177–8
  It has been suggested that the application of Island Biogeography theory to practical conservation is premature, since the theory has not been fully validated. See: D. S. Simberloff and L. G. Abele, 'Island Biogeography theory and conservation practice', *Science*, **191** (1976), 285–6
7 Diamond, 'The island dilemma'
8 For details of legal regulations regarding British birds see: *Wild Birds and the Law*, R.S.P.B. (1971)
9 Zimmerman, *To Save a Bird in Peril*, ch. 7
10 R. D. Martin, Introduction to *Breeding Endangered Species in Captivity*, R. D. Martin (ed.), Academic Press (London, 1975)
11 G. V. T. Matthews, 'Some problems facing captive breeding and restoration programmes for waterfowl', *Int. Zoo. Yearbook*, **13** (1973), 8–11
12 J. Kear, 'Returning the Hawaiian Goose to the Wild', in *Breeding Endangered Species in Captivity*
  Zimmerman, *To Save a Bird in Peril*, ch. 5
13 Matthews, 'Some problems facing captive breeding and restoration programmes for waterfowl'
14 Ibid.
15 Zimmerman, *To Save a Bird in Peril*, ch. 4
16 T. J. Cade, 'Falcon farming', *Animal Kingdom*, **78** (1975), 3–9
  P. Wayre, 'Conservation of Eagle Owls and other captors through captive breeding and return to the wild, in *Breeding Endangered Species in Captivity*
17 G. Durrell, Foreword to *Breeding Endangered Species in Captivity*
18 D. D. Bridgwater, 'Status of rare and endangered birds in captivity with a general reference to mammals', *Zoologica*, **57** (1972), 119–25
19 P. Wayre, 'Breeding endangered pheasant species in captivity as a means of ensuring their survival', in *Breeding Endangered Species in Captivity*, 87–97
20 J. Terborgh, 'Preservation of natural diversity: the problem of extinction-prone species', *Bioscience*, **24** (1974), 715–22
21 G. Mountfort, 'The need for research concerning endangered species', *Ibis*, **112** (1970), 445–7
22 Zimmerman, *To Save a Bird in Peril*, ch. 11

American editions of books cited above (where applicable)

Campbell B., *The Dictionary of Birds in Color*, Viking Press (New York, 1974), 229
Cox C. B., Healey I. N. and Moore P. D., *Biogeography: an ecological and evolutionary approach*, Halsted Press (New York, 1976), ch. 6
Delacour J., *The Waterfowl of the World*, Arco (New York, 1954), vol. 2, 197
Diamond J. M. and May R. M., 'Island biogeography and the design of nature reserves', in *Theoretical Ecology: principles and applications*, R. M. May (ed.), Lippincott (Philadelphia, 1976), ch. 9
Dorst J. *The Life of Birds*, Columbia University Press (New York, 1974), vol. 2, ch. 23
Falla R. A., 'Moa', in *A New Dictionary of Birds*, A. Landsborough Thomson (ed.), McGraw-Hill (New York, 1964)

Fisher J. and Lockley R. M., *Sea Birds*, Houghton Mifflin (Boston, 1954), 65

Fisher J., (1964) 'Extinct birds', in *A New Dictionary of Birds*, A. Landsborough Thomson (ed.), McGraw-Hill (New York, 1964), 259–64

Fisher J., Simon N. and Vincent J., *Wildlife in Danger*, Viking Press (New York, 1969)

Forshaw J. M., *Parrots of the World*, Doubleday (New York, 1973), 414–18

Kear J., 'Returning the Hawaiian Goose to the wild', in *Breeding Endangered Species in Captivity*, R. D. Martin (ed.), Academic Press (New York, 1975), 115–23

Lack D., *Darwin's Finches*, Harper (New York, 1961), and reissued by Peter Smith, Magnolia (Mass., 1968)

Martin R. D., Introduction to *Breeding Endangered Species in Captivity*, R. D. Martin (ed.), Academic Press (New York, 1975)

Mayr E., 'Nearctic region,' in *A New Dictionary of Birds*, A. Landsborough Thomson (ed.), McGraw-Hill (New York, 1964), 514–16

Meinertzhagen R. and Voous K. H., 'Palaearctic region', in *A New Dictionary of Birds*, A. Landsborough Thomson (ed.), McGraw-Hill (New York, 1964), 583–8

Merton D. V., 'The Saddleback: its status and conservation', in *Breeding Endangered Species in Captivity*, R. D. Martin (ed.), Academic Press (New York, 1975), 61–74

Peattie D. C., *Green Laurels: the lives and achievements of the great naturalists*, Simon and Schuster (New York, 1936), ch. 10

Phillips J. C., *A Natural History of Ducks*, Houghton Mifflin (Boston, 1923), vol. 1, 90

Ricklefs R. E., *Ecology*, Chiron Press (Portland [Oregon], 1973), 570–2

Rowley I., *Bird Life*, Taplinger (New York, 1974)

Singer P., *Animal Liberation*, Random House (New York, 1976)

Southwood T. R. E., 'Bionomic strategies and population parameters', in *Theoretical Ecology: principles and applications*, R. M. May (ed.), Lippincott (Philadelphia, 1976) ch. 3

Sparks J. and Soper T., *Penguins*, Taplinger (New York, 1967)

Teale E. W., *Audubon's Wildlife, with Selections from the Writings of John James Audubon*, Viking Press (New York, 1964)

Turbott E. G., *Buller's Birds of New Zealand*, University Press of Hawaii (Honolulu, 1967)

Wayre P., 'Conservation of Eagle Owls and other raptors through captive breeding and return to the wild', in *Breeding Endangered Species in Captivity*, R. D. Martin (ed.), Academic Press (New York, 1975), 125–31

Wright E. N., 'Modification of the habitat as a means of bird control', in *The Problems of Birds as Pests*, R. K. Murton and E. N. Wright (eds.), Academic Press (New York, 1968), 97–105

Appendix

Latin names of bird species mentioned in the text

Abbott's Booby	*Sula abbotti*
American Egret	*Casmerodius albus*
Attwater's Prairie Chicken	*Tympanuchus cupido attwateri*
Auckland Island Merganser	*Mergus australis*
Audouin's Gull	*Larus audouinii*
Australian Bustard	*Ardeotis australis*
Australian Silvereye	*Zosterops lateralis*
Avocet (European)	*Recurvirostra avosetta*
Bachman's Warbler	*Vermivora bachmani*
Bald Eagle	*Haliaetus leucocephalus*
Bald Ibis	*Geronticus eremita*
Bank Swallow	*Riparia riparia*
Bearded Vulture	*Gypaetus barbatus*
Beautiful or Paradise Parrot	*Psephotus pulcherrimus*
Bittern (European)	*Botaurus stellaris*
Black Duck	*Anas superciliosa*
Black Grasswren	*Amytornis housei*
Black-headed Gull	*Larus ridibundus*
Black-tailed Godwit	*Limosa limosa*
Black-tailed Native Hen	*Tribonyx ventralis*
Black Vulture	*Coragyps barbatus*
Blue Chaffinch	*Fringilla teydea*
Blue Duck	*Hymenolaimus malacorhynchos*
Blue Tit	*Parus caeruleus*
Blue-winged Grass Parakeet	*Neophema chrysostoma*
Brown-headed Cowbird	*Molothrus ater*
Brown Pelican	*Pelecanus occidentalis*
Brown Teal	*Anas aucklandica*
Budgerigar	*Melopsittacus undulatus*

Bush Canary	*Mohoua ochrocephala*
Bush Wren	*Xenicus longipes*
Cahow	*Pterodroma cahow*
California Condor	*Gymnogyps californianus*
Canvasback Duck	*Aythya valisneria*
Cape Barren Goose	*Cereopsis novaehollandiae*
Carolina Duck	*Aix sponsa*
Carolina Parakeet	*Conuropsis carolinensis*
Carrion Crow	*Corvus corone*
Cassowary	*Casuarius* (3 species)
Chaffinch	*Fringilla coelebs*
Chatham Islands Black Robin	*Petroica traversi*
Cock of the Rock	*Rupicola peruviana*
Cocos Island Finch	*Pinaroloxias inornata*
Collared Dove	*Streptopelia decaocto*
Crested Coot	*Fulica cristata*
Crested Honeycreeper	*Palmeria dolei*
Dalmatian Pelican	*Pelecanus crispus*
Dartford Warbler	*Sylvia undata*
Darwin's Large-billed Ground Finch	*Geospiza magnirostris*
Dodo	*Raphus cucullatus*
Duck Hawk	*Falco peregrinus*
Eagle Owl	*Bubo bubo*
Eastern Bristlebird	*Dasyornis brachypterus*
Egyptian Vulture	*Neophron percnopterus*
Eider Duck	*Somateria mollissima*
Elephant Bird	*Aepyornis* and *Mullerornis* (several species)
Emperor Penguin	*Aptenodytes forsteri*
Emu	*Dromaius novaehollandiae*
Eskimo Curlew	*Numenius borealis*
Everglade Kite	*Rostrhamus sociabilis*
Eyrean Grasswren	*Amytornis goyderi*
Fieldfare	*Turdus pilaris*
Flock Pigeon	*Phaps histrionica*
Freckled Duck	*Sticitonetta naevosa*
Fulmar	*Fulmarus glacialis*
Gannet	*Sula bassana*
Gentoo Penguin	*Pygoscelis papua*
Glossy Ibis	*Plegadis falcinellis*
Golden-shouldered Parrot	*Psephotus chrysopterygius*
Goshawk	*Accipiter gentilis*

Great Auk	*Alca impennis*
Great Bustard	*Ortis tarda*
Great Crested Grebe	*Podiceps cristatus*
Great Indian Bustard	*Choriotis nigriceps*
Great Northern Diver	*Gavia immer*
Great Tit	*Parus major*
Great White Egret	*Egretta alba*
Greater Flamingo	*Phoenicopterus ruber*
Greater Prairie Chicken	*Tympanuchus cupido pinnatus*
Greater Spotted Kiwi	*Apteryx haasti*
Grey Duck	*Anas superciliosa*
Grey Grasswren	*Amytornis barbatus*
Grey Teal	*Anas gibberifrons*
Griffon Vulture	*Gyps fulvus*
Ground Parrot	*Pezoporus wallicus*
Guillemot	*Uria aalge*
Hawaiian Goose	*Branta sandvicensis*
Heath Hen	*Tympanuchus cupido cupido*
Helmeted Honeyeater	*Meliphaga cassidix*
Hermit	*Geronticus eremita*
Herring Gull	*Larus argentatus*
Himalayan Mountain Quail	*Ophrysia superciliosa*
Hoatzin	*Opisthocomus hoazin*
Hooded Crow	*Corvus cornix*
Hooded Parrot	*Psephotus dissimilis*
House Sparrow	*Passer domesticus*
Huia	*Heteralocha acutirostris*
Imperial Eagle (Spanish race)	*Aquila heliaca adalberti*
Ivory-billed Woodpecker	*Campephilus principalis*
Jackass Penguin	*Spheniscus demosus*
Jerdon's Courser	*Rhinoptilus bitorquatus*
Kakapo	*Strigops habroptilus*
Kaui Oo	*Moho braccatus*
Kea	*Nestor notabilis*
Kestrel (European)	*Falco tinnunculus*
Kirtland's Warbler	*Dendroica kirtlandii*
Kiwi	*Apteryx* (3 species)
Kokako	*Callaeas cinerea*
Labrador Duck	*Captorhynchus labradorius*
Lammergeier	*Gypaetus barbatus*
Laughing Owl	*Sceloglaux albifacies*

Laysan Duck	*Anas platyrhynchos laysanensis*
Laysan Finch	*Psittirostra cantans cantans*
Laysan Honeycreeper	*Himatione sanguinea freethi*
Lesser Prairie Chicken	*Tympanuchus pallidicinctus*
Lesser Spotted Eagle	*Aquila pomarina*
Lesser Spotted Woodpecker	*Dendrocopos minor*
Little Spotted Kiwi	*Apteryx oweni*
Long-eared Owl	*Asio otus*
Long-tail	*Phaëthon lepturus*
Lord Howe Island Silvereye	*Zosterops tephropleura*
Lord Howe Island Wood Rail	*Tricholimnas sylvestris*
Lyrebird	*Menura alberti*
Mackinlay's Cuckoo Dove	*Macropygia mackinlayi*
Mallard Duck	*Anas platyrhynchos*
Mallee Fowl	*Leipoa ocellata*
Mauritius Kestrel	*Falco punctatus*
Moa	6 genera: *Dinornis, Anomalopteryx, Megalapteryx, Pachyornis, Emeus, Euryapteryx*
Muttonbird	*Puffinus tenuirostris*
Mynah Bird	*Acridotheres tristis*
Néné	*Branta sandvicensis*
New Zealand Robin	*Petroica australis*
New Zealand Thrush	*Turnagra capensis*
New Zealand Tit	*Petroica macrocephala*
Night Heron	*Nycticorax nycticorax*
Night Parrot	*Geopsittacus occidentalis*
Noisy Scrub-Bird	*Atrichohrnis clamosus*
Orange-bellied or Orange-chested Grass Parakeet	*Neophema chrysogaster*
Osprey	*Pandion haliaetus*
Ostrich	*Struthio camelus*
Passenger Pigeon	*Ectopistes migratorius*
Peregrine Falcon	*Falco peregrinus*
Pied Flycatcher	*Ficedula hypoleuca*
Pied Goose	*Anseranas semipalmata*
Pink-headed Duck	*Rhodonessa caryophyllacea*
Piopio	*Turnagra capensis*
Pukeko	*Porphyrio porphyrio*
Puffin	*Fratercula arctica*
Purple Gallinule	*Porphyrula martinica*
Pygmy Cormorant	*Phalacrocorax pygmaeus*

Red-breasted Goose	*Branta ruficollis*
Red-cheeked Ibis	*Geronticus eremita*
Rhea	*Rhea* (2 species)
Ring-necked Parakeet	*Psittacula krameri echo*
Robin (European)	*Erithacus rubecula*
Robust Silvereye	*Zosterops strenua*
Rock Wren	*Xenicus giliventris*
Rufous Scrub-bird	*Atrichornis rufescens*
Sacred Ibis	*Threskiornis aethiopicus*
Saddleback	*Creadion carunculatus*
Savi's Warbler	*Locustella luscinoides*
Short-tailed Albatross	*Diomedea albatrus*
Silver Gull	*Larus novaehollandiae*
Snowy Owl	*Nyctea scandiaca*
Solitaire (Réunion)	*Raphus solitarius*
Solitaire (Rodriguez)	*Pezophaps solitaria*
Splendid or Scarlet-chested Grass Parakeet	*Neophema splendida*
Starling (European)	*Sturnus vulgaris*
Steller's Albatross	*Diomedea albatrus*
Stephen Island Wren	*Xenicus lyalli*
Swallow	*Hirundo rustica*
Swinhoe's Pheasant	*Lophura swinhoei*
Takahe	*Notornis mantelli*
Tasmanian Native Hen	*Tribonyx mortierii*
Thick-billed Murre	*Uria lomvia*
Tooth-billed Pigeon	*Didunculus strigirostris*
Turquoise Grass Parakeet	*Neophema pulchella*
Waldrapp	*Geronticus eremita*
Welcome Swallow	*Hirundo neoxena*
Western Bristlebird	*Dasyornis longirostris*
Western Tragopan	*Tragopan melanocephalus*
White-crowned Pigeon	*Columba leucocephala*
White Gallinule	*Porphyrio porphyrio albus*
White Pelican	*Pelecanus onocrotalus*
White-tailed Eagle	*Haliaetus albicilla*
White-tailed Tropic-Bird	*Phaëthon lepturus*
Whooping Crane	*Grus americana*
Wild Turkey	*Meleagris gallopavo*
Wood Duck	*Aix sponsa*
Yellowhead	*Mohoua ochrocephala*

Index

Page numbers in italics indicate illustrations.

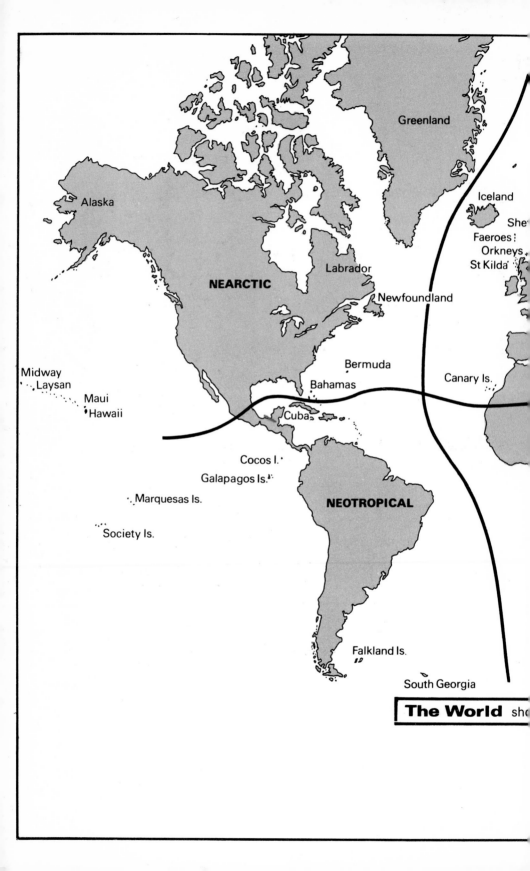

Greenland

Iceland

She

Faeroes

Orkneys

St Kilda

Alaska

NEARCTIC

Labrador

Newfoundland

Bermuda

Midway

Laysan

Bahamas

Canary Is.

Maui

Hawaii

Cuba

Cocos I.

Galapagos Is.

Marquesas Is.

NEOTROPICAL

Society Is.

Falkland Is.

South Georgia

The World sh